STEAM

AROUND NORTH WALES

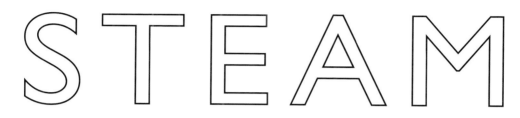

STEAM

AROUND NORTH WALES

THE NORTH WALES COAST
& THE LLEYN PENINSULA

MIKE HITCHES

AMBERLEY

Cover illustrations: Front: BR Britannia Pacific *Byron* leaving Penmaenbach tunnel. (P. Owen) *Back:* 57xx 0-6-0PT No. 5742 approaching Bala station. (H. Casserley)

First published 2013

Amberley Publishing
The Hill, Stroud
Gloucestershire, GL5 4EP

www.amberley-books.com

British Library Cataloguing in Publication Data.
A catalogue record for this book is available from the British Library.

ISBN 978 1 4456 0765 8

Typeset in 10pt on 12pt Sabon.
Typesetting and Origination by Amberley Publishing.
Printed in the UK.

CONTENTS

INTRODUCTION

Contrasts in the landscape in North Wales influenced the economy of the area and provide evidence for the network of railways in the locality. The eastern section of North Wales, around Flintshire, was scattered with steelworks at Brymbo and collieries at places like Gresford and Point of Air. Along with the industrial landscape in the Wrexham area, the west of North Wales had its extraction industries of granite in Penmaenmawr and Llanfairfechan, and its famous slate quarries in Snowdonia at Bethesda, Nantlle and, famously, at Blaenau Ffestiniog. North-west Wales is also noted for its tourist trade along the coast in resorts at Prestatyn, Rhyl, Colwyn Bay and Llandudno, as well as others. The area is also home to the Snowdonia National Park, with Mount Snowdon as its centrepiece, which brings in tourists and also has its quarries at places like Llanberis. Cardigan Bay also has its seaside resorts at Barmouth, Portmadoc and Pwllheli. The locality also has its famous castles at Harlech and Criccieth, along with those at Caernarfon, Conwy and Flint, which also bring in visitors. Thus, there was plenty of traffic to interest the various railway companies that would be established within North Wales. Impetus for a railway in North Wales, however, was to create speedier links between the seat of government at Westminster and Ireland, which was still part of the United Kingdom at this time.

Although the most important railway in North Wales was the Chester & Holyhead, the first to enter the locality was the Shrewsbury and Chester Railway, opened in 1846 and reaching Chester from Saltney Junction, in north-east Wales, via the Roodee Viaduct, which had been constructed to carry the C&HR into Chester. The C&HR was opened two years later, in 1848, having received royal assent in 1844. The C&HR, along with the Crewe and Chester Railway, became part of the powerful London & North Western Railway in the 1850s and this spelt trouble for the small, but resilient, Shrewsbury & Chester Railway. The little company had entered into an agreement with the Shrewsbury & Birmingham Railway over the handling of through traffic between the industrial heartland of the West Midlands and the North West of England, which struck at the very heart of the LNWR monopoly. Alarmed by the prospect of fierce competition from the little Shrewsbury companies, the aggressive general manager of the LNWR, Captain Mark Huish, issued several written threats about incursions into LNWR territory but the Shrewsbury companies chose to ignore them. Thus, Huish then used force by gaining a majority on the management of Chester station. Having gained control, a ban was placed on the sale of through tickets to Birmingham via Shrewsbury. The LNWR even had the temerity to have the resistant booking clerk physically ejected from the station, his tickets being thrown after him. The Birkenhead, Lancashire & Cheshire Junction Railway, a satellite of the LNWR, was then forced to boycott as much S&C traffic as it could legally dare. This belligerence by the LNWR was to eventually fail, when the two Shrewsbury companies sought an alliance with Huish's deadly enemy, the Great Western Railway, the S&B also having problems with the LNWR at Wolverhampton. Thus, two of the greatest railway rivals were forced to come to terms with each other at Chester. Indeed, the line to Birkenhead became jointly owned by the LNWR and GWR. Events at Chester brought the GWR into North Wales around the Wrexham area to capture freight and local traffic as well as through trains between Birkenhead and Paddington, taking some Mersey dock trade from the LNWR at Liverpool.

The Chester & Holyhead Railway was constructed to connect London with Ireland, via the sea packet port at Holyhead, the capital also being the administrative centre for Ireland as well as Great Britain. Holyhead had for centuries been the main port for Ireland as it provided the shortest crossing, but travel by road could be difficult and dangerous. The coast road meant crossing the twin headlands at Penmaenbach and Penmaenmawr; the road around the latter would often collapse and travellers risked life and limb using this route. Indeed, many would stay overnight before crossing Penmaenmawr. At Conwy, the river had to be traversed by ferry; the ferrymen were noted for their rudeness and would often force passengers to wade through part of the river to reach the opposite shore, the tide actually being quite rapid at this point, so wading could present its own dangers. Even using the A5, Thomas Telford's 1805-built Holyhead Road, through Snowdonia had its risks and clamour for a railway was made when an Irish Minister, on his way back to his constituency, was involved in a stagecoach accident in the 1830s. Such were the dangers of the roads to Holyhead that many travellers chose to risk the longer sea crossing from Parkgate, on the Dee Estuary, to Ireland.

As early as 1836, commissioners were appointed to investigate the possibilities for a general railway system in Ireland. These commissioners appointed Charles Vignoles as engineer and asked him to report on plans for connecting railways in England and Wales. By 1837, he reported in favour of a railway from London, via Mid Wales and through Llangollen, Bala and Barmouth to Porth Dinllaen, near Caernarfon. He did not favour an alternative proposal from Chester and along the North Wales coast to Holyhead due to engineering problems associated with crossing the River Conwy and Menai Strait, along with having to solve difficulties of going around the twin headlands at Penmaenbach and Penmaenmawr, 5 miles west of Conwy. However, the port at Holyhead was well-established and a port at Porth Dinllaen would have to be fully developed. A line through Llangollen and Bala would eventually run from Ruabon by the GWR, which would connect with the Cambrian Railways line to Barmouth and Pwllheli at Barmouth Junction.

While the two main contenders were under consideration, another alternative was offered by the St George's Harbour & Railway Company. This new alternative envisaged a railway from Chester, an increasingly important junction, along the North Wales coast to Orme's Bay, to be called Port Wrexham. This project was quickly rejected as it was believed that passengers would prefer to sail from Liverpool rather than travel by rail to Port Wrexham. Orme's Bay itself became the fashionable seaside resort of Llandudno and it is interesting to speculate what may have happened had the railway come to Orme's Bay and a harbour been built here. The resort of Llandudno would certainly not have existed, the locality may well have developed like the port at Holyhead. As far as the railway was concerned, track may not have gone further west than Llandudno Junction because of the problems crossing the River Conwy and Menai Strait, although the suspension bridge was already in existence, giving access to Anglesey from the mainland, and the A5 road was in use. The twin headlands previously mentioned would have retained their roads. Having said that, most of the granite and slate quarries lie west of Conwy, so some sort of branch lines, probably narrow gauge as such railways were popular with the quarry companies, would have appeared to serve these quarries, standard gauge tracks probably running inland from Cardigan Bay, which would have increased revenue to the Cambrian Railways lines at the expense of the LNWR. Populations west of Conwy would probably have remained small and Welsh-speaking.

These events did not occur thanks to the great railway engineer, Robert Stephenson, who presented plans that would overcome engineering problems associated with the route west of Llandudno Junction. He suggested construction of tubular bridges over the River Conwy and Menai Strait along with driving tunnels through Penmaenbach and Penmaenmawr rather than going round the headlands, a policy which later road builders would follow. These plans were accepted and royal assent for construction of the Chester & Holyhead Railway was given on St David's Day 1844. The LNWR applied pressure on the C&HR to have its line opened as soon as possible because the Euston company's great rival, the GWR, was attempting to win the mail contract to Ireland using their own harbour at Milford Haven in South Wales. The C&HR finally opened as far as Bangor in 1848; the rail link to Holyhead was not completed for another two years when the tubular Britannia Bridge was opened. Thus, the C&HR, in association with the LNWR, won a mail contract that had been inaugurated by the London & Birmingham Railway in 1837. The L&B, by now, was part of the LNWR empire. Despite being the most important railway for services to Ireland, the C&HR was never financially sound, no doubt due to construction costs, and it was finally absorbed into the LNWR empire in 1859.

Although Vignoles's plan for a railway to Porth Dinllaen ultimately failed, Cardigan Bay was eventually served by a railway from 1867, when the Aberystwyth & Welsh Coast Railway was opened, by then part of the Cambrian Railways from 1865. The A&WCR planned a line that left the Newtown & Machynlleth Railway, running via the Dyfi (Dovey), Mawddach and Glaslyn estuaries to Pwllheli and on to Porth Dinllaen. Royal assent for the line was granted in 1861 and the first section between Machynlleth and Borth was opened on 1 July 1863, engineered by David Davies and Thomas Savin. It was Cambrian Railways who completed the line to Pwllheli, which opened without ceremony on 10 October 1867. The extension to Porth Dinllaen was never built; thus Cambrian Railways never realised their ambitions to compete with Holyhead for traffic to Ireland.

The A&WCR was built through picturesque and mountainous country, which caused problems for its engineers. From Aberystwyth, the first major problem was the Dyfi Estuary. The original intention was for the railway to cross the estuary by constructing a viaduct. Unfortunately, unsound foundations meant that the railway had to follow the shore and cross the Dyfi further upstream. Further north, the mountains around the Cader Idris sweep down to the sea, precipitous cliffs at Friog being a major feature. The railway company was, therefore, forced to carve a route through the rocks. The final obstacle was the wide sandbank estuary of the Mawddach, near Barmouth, which also has strong sea currents. This problem was solved by construction of a timber viaduct of 113 spans supported by more than 500 piles. On the Barmouth side of the estuary, an iron section of 8 spans was built, one of which drew back over the others to allow the passage of ships. In 1909, this was replaced by a swing bridge. The Barmouth Bridge was opened on 3 June 1867 and is still considered to be the finest structure on the whole of the Cambrian Coast line.

The railway remained mostly single-track throughout its existence and was never the great success that its promoters had hoped. Its major problem was that the areas that it served were sparsely populated and the Cambrian was often faced with bankruptcy through lack of traffic. The railway did, however, open up Merionethshire and the Lleyn Peninsula to tourism in much the same way that the C&HR had done for the North Wales coast, the Cambrian Railways line benefiting from a growing tourist trade which peaked in the 1950s.

After the First World War, the railways in North Wales became part of two major groups. The financially destitute Cambrian Railways became part of the Great Western Railway in 1922, pre-empting the 1923 Grouping. The lines around Wrexham and Shrewsbury were already part of the Paddington organisation and it made sense for the Cambrian, whose headquarters were at Oswestry in Shropshire, to become part of this group; having said that, even the GWR could not make the Cambrian pay. The LNWR was merged with the Midland Railway, among others, to become the new London, Midland & Scottish Railway at the 1923 Grouping. The railways suffered badly during the Great Depression of the 1930s and overuse during the Second World War left them in a poor state of repair. Election of a Labour government in the first post-war ballot of 1945 meant a policy of nationalisation of key industries, including the railways. Thus, at the beginning of 1948, the railways became state-owned, the North Wales Coast line becoming part of the London-Midland Region of British Railways and the Cambrian, along with railways in the Wrexham area, became part of the new Western Region. An anomaly was the line between the Wirral and Wrexham, which was operated by the Manchester, Sheffield & Lincolnshire Railway, later the Great Central Railway, which became part of the London & North Eastern Railway (the furthest point west reached by the King's Cross Company).

Over the years, famous trains operated through North Wales, the most famous being the Irish Mail, the oldest named train in the world, having been inaugurated with the opening of the C&HR in 1848, which ran from Euston to Holyhead and was unusual in that it carried both mails and passengers. Perhaps the locomotives most associated with this train were LMS Fowler and Stanier Royal Scot Class 4-6-0s, these operating the service from the 1930s to the 1960s, when they were replaced by BR Britannia Pacifics and diesel-electric engines. At times, the train was also in the hands of LMS Princess Coronation and Princess Royal Pacifics. Back in LNWR days, many famous classes operated the Irish Mail over the years, including Lady of the Lake or Problem Class 2-2-2s, often double-headed as trains became heavier. Later, George V Class 4-4-0s and Claughton 4-6-0s were often seen on the service. Other expresses on the North Wales Coast included the Emerald Isle Express and the Welshman, the latter running from Euston to Bangor, thence through Caernarfon to Pwllheli, via Afonwen. In the 1950s, the Welsh Dragon, usually hauled by an Ivatt 2-6-2 tank loco, operated a local service during the summer between Rhyl and Llandudno.

Over at Wrexham, the famous GWR Paddington–Birkenhead expresses were a feature, often hauled by Churchward Star or Saint Class 4-6-0s until replaced by the famous Collett Castle Class 4-6-0s from the late 1920s. After nationalisation, Hawksworth County Class 4-6-0s could often be seen on these trains. The other GWR line, the Cambrian, had its own named express, the Cambrian Coast Express. In July 1921, the Cambrian introduced a through restaurant-car service from Paddington to Aberystwyth, Barmouth and Pwllheli. It was this train which would become the Cambrian Coast Express under Western Region auspices in 1951. The train ran through to Dovey Junction where it was divided, the front portion continuing to Aberystwyth while the rear portion went to Pwllheli. In the 1950s, the train was headed by a King or Castle 4-6-0 as far as Shrewsbury, the train then being handed over to a lightweight Collett Manor Class 4-6-0, which ran to Dovey Junction and Aberystwyth, while the portion for Pwllheli could be hauled by anything from double-framed Dukedog 4-4-0s to BR Standard Class 4-6-0s, 2-6-4 and 2-6-2 tank engines.

Along with famous trains, there were plenty of summer excursion trains that could be hauled by anything from ex-MR Compound 4-4-0s through to the famous Stanier Black Five 4-6-0s, Jubilee 4-6-0s and even 4F 0-6-0s. Over on the Cambrian, excursions could be operated by Dukedogs, BR Class 4 4-6-0s, Manors and BR 2-6-4 tanks. There were also plenty of freight trains, hauling slate and granite, often headed by anything from humble 0-6-0s to BR 9F 2-10-0s. Local trains were operated by 2-4-2, 0-6-0, 2-6-2 and 2-6-4 tank engines, such was the variety of motive power in North Wales.

The 'Modernisation Plan' of 1955, followed by the infamous Beeching Report of 1963, did much to decimate steam traction in North Wales. By the late 1950s, diesel multiple units were replacing steam on local and branch services. Many of these branches were to close under Beeching, and diesel-electric locomotives would see the demise of steam traction – by the mid-1960s the romance of the steam railway was to have disappeared forever. However, the lines to Holyhead and the Cambrian would, once again, see steam as preserved locos headed excursions from 1989 between Crewe and Holyhead and to Aberystwyth from Shrewsbury, once again reliving those wonderful steam days.

ONE

THE LNWR ON THE NORTH WALES COAST

Along with the main Chester & Holyhead line, several branch lines were opened to serve small villages and quarries that were some distance from the main line. Some of these branches were quite important, serving towns such as Mold, Denbigh and Caernarfon, while others served small locations, such as Dyserth and Nantlle. Some of these branches were long and had branches of their own, like the line from Rhyl to Corwen (where it met the GWR line from Ruabon to Barmouth), via Denbigh, where there was also a branch from the town to Saltney Ferry, at which point it rejoined the C&HR just west of Chester, via Mold. West of Bangor, there was the long branch from Menai Bridge station to Afonwen, where the LNWR met the Cambrian, which allowed through services to operate between Euston and Pwllheli, via Chester, Bangor and Caernarfon (county town of Caernarfonshire, now Gwynedd), situated about a third of the way along the branch from Menai Bridge. There were a few short branches from the Menai Bridge–Afonwen line, at Caernarfon where there was a line to Llanberis for slate traffic, but it also made a connection with the Snowdon Mountain Railway. At Pen-y-Groes, there was another short branch to Nantlle to serve slate quarries there. There was also a connection with the narrow gauge Welsh Highland Railway at Dinas Junction. There were short branches from Holywell Junction to Holywell Town, Llandudno Junction to Llandudno, which was a fast-growing and fashionable seaside resort, and from the C&HR between Aber and Bangor to the slate-quarrying town of Bethesda.

To serve the C&HR and the branches, several loco sheds were established at Mold Junction (to serve a large goods yard here), Rhyl, Denbigh, Llandudno Junction and Bangor. Loco sheds were also established in Chester to serve both the LNWR/LMS and the GWR.

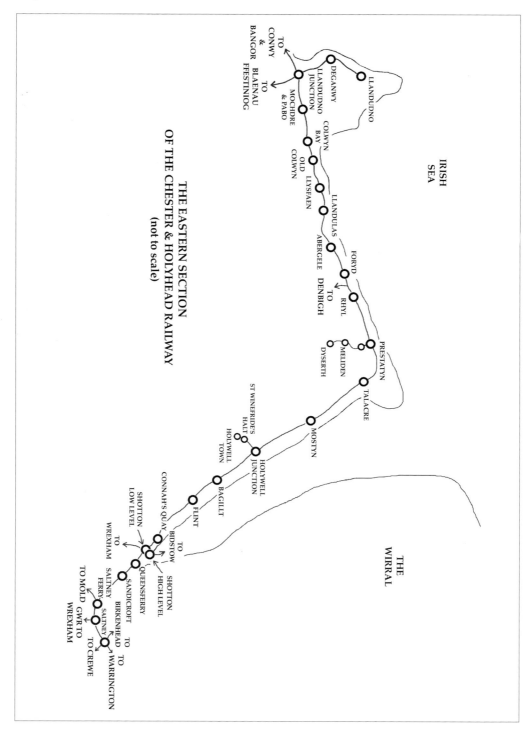

The eastern section of the Chester & Holyhead Railway from Chester to Llandudno Junction showing, where possible, the branches from Saltney Ferry, Holywell Junction, Prestatyn, Rhyl and Llandudno Junction. The Great Central line from Bidston, on the Wirral, to Wrexham on Shotton High Level is also shown. (Author's Collection)

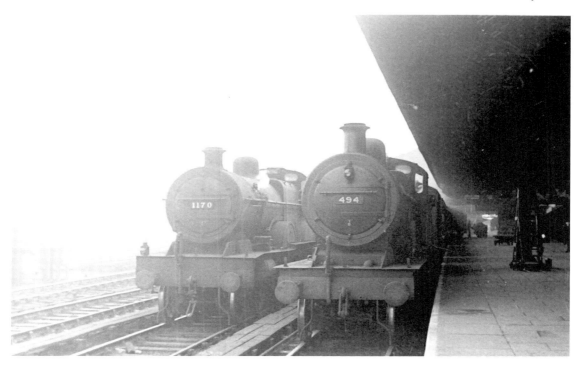

Although just over the border in England, Chester station was the meeting point of LNWR and GWR services into North Wales. Chester was of interest to the railway companies as early as the 1830s, but it was not until 1840 that the Chester & Birkenhead and Chester & Crewe railways opened their respective lines with their stations facing each other at Brook Street. A third company, the Shrewsbury & Chester, arrived six years later over the, as yet, incomplete Chester & Holyhead Railway. There was general agreement by 1845 that a joint station was required at Chester and authorisation for a new station, some 17 chains west of Brook Street, was approved. The first Chester & Holyhead trains used Brook Street for around five months until the, as yet, incomplete station was formally opened on 1 August 1848. The facade of the new Chester station, which faced the town, was one of the best works by C&HR architect, Francis Thompson. A 1,050-foot-long building was constructed, which fronted a 750-foot-long platform that handled all through traffic, with adjacent 290-foot bays to accommodate terminating trains. The Italianate-style main building was built in dun-coloured brick, relieved by stone facings. The two-storey section in the middle contained the usual station facilities with offices above. The effect of the length of the building was offset by pavilions with towers at the corners. Inside, a 60-foot-span iron roof was supported on the opposite platforms on a brick arcade, behind which stood a large carriage-storage shed. This original station worked for many years, but increasing traffic meant that the station was unable to cope. Discussions regarding extension of the station between the LNWR and GWR, two companies who had been bitter enemies since early railway days, were difficult, each coming up with proposals that were not suitable for the other. By 1890, a plan was finally agreed and, in July of that year, a new side of the station was brought into use so that Up trains could be dealt with on the new platform and Down trains using the original platform, scissors crossings built halfway along so that two trains could be accommodated on one platform face at any one time. Here, on 22 April 1947, just under a year before nationalisation, ex-MR 4-4-0s are seen at Chester. On the right is 2P 4-4-0 No. 494 having just brought in a train from Crewe, while waiting to take over, on the left is 4P Compound 4-4-0 No. 1170, then still under LMS auspices. (H. Casserley)

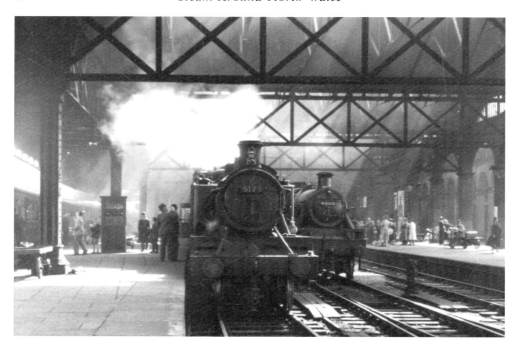

Under the roof at Chester are examples of both GWR and LMS tank locos that were used on local passenger services. On the left is ex-GWR Churchward 2-6-2 Prairie tank No. 5179, and on the right is ex-LMS Stanier 2-6-2 tank No. 40110. The GWR loco is at the head of a train for Birkenhead, while the LMS engine is awaiting its turn of duty, probably on a Mold-branch train. (D. Ibbotson)

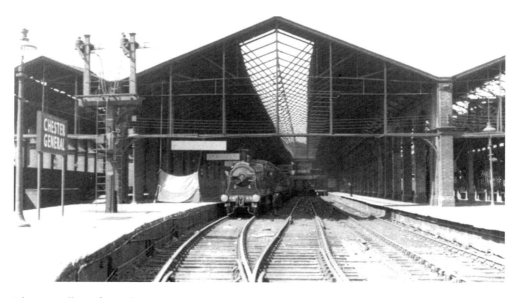

The overall roof at Chester station on 10 August 1963 with ex-Caledonian Railway 4-2-2, preserved in its Caledonian blue livery, on exhibition at the station. During this decade, some of the overall roof was removed and umbrella canopies replaced it. The glazing at the end of the roof had been removed by 1951. (H. Casserley)

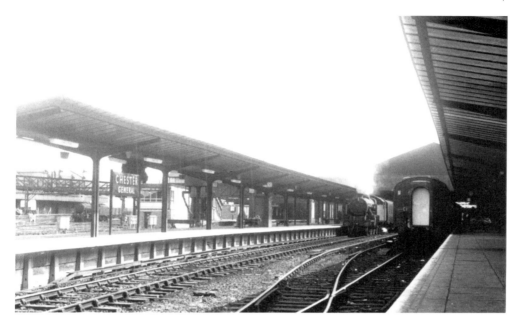

Waiting at Chester on 27 August 1964 is ex-LMS Stanier 2-6-4 tank No. 42459 at the head of a local service for Birkenhead. In view are the platform canopies which replaced the overall roof here. In the left background, a Stanier Black Five can be seen in the goods yard at the head of a freight train. (H. Casserley)

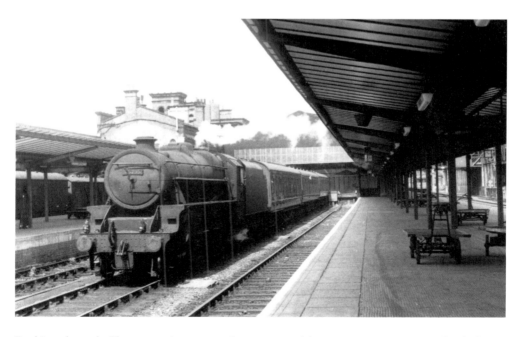

Rushing through Chester station, on 21 June 1966, with an excursion train to Llandudno is ex-LMS Black Five 4-6-0 No. 45295. The roofline of the main station building can be seen above the canopies on the left and glazing at the end of the overall roof here is still *in situ*. (H. Casserley)

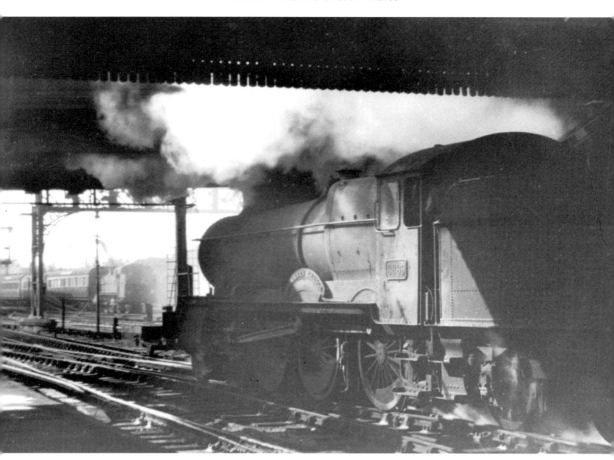

Departing from Chester with a train for Shrewsbury, where it will connect with the Cambrian Railways line to Aberystwyth and Pwllheli, is ex-GWR two-cylinder Grange Class 4-6-0 No. *6869 Resolven Grange*. The train will leave the C&HR line at Saltney and then call at Wrexham before entering Shropshire on its way to its destination at Shrewsbury. In the background is an ex-GWR Prairie tank at the head of a local train from Birkenhead Woodside. Shortly after the Shrewsbury & Chester Railway had opened, the Roodee Viaduct, which carries the railway over the River Dee before entering Chester, collapsed in May 1847 while an S&C train was crossing, killing six people. Stephenson's bridge, built of cast iron on stone abutments and piers, was found to be of poor design. The bridge was demolished later in the same year and was extensively rebuilt in wrought iron and brick in 1870–71. (D. Ibbotson)

Opposite page: A 1910 LNWR timetable for trains running from Crewe and Chester to Holyhead over the C&HR and connecting with packet boats to Ireland – the reason that this line was originally built. (Author's Collection)

CREWE, CHESTER, RHYL, COLWYN BAY, LLANDUDNO, CONWAY, BANGOR, HOLYHEAD, and DUBLIN.—L. & N. W.

Week Days.

Miles from Crewe.	Down.	aft	aft	aft	ngt.	mrn	mrn	ngt.	mrn	mrn	mrn	mrn	mrn	mrn	mrn	mrn
	Euston Station, 404 **London** .... dep.	8 45	1015	10 0	12r0	...	...	12h0	...	...	5 0	...	...	...	7 10	8 30
	404 Birmingham (New St.). "	1015	11 0	11o0	2A50	...	...	3l10	6 0	...	7 20	...	...	...	9 15	9 55
	517 Manchester (Lon. Rd.). "	1045	12v5	12r5	v	...	...	...	6 40	...	8 25	...	...	...	1010	1040
	Crewe .... dep.	12 7	1 25	2 5	5A0	...	...	7 20	8 15	...	9 25	...	...	...	1120	1148
3¾	Worleston	mrn	mrn	mrn	...	...	...	7 27	8 24	...	...	...	...	...	1127	...
8	Calveley	...	...	...	...	...	...	7 35	8 32	...	...	...	...	...	1134	...
10¾	Beeston Castle and Tarporley †	...	...	...	...	...	...	7 50	8 38	...	9 39	...	...	...	1139	...
14½	Tattenhall Road	...	...	...	...	...	...	7 58	8 47	...	...	...	...	...	1145	...
18	Waverton **456** .... [493	...	...	...	...	...	...	8 5	8 53	...	...	...	...	...	c	...
21¼	**Chester** ‖ **80, 478, 480, 482**, ar	1234	...	2 33	5A30	...	...	8 13	9 3	...	9 57	...	...	...	12 0	1215
—	492 Manchester (Exch.) .. dep.	1035	...	...	...	...	...	6 45	7 40	...	8 5	...	9 45	...	Stop	1045
—	492 Warrington (Bank Qy.) "	1157	t	...	...	...	...	7 34	8 17	...	9 5	...	1028	...	...	1130
—	482 Liverpool (Lime St.). " t	1055	j	1055 t	...	...	...	7 25	...	...	8 35	...	...	...	...	1110
—	481 Birkenhead (W'dside) "	1120	t	...	...	...	7 0	7 45	8 15	...	9 10	...	1035	1045	...	1115
—	**Chester** (General) .... dep.	1241		2 48	6 0	...	7 55	8 40	9 15	...	10 5	...	1110	1135	...	1223
27	Sandycroft	Irish Mail. Sleeping Saloons.	Irish Night Express. Sleeping Saloons.	...	6 10	...	8 5	8 50	9 25	...	...	...	...	1145	...	Breakfast and Luncheon Cars, London to Holyhead. Irish Mail.
28½	Queen's Ferry			...	6 14	...	8 9	8 54	9 29	...	...	...	...	1149	...	
29½	Shotton			...	6 17	...	8 12	Stop	9 32	...	...	...	...	1152	...	
30½	Connah's Quay **670**			...	6 21	...	8 16		9 36	...	...	...	...	1156	...	
33½	Flint			3 5	6 27	...	8 22	...	9 42	...	1022	...	...	12 1	...	
35½	Bagillt			...	6 34	...	8 29	...	9 49	...	...	...	...	12 9	...	
38	Holywell ††			...	6 39	...	8 34	...	9 55	...	...	...	1130	1213	...	
41½	Mostyn			...	6 45	...	8 42	...	10 2	...	...	...	...	1221	aft	
44½	Talacre			...	6 54	m	8 49	...	10 9	m	...	...	...	1229	m	
47½	Prestatyn **483**			...	7 0	8 30	8 55	...	1015	1030	...	...	1145	1235	1 17	
51¼	**Rhyl 476** .... arr.			3 30	7 8	8 38	9 3	...	1022	1038	1047	...	1153	1243	1 25	
	Rhyl dep.			3 35	7 12	Stop	9 7	...	1030	...	1050	...	1157	...	...	
52½	Foryd			...	7 16		9 11	...	1034	...	...	...	...	...	...	
55½	Abergele and Pensarn			...	7 22	...	9 17	...	1040	...	1057	...	12 5	...	...	
58	Llandulas			...	7 31	...	9 25	...	1047	...	11 4	...	...	...	...	
59	Llysfaen			...	7 35	mrn	9 30	mrn	1051	...	11 8	...	...	...	...	
60	Old Colwyn			...	7 40	m	9 34	m	1055	...	...	m	1215	...	...	
61½	**Colwyn Bay**			a	7 43	9 5	9 37	1010	1058	...	1113	1135	1219	...	...	
63½	Mochdre and Pabo .... [476			...	7 51	...	9 45	...	11 6	...	...	...	...	...	...	
65½	Llandudno Junction **471**, arr.			4 1	7 57	9 13	9 51	1018	1111	...	1122	1143	1228	...	...	
80½	471 Bettws-y-Coed ‡ .... arr.	...	...	5 20	9 10	...	1055	1055	...	...	12 4	...	1 10	...	...	...
69	**Llandudno** .... arr.	Arrives at Greenore at 6 55 mrn. on Mondays.	Except Monday Mornings.	6 50	8 25	9 25	1010	1030	1125	...	1137	1155	1240	...	...	...
	Llandudno dep.			...	7 50	Stop	9 35	Stop	...	...	11 5	...	1215	...	...	...
—	Llandudno Junction .... dep			4 8	8 7		9 56		...	...	1125	...	1235	...	...	...
66½	Conway			...	8 11	...	10 1	...	...	...	1128	...	1238	...	...	...
71	Penmaenmawr			...	8 20	...	1010	...	...	...	1137	...	1247	...	...	...
73¾	Llanfairfechan			...	8 26	...	1016	...	...	...	1144	...	1254	...	...	...
75½	Aber .... [471, 501			...	8 32	...	1022	...	...	...	1150	...	...	...	...	...
81	**Bangor**, for Beaumaris ¶. arr.			4 29	8 42	...	1032	...	...	...	12 0	...	1 6	...	...	...
89½	471 Carnarvon .... arr.			5 5	9 27	...	11 0	...	...	...	1228	...	1 37	...	...	...
108½	471 Afonwen .... "			5 56	1040	...	...	...	...	...	1 30	...	...	...	...	...
112½	471 Pwllheli .... "			6 10	1055	mrn	...	mrn	...	...	1 55	...	...	...	...	...
—	**Bangor** .... dep.			4 40	8 51	9 8	...	11 0	...	...	1210	...	...	...	...	...
82½	Menai Bridge ¶			...	8 54	9 12	...	11 4	...	...	1214	...	...	...	...	...
84½	Llanfair			...	9 1	9 19	...	1111	...	...	1220	...	...	...	...	...
87½	Gaerwen **476**			4 55	9 6	9 24	...	1118	...	...	1225	...	...	...	...	...
93¾	Bodorgan			...	9 24	One class only.	...	Thurs. only.	...	...	1239	...	...	...	...	...
96½	Ty Croes			...	9 32		...		...	...	1246	...	...	...	...	...
98½	Rhosneigr			...	9 36		...		...	...	1250	...	...	...	...	...
102½	Valley			...	9 45		...		...	...	1 0	...	...	...	...	...
105½	**Holyhead 920** .... arr.	2 17	3 30	5 35	9 54		...		...	...	1 8	...	...	...	...	2 5
165½	Kingstown Pier § .... arr.	5 30	...	...	...	...	...	...	...	...	...	...	...	...	...	5 0
170½	Dublin (by Steamer) .. "	6k0	7n30	...	...	...	...	...	...	...	...	...	...	...	...	5k30

Down.	aft	mrn	mrn	aft	aft	mrn	mrn	aft	aft	aft	aft	aft	aft	aft	aft
Euston Station, 404 **London** .... dep.	...	...	...	...	...	10v0	1037	...	...	...	1210	...	...	...	1 20
404 Birmingham (New St.). "	...	...	1115	...	...	...	1210	...	...	1 0	...	...	2 20	...	2 55
517 Manchester (Lon. Rd.). "	v	...	1150	...	...	1215	...	...	1240	s	2 10	...	2 45	...	...
Crewe .... dep.	...	...	1 0	...	...	1 15	...	...	2 3	...	3 15	...	3 55	...	...
Worleston	...	...	...	...	...	1 22	...	...	...	...	...	...	...	...	...
Calveley	...	...	...	...	...	1 29	...	...	...	...	...	...	...	...	...
Beeston Castle and Tarporley †	...	...	1 14	...	...	1 34	...	...	...	...	h	...	k	...	...
Tattenhall Road	...	...	...	...	...	1 40	...	...	...	...	...	...	...	...	...
Waverton **456** .... [493	...	...	...	...	...	f	...	...	...	...	...	...	...	...	...
Chester ‖ **80, 478, 480, 482**, ar	...	...	1 30	...	...	1 55	2 7	...	2 30	...	3 46	...	4 25	...	5 0
492 Manchester (Exch.) .. dep.	...	...	...	1225	...	Stop	1 5	...	...	...	Stop	...	2 40	...	3 40
492 Warrington (Bank Qy.) "	...	...	...	1230	1230		1 40	...	...	...		2 0	3 19	...	4 22
482 Liverpool (Lime St.). " t	...	...	...	1235	...	...	...	...	1 35	...	...	...	3 15	4 0	4 0
481 Birkenhead (W'dside) "	...	1155	...	1255	1255	...	1 35	...	...	...	...	2 35	3 38	...	4 35
Chester (General) .... dep.	1230	1240	...	1 40	1 40	...	2 15	...	2 40		...	3 5	4 30	4 42	5 10
Sandycroft	...	1250	...	Saturdays only.	1 50	...	Luncheon Car, London to Chester.	...	...	Saturdays only.	...	3 15	4 40	...	Irish Day Express.—Via Kingstown. Luncheon and Tea Cars, London to Holyhead.
Queen's Ferry	...	1254	...		1 54	...		...	...		...	3 19	4 44	...	
Shotton	...	1257	...		1 57	...		...	...		...	3 22	4 53	...	
Connah's Quay **670**	...	1 1	...		2 1	...		...	...		...	3 26	4 57	...	
Flint	...	1 6	...		2 7	...		...	...		...	3 31	5 2	...	
Bagillt	...	1 14	...		2 14	...		...	...		...	3 39	5 9	...	
Holywell ††	...	1 19	...		2 19	...		...	...		...	3 44	5 14	...	
Mostyn	...	1 26	...		2 26	...		...	...		...	3 52	5 21	...	
Talacre	...	1 34	...		2 34	...		m	...		...	3 59	5 29	b	
Prestatyn **483**	...	1 40	...	n	2 40	...		2 47	3 12		...	4 5	5 35	...	
Rhyl 476 .... arr.	1 10	1 48	...	2 15	2 48	...	2 50	2 55	3 20	3 25	...	4 13	5 43	5 19	
Rhyl dep.	1 14	1 53	...	2 17	...	...	2 53	Saturdays only.	3 23	3 28	...	4 28	Stop	5 21	
Foryd	...	1 57	...	...	...	...	...		...	...	...	4 32		...	
Abergele and Pensarn	1 21	2 3	...	...	...	...	3 0		...	...	...	4 38	...	5 27	
Llandulas	...	2 10	...	...	...	...	...		...	...	...	4 45	...	...	
Llysfaen	...	2 14	...	...	...	aft	...		...	...	aft	4 49	aft	...	
Old Colwyn	1 31	2 18	...	...	...	m	3 10		...	...	m	4 53	m	...	
Colwyn Bay	1 35	2 21	...	2 32	...	3 0	3 14		3 35	3 43	4 15	5 0	5 55	5 36	
Mochdre and Pabo .... [476	...	2 28	...	...	...	...	...		...	...	...	5 8	...	...	
Llandudno Junction **471**, arr.	1 44	2 33	...	...	...	3 8	3 23		3 45	3 53	4 23	5 13	6 3	5 45	
471 Bettws-y-Coed ‡ .... arr.	2 50	...	...	...	...	...	...	...	4 34	4 34	...	...	...	6 37	
Llandudno .... arr.	2 2	2 45	...	2 50	...	3 20	3 40	...	4 5	4 5	4 35	5 40	6 15	5 57	
Llandudno dep.	1 30	...	...	...	...	...	2 55	...	3 25	...	...	4 55	...	...	
Llandudno Junction .... dep	1 48	...	...	...	...	...	3 25	...	3 49	...	...	5 16	...	...	
Conway	1 52	...	...	...	...	...	3 29	...	3 53	...	...	5 20	...	...	
Penmaenmawr	2 1	...	...	...	...	...	3 38	...	4 2	...	...	5 29	...	...	
Llanfairfechan	2 7	...	...	...	...	...	3 44	...	4 8	...	...	5 35	...	...	
Aber .... [471, 501	2 13	...	...	...	...	...	...	...	4 14	...	...	5 41	...	...	
Bangor, for Beaumaris ¶. arr.	2 23	...	...	...	...	...	3 56	...	4 24	...	...	5 51	...	6 7	
471 Carnarvon .... arr.	2 51	...	...	...	...	...	4 30	...	5 1	...	...	...	...	6 32	...
471 Afonwen .... "	3 53	...	...	...	...	...	...	...	6 4	...	...	...	...	...	...
471 Pwllheli .... "	4 20	...	...	...	...	...	...	...	6 20	...	...	...	...	...	...
Bangor .... dep.	2 33	...	...	...	...	...	4 0	...	4 34	...	...	...	...	6 25	...
Menai Bridge ¶	2 36	...	...	...	...	...	4 4	...	4 38	...	...	...	...	6 29	...
Llanfair	2 42	...	...	...	...	...	4 10	...	4 45	...	...	...	...	6 36	...
Gaerwen **476**	2 47	...	...	...	...	...	4 15	...	4 50	...	...	...	...	6 41	...
Bodorgan	3 0	...	...	...	...	...	...	...	5 6	...	...	...	...	6 58	...
Ty Croes	3 6	...	...	...	...	...	...	...	5 12	...	...	...	...	7 6	...
Rhosneigr	3 10	...	...	...	...	...	...	...	5 16	...	...	...	...	7 10	...
Valley	3 20	...	...	...	...	...	...	...	5 26	...	...	...	...	7 20	...
Holyhead 920 .... arr.	3 28	...	...	...	...	...	...	...	5 34	...	...	...	...	7 28	6 55
Kingstown Pier § .... arr.	...	...	...	...	...	...	...	...	...	...	...	...	...	...	9 50
Dublin (by Steamer) .. "	...	...	...	...	...	...	...	...	...	...	...	...	...	...	k1020

☞ For Through Communication to the Interior of Ireland, see page 942.

CREWE, CHESTER, RHYL, COLWYN BAY, LLANDUDNO, CONWAY, BANGOR, HOLYHEAD, and DUBLIN.—L. & N. W.

Down.	Week Days—*Continued.* aft	aft	aft	aft	aft	aft	aft	aft	aft	aft	aft	aft	aft	aft	aft	aft	Sundays. Sat.	Sat.	Sat.	mrn	mrn	non	aft
Euston Station, 404 **London** .... dep.	...	...	...	1225	...	1 30	...	2 40	...	4 10	5 30	5 35	...	Saturdays only.	7 30	Breakfast Cars, Greenore to Belfast.	8 45	1015	10 0	...	...	12 0	6 15
404 Birmingham (New St.) "	...	...	...	...	...	3 30	...	...	...	5 50	6 50	7 55	8 40		...		1015	11 0	11 0	...	8 45	1 40	7 10
517 M'chester (Lon. Rd.) "	...	...	...	3 0	...	4 10	...	4 20	4e45	6 25	7 10	8 5	...		...		1045	12v5	12v5	...	9 0	1 0	4 25
Crewe .... dep	...	...	...	4 35	...	5 14	...	5 46	6 20	8 0	8 36	9 44	1021		...		12 7	1 25	2 5	...	1045	3 40	9 25
Worleston	...	...	...	4 42	...	5 24	...	...	6 27	...	...	9 51	...		...		Sun	Sun	Sun	...	...	3 48	...
Calveley	...	...	...	4 51	...	...	...	...	6 36	...	...	9 58	...		...		mrn	mrn	mrn	...	...	3 56	...
Beeston Castle & Tarporley †	...	...	...	4 58	...	5 34	...	...	6 43	8 15	...	10 4	...		...		...	...	...	...	...	4 4	9 39
Tattenhall Road	...	...	...	5 5	...	...	...	...	6 50	...	...	1011	...		...		...	...	...	...	...	4 11	...
Waverton **456** .... [482, 493	...	...	...	5 11	...	c	...	...	6 56	...	...	1017	...		...		...	...	...	...	...	4 18	...
Chester ‖ **80, 478, 480**, arr.	...	...	...	5 21	...	5 55	...	6 16	7 5	8 32	9 4	1026	1049		11 7		1234	...	2 33	...	1115	4 30	9 55
492 Manchester (Ex.) dep.	...	...	...	4 55	...	...	...	...	5 10	7 15	...	Stop	...	9 30		9 30	1035	i	...	7 50	...	...	...
492 Warrington (B.Q.) "	...	...	...	4 40	...	...	...	5e30	6 4	7 57	8 10		...	1018		1018	1157	i	...	8 42	...	...	...
482 Liverpool (Lime St.) "	...	...	...	...	...	5 5	...	...	6 20	7 20	...	...	9 40	9 40		9 40	1055	j	1055 i	...	...	...	...
481 Birkenhead* .... "	...	...	...	4 45	...	5 25	...	5 55	6 35	7 35	8 30	...	10 0	10 0		10 0	1120	i	...	8 35	...	4 15	...
Chester (General) ..... dep.	...	5 15	5 20	5 46	...	6 10	...	6 40	8 0	8 40	9 25	...	1038	1110		1118	1241	...	2 48	9 45	1125	6 0	...
Sandycroft	...	...	5 30	...	...	...	...	6 50	8 10	...	9 35	...	Except Saturdays between Chester and Holyhead.	1120	Except Saturdays. Dining Car from London.	Greenore Boat Express.	Irish Mail. Sleeping Saloons.	Irish Night Express. Sleeping Saloons.	...	9 56	...	6 10	...
Queen's Ferry	...	...	5 34	...	...	...	...	6 54	8 15	...	9 40	...		1125					...	10 0	...	6 15	...
Shotton	...	...	5 37	...	...	...	...	6 58	8 19	...	9 43	...		1132					...	10 3	...	6 18	...
Connah's Quay **670**	...	...	5 41	...	...	...	...	7 2	8 23	...	9 47	...		1136					...	10 7	...	6 22	...
Flint	...	5 30	5 46	...	...	...	...	7 7	8 30	...	9 52	...		1141					3 5	1015	...	6 27	...
Bagillt	...	...	5 54	...	...	...	...	7 15	8 37	...	10 0	...		1149					...	1021	...	6 36	...
Holywell ††	...	...	5 59	...	...	...	...	7 19	8 42	9 0	10 5	...		1154					...	1027	...	6 41	...
Mostyn	...	d	6 7	...	...	...	...	7 26	8 50	...	1013	aft		12 2					...	1037	...	6 50	...
Talacre	...	...	6 14	...	...	...	m	7 35	8 57	...	...	m		...					...	...	...	...	...
Prestatyn **483**	...	5 51	6 19	...	...	6 45	7 35	7 41	9 4	9 15	1023	9 57		1212					...	1049	...	7 0	...
Rhyl 476 .... arr.	...	5 58	6 28	6 20	...	6 54	7 43	7 49	9 12	9 23	1031	10 5		1220		1155			3 30	1059	12 2	7 9	...
Rhyl dep.	...	6 1	...	6 22	...	6 59	Stop	...	...	9 28	...	☞ Saturdays only.		...		1158			3 35	...	12 5	7 10	...
Foryd	...	...	...	...	...	7 4		...	...	...	...			...		...			...	...	...	...	...
Abergele and Pensarn	...	6 7	...	6 28	...	7 9	...	...	...	9 36	...			...		...			...	...	...	7 18	...
Llandulas	...	6 14	...	...	...	7 17	...	...	...	9 45	...			...		...			...	...	...	...	...
Llysfaen	...	...	...	...	...	7 21	aft	...	...	...	...			...		...			...	...	...	...	...
Old Colwyn	...	6 20	...	...	...	7 25	m	...	...	9 50	...			...		...			...	...	...	7 31	...
Colwyn Bay	...	6 24	...	6 38	6 46	7 28	7 50	...	...	9 53	...			...		...			a	...	1220	7 34	...
Mochdre and Pabo .... [476	...	...	...	...	...	7 36	...	...	...	...	...			...		...			...	...	...	...	...
Llandudno Junc. **471**, arr.	...	6 33	...	...	6 54	7 42	7 58	...	...	10 5	...			...		...			4 1	...	1229	7 45	...
471 Bettws-y-Coed ‡ .. arr.	...	...	...	...	7 35	...	8 56	...	...	...	...		...	...	...	...	...	...	5 44	...	...	...	...
Llandudno .... arr.	...	6 45	...	6 55	...	8 0	8 10	...	...	1025	...		...	...	...	Arrives at Greenore at 6 mrn. (except on Sundays).	...	...	...	...	1245	8 0	...
Llandudno dep.	5 45	...	...	...	6 35	7 25	...	...	...	9 50	...		...	...	...		...	...	...	...	...	7 30	...
Llandudno Junction .. dep.	6 5	...	...	...	6 57	7 47	...	...	...	1010	...		...	...	...		...	...	4 8	...	1222	7 48	...
Conway	6 9	...	...	...	7 1	7 51	...	...	...	1014	...		...	...	...		...	...	...	...	1236	7 52	...
Penmaenmawr	6 18	...	...	...	7 10	8 1	...	...	...	1024	...		...	...	...		...	...	...	...	...	8 2	...
Llanfairfechan	6 24	...	...	...	7 15	8 8	...	...	...	1030	...		...	...	...		...	...	...	...	...	8 8	...
Aber .... [471, 501	6 30	...	...	...	...	8 14	...	...	...	...	...		...	...	...		...	...	...	...	...	...	...
Bangor, for Beaumaris ¶ arr.	6 40	...	...	...	7 27	8 24	...	...	...	1045	...		...	...	...	1237	...	...	4 29	...	1 3	8 28	...
471 Carnarvon .... arr.	...	...	...	...	7 52	8 50	...	...	s	1111	...	...	...	...	...	...	...	...	5 5	...	...	9 26	...
471 Afonwen .... "	...	...	...	...	8 54	...	...	...	...	...	...	...	...	...	...	...	...	...	8 47	...	...	...	...
471 Pwllheli .... "	...	...	...	...	9 12	...	...	...	...	...	...	...	...	...	...	...	...	...	8 58	...	...	...	...
Bangor .... dep	...	...	...	...	...	8 36	...	...	...	...	...	...	...	...	...	1240	...	...	4 40	...	1 8	8 40	...
Menai Bridge ¶	...	...	...	...	...	8 41	...	...	...	...	...	...	...	...	...	...	...	...	...	...	...	8 44	...
Llanfair	...	...	...	...	...	8 49	...	...	...	...	...	...	...	...	...	...	...	...	...	...	...	...	...
Gaerwen **476**	...	...	...	...	...	8 54	...	...	...	...	...	...	...	...	...	...	...	...	...	...	...	...	...
Bodorgan	...	...	...	...	...	9 8	...	...	...	...	...	...	...	...	...	...	...	...	...	...	...	...	...
Ty Croes	...	...	...	...	...	9 16	...	...	...	...	...	...	...	...	...	...	...	...	...	...	...	...	...
Rhosneigr	...	...	...	...	...	9 20	...	...	...	...	...	...	...	...	...	...	...	...	...	...	...	...	...
Valley	...	...	...	...	...	9 30	...	...	...	...	...	...	...	...	...	...	...	...	...	...	...	...	...
Holyhead 920 .... arr.	...	...	...	...	...	9 38	...	...	...	...	...	...	1240	...	...	1 15	2 17	3 30	5 35	...	1 48	9 20	...
Kingstown Pier § .. arr.	...	...	...	...	...	...	...	...	...	...	...	...	...	...	...	...	5 30	...	...	...	4 45	...	...
Dublin (by Steamer) "	...	...	...	...	...	...	...	...	...	...	...	...	...	...	...	...	6k0	7n30	...	...	5k30	...	...

SUNDAY TRAINS.
Special attention is directed to the **NOTE on page 1**, referring to long distance journeys commenced on the evening of Saturday or Sunday.

NOTES.

- **a** Stop to set down.
- **A** Except Mondays.
- **b** Stops to set down from Liverpool on notice being given to the Guard.
- **c** Stop to set down from beyond Crewe on notice being given to the Guard.
- **d** Stops to set down from London and Manchester on informing the Guard.
- *e* Except Saturdays.
- **f** Stops to set down on notice being given to the Guard.
- **h** Stops to set down from London on informing the Guard.
- *h* Sunday nights only.
- *i* Saturday night times.
- **j** Leaves Liverpool at 11 55 aft., via Crewe.
- **k** Stops on Mondays and Saturdays.
- *k* Westland Row.
- *l* Mondays only.
- **m** Motor Car, one class only.
- **n** Stop to set down from Liverpool or Manchester on notice being given to the Guard.
- *n* North Wall.
- *o* Leaves at 10 15 aft. on Sundays.
- *r* Leaves at 11 55 aft. on Sundays.
- *s* Saturdays only.
- *t* Leaves Warrington at 11 37, Liverpool at 10 45, and Birkenhead at 10 aft. on Sundays.
- *v* 1st and 3rd class.
- *z* Except Sunday nights.
- * Woodside Station.
- † Station 2 miles from Tarporley.
- ‡ Station for Capel Curig.
- § By Steamer.
- ‖ General Station; about ¾ mile to Northgate Station (Cheshire Lines).
- ¶ Station for Beaumaris (5 miles).—For **Omnibus Service** between Bangor and Beaumaris see page 479.
- †† Station 1½ miles from Holywell.

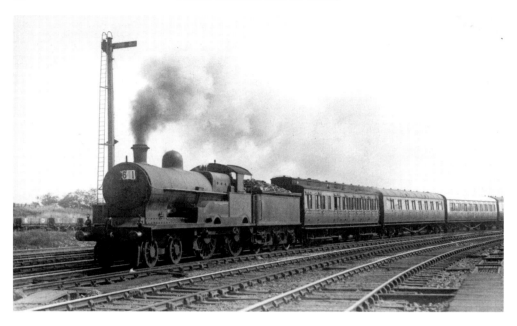

Departing from Chester with an excursion for Llandudno is ex-LNWR George V Class 4-4-0, as LMS No. 5303. From Chester station, the train would run through two tunnels then pass the three-rise lock of the Shropshire Union Canal on the left, then over a high embankment and forty-nine-arch Roodee Viaduct, which also gives a good view of Chester racecourse to the left. Widening of the railway from Saltney Junction, authorised by an Act of 1893, allowed the GWR to build a widening structure next to Roodee Viaduct, which was opened in 1904. This section, nearest to the racecourse, is still open while the original was closed to traffic under rationalisation at Chester in 1979. (Author's Collection)

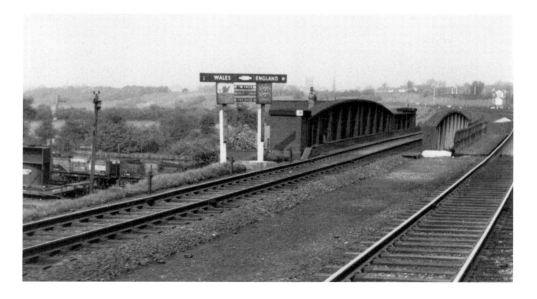

The sign that shows the border between England and Wales, seen here on 23 April 1959. This signpost has since disappeared. (Author's Collection)

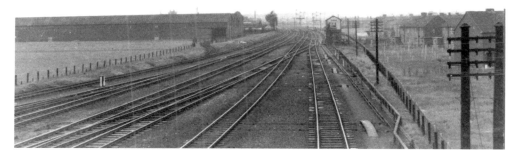

Saltney Ferry, seen here, is the junction of the C&HR and the S&C (the LNWR and GWR), the latter line running to Wrexham and Shrewsbury and then to Wolverhampton, Birmingham and Paddington, while the former route incorporates the line from Holyhead to Chester, thence to Crewe, Stafford and Euston. Thus, strong competition existed between the Euston and Paddington rivals until the old GWR line was closed in the 1960s. (Author's Collection)

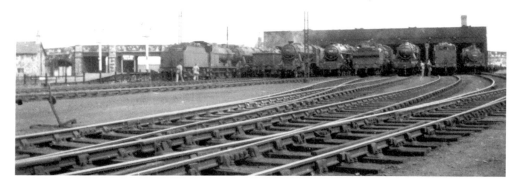

The loco shed at Mold Junction as it appeared in the mid-1950s. The shed here served the large marshalling yard at Mold Junction, which was also the point where the branch to Mold and Denbigh left the main C&HR, which will be discussed later. Mold Junction marshalling yard was responsible for sorting freight traffic from all parts of North Wales, including slate from the quarries in the north-west of Wales, and its sidings could hold up to 900 wagons. The eight-road loco shed had an allocation of engines that were suited to its role as this sample allocation for January 1960 indicates. At this time, the shed was coded 6B:

Ex-LMS Stanier 2-6-0	42945, 42965, 42967, 42971, 42973, 42976, 42981, 42982
Ex-LMS 4F 0-6-0	44065, 44445, 44493
Ex-LMS Black Five 4-6-0	44800, 44917, 44935, 45028, 45031, 45042, 45043, 45055, 45070, 45072, 45225, 45247, 45275, 45325, 45345
Ex-LMS Patriot 4-6-0	45501 *St Dunstans**, 45511 *Isle of Man**, 45546 *Fleetwood**, 4548 *Lytham St Annes**
Ex-LMS Jinty 0-6-0T	47269, 47615, 47646, 47650
Ex-LMS 8F 2-8-0	48054, 48074, 48166, 48175, 48246, 48259, 48264, 48323, 48458, 48697, 48749, 48753, 48754, 48771
Ex WD 2-8-0	90147, 90187, 90227, 90532, 90566, 90606, 90702
	Total: 55

*The Patriot Class 4-6-0s only stayed at Mold Junction for four months and were the only named locos allocated to the shed. (R. Carpenter)

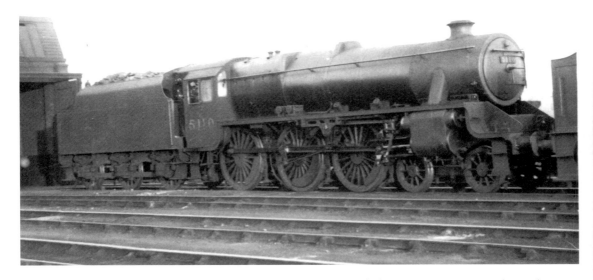

Outside Mold Junction shed on 6 July 1935 is LMS Stanier Black Five 4-6-0 No. 5110, then only a few years old. The engine stayed in North Wales for most of its working life and retired from Holyhead shed in March 1964. As 45110, the engine found her way into preservation on the Severn Valley Railway at Bridgnorth, Shropshire, who renamed her *RAF Biggin Hill*, and she can still be found on steam excursions on the main line. (A. G. Ellis Collection)

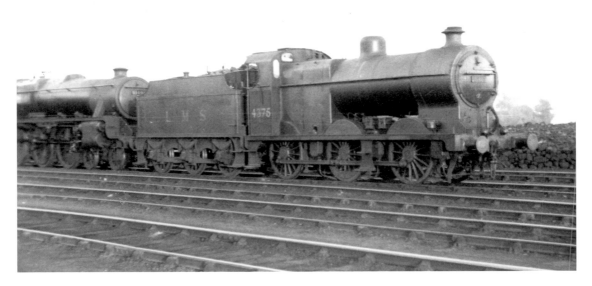

On the same day, LMS Fowler 4F 0-6-0 No. 4375 awaiting her turn of duty. These engines, along with Black Five 4-6-0s, Stanier 8F 2-8-0s and the ubiquitous 3F Jinty shunting tanks, were the mainstay of locos at Mold Junction shed. (A. G. Ellis Collection)

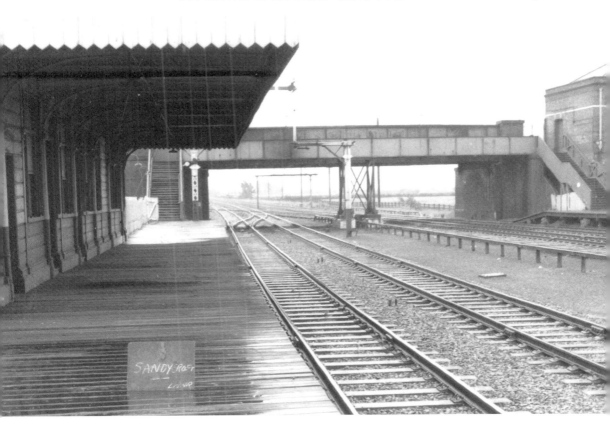

A view of Sandycroft station looking in the direction of Chester shortly before closure in 1966. An experimental station was opened at Sandycroft on 1 March 1884, which consisted of basic two-sleeper platforms with small wooden shelters and a cast-iron footbridge. It stood on the Queensferry side of a level crossing that was formed as part of the Hawarden–Sandicroft Quay road. The station here remained in existence until the C&HR line was quadrupled as far as Llandudno Junction in 1900. As part of this quadrupling, a new, much-enlarged station was opened at Sandycroft. A road overbridge, seen in this view, replaced the level crossing and on 1 June 1899 longer platforms were provided on the outer slow lines and standard LNWR wooden buildings were placed on the platforms. A brick-built booking office was provided at road level, on the right as seen here. From the booking office, a long footbridge connected the platforms. The LNWR also provided a timber- and brick-built signal box, which was built between the Up and Down main lines, opposite the platforms, and a row of employees' cottages were situated behind the Chester-bound platform. Less than a mile west of Sandycroft station were Dundas Sidings, which served the coal mines of Admiral Dundas. These sidings were greatly increased in size during the 1900 track-widening scheme and became important during the First World War as munitions production expanded in the area. (Author's Collection)

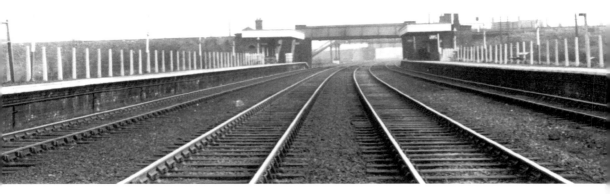

From Sandycroft, the C&HR passed through the small station at Queensferry. The little station opened with the line in 1848 and its Thompson-designed main building was situated on the Up side. When the line was quadrupled here, the Thompson building was demolished and a new booking office was provided at the roadside on the Down side of the line. After Queensferry, the line enters Shotton (Low Level). The High-Level station at Shotton, the bridge of which can be seen in the background, served the Manchester, Sheffield & Lincolnshire Railway, later the Great Central Railway, line between Bidston and Wrexham. The Low-Level LNWR Shotton station was one of the last opened on the C&HR when it came into existence on 1 April 1907 and was placed immediately west of the GCR High-Level station. The station consisted of platforms to the outer lines, which were connected via a footbridge. The platforms were of brick construction with station buildings of timber, but there was no road access, passengers reaching the LNWR station via the GCR High-Level station. The station was closed in 1966 as Chester and Holyhead rationalisation took effect, but it was reopened in 1972 to serve the British Steel (ex-John Summers Ltd) works nearby. The C&HR rationalisation had meant that the old four-track formation had been reduced to two and timber platforms for the new station were constructed on the old trackbed. The timber platforms have since been replaced by ones of concrete. The preserved BR 9F 2-10-0 No. 92203, now named *Black Prince*, was working at the steelworks when she was withdrawn in 1967. She now works on the East Somerset Railway and is owned by the artist David Shepherd. Back in 1937, there was a major strike at Shotton steelworks, and the management brought in 'blackleg' labour from along the coast. In an attempt to deter such labour from turning up for work, the strikers lined the railway near the station and stoned trains bringing in 'blackleg' labour to the works. Even the stationmaster was pelted as he closed the train doors. Eventually, police were brought in to quell the trouble. (H. Casserley)

Opposite above: Connah's Quay station when first opened on 25 May 1906. The station in this view replaced the original, which had opened on 1 September 1870. The replacement station, seen here, had brick buildings, which had been designed by C&HR architect Francis Thompson. Connah's Quay itself was developed by the Wrexham, Mold & Connah's Quay Railway Company, later to become part of the GCR, and became a customer of the LNWR with the opening of Connah's Quay station. Just west of the station, a branch curved away to Connah's Quay that was controlled by Connah's Quay No. 2 signal box. The station closed to passengers in 1966 and was soon demolished. (Author's Collection)

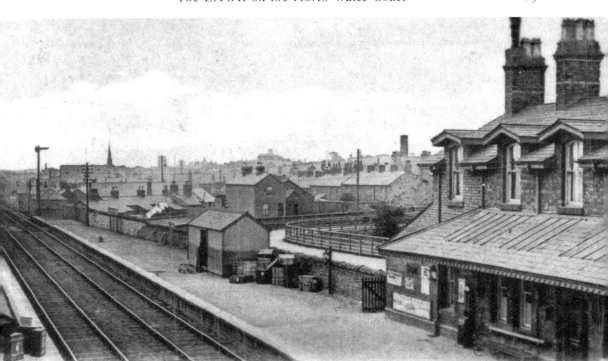

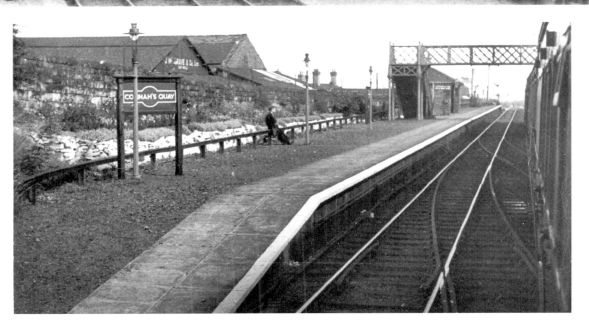

Another view of Connah's Quay station as it appeared on 10 August 1953 and looking towards Chester. Just west of the station stands Rockliffe Hall power station, which had its own sidings to supply the power station with coal from local collieries. From Connah's Quay to Bagillt, the four-track formation was reduced to two tracks. The power station now no longer exists; its cooling towers have been demolished. From the power station, the line passes through a wooded cutting and then through the 98-yard Rockliffe Tunnel on its way to Flint. (R. Casserley)

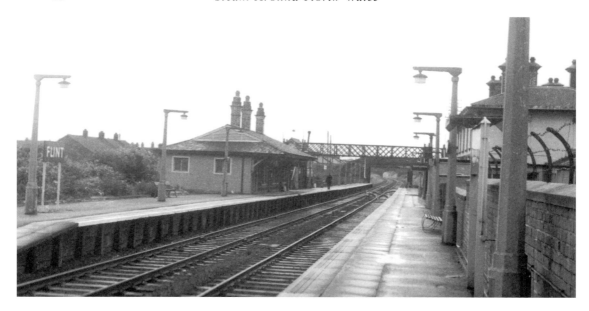

Flint station looking towards Chester as it appeared on 21 June 1966. On entering the station from Chester, the remains of the Plantagenet castle, once on the bank of the Dee Estuary, to which the line has run parallel since leaving Connah's Quay, is visible on the right. During the nineteenth century, Flint was a very busy port and in the 1880s it supplied Muspratt's chemical works, which in those days was the largest employer in the area. The works was situated just west of the station and had become part of the Courtalds group. Like many industries in the locality, the works had gone by the 1990s. In 1979, Flint station (now spelt Fflint) acquired a park-and-ride facility and its Down platform was extended. (H. Casserley)

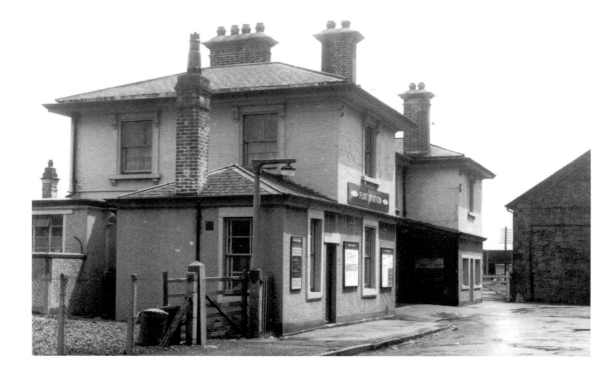

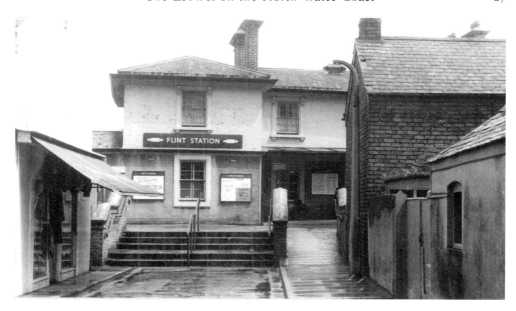

Opposite below and above: Two views of the exterior of Flint station, whose main building seen here was designed by the C&HR architect Francis Thompson and was opened with the station in 1848. The building is still *in situ* at the present time. (H. Casserley)

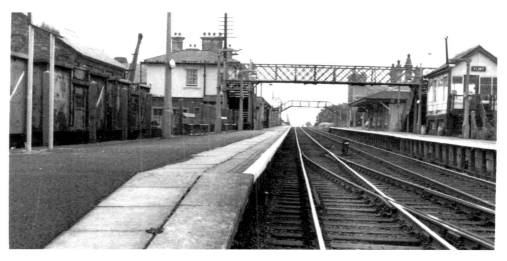

Flint station facing west showing the station footbridge in the distance and a footbridge in the foreground that provided a public right of way over the railway. The goods shed, just visible on the left and behind the main station building, was built in 1860. Just beyond Flint, the line was quadrupled to Llandulas, a distance of some 24 miles, between 1896 and 1915 and runs on a straight course past marshland at the mouth of the Dee, and the Wirral can also be seen in the distance on the right. On the right, in this view, is the signal box built by the LMS in 1932, which controlled movements at Flint. It replaced an original C&HR example which controlled a level crossing that was once situated here until replaced by a road overbridge. Once this overbridge had made the level crossing redundant, the station platforms were extended across the old crossing site. The station footbridge at Flint was originally located at Sandycroft and was moved here in 1901. (Author's Collection)

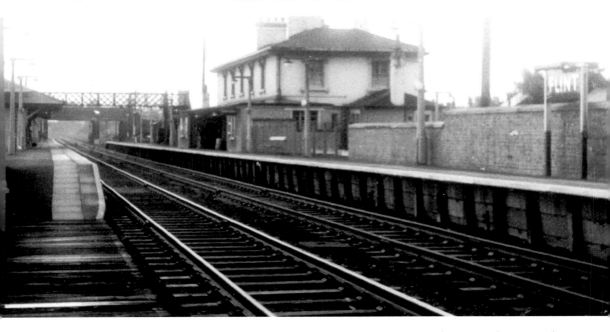

Another view of Flint station, looking towards Chester as it appeared on 11 July 1960. The road overbridge that replaced the level crossing can be seen in the distance beyond the lattice footbridge serving the station platforms. To the left is the waiting shelter on the Up side, which was built in 1883. (R. Casserley)

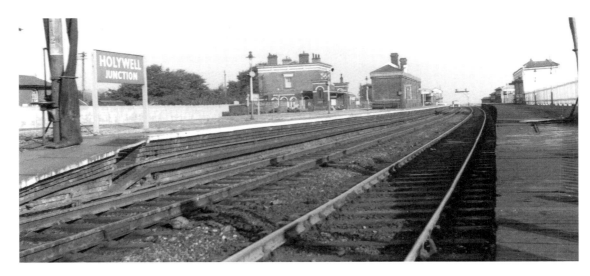

The substantial station of Holywell Junction as it appeared on 10 July 1960. Between Flint and Holywell Junction, the C&HR line passed through the station at Bagillt, which lay in the middle of what was once Bettinsfield Colliery and was the reason for its existence. Bagillt station itself was closed in 1966 and only the remains of the Up platform are a reminder that it once existed. The station at Holywell Junction was opened in 1848 and its Italianate-style main building was designed by Francis Thompson and is the subject of a preservation order since closure in 1966. The station became a junction with the opening of the short branch to Holywell Town in 1912. (R. Casserley)

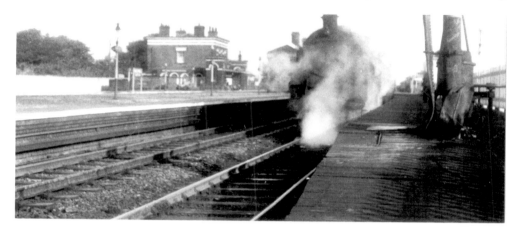

On 10 July 1960, an unidentified ex-LMS tank loco heads a local train to Chester and has just arrived from Rhyl. The station at Holywell had undergone several changes since opening in 1848, not least when the line was quadrupled, which necessitated two extra platforms. A subway, with inclined footways, connected all of the platforms, so there was no need for a footbridge. New buildings were provided for the newly added platforms, in brick on the island platform and timber on the Up platform, all being of standard LNWR design. The station was also provided with substantial goods facilities, complete with a goods shed. Since closure nothing, except the main station building, remains of what was a substantial C&HR station. (R. Casserley)

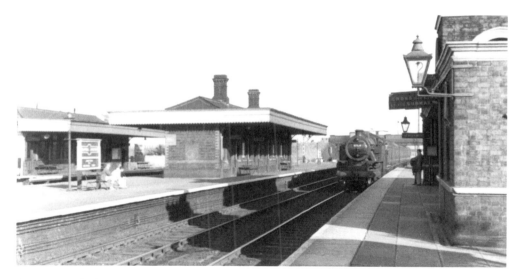

Arriving with the Chester–Rhyl train on 10 August 1953 is ex-LMS Fairburn 2-6-4 tank No. 42159. The original Italianate main building is just visible on the Down platform and the LNWR building can be seen on the island platform. Until 1877, when the station area was redeveloped, there was a right-angled crossing that ran right through the centre of the station and gave access to the goods yard by way of a reversal from the main line, with a small signal box on the Up side also controlling a level crossing with five lines, which must have created many problems for road traffic when shunting operations were going on. After 1877, goods traffic approached the yard from the Mostyn end of the station thereby getting rid of the right-angled crossing. The level crossing was rationalised at the same time, but finally disappeared when a road overbridge, seen in the background, was opened in 1878. (R. Casserley)

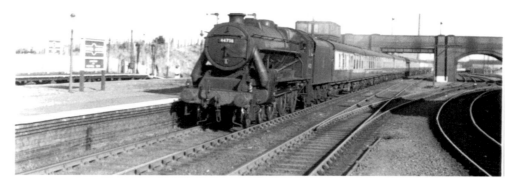

Caprotti valve-geared ex-LMS Stanier Black Five 4-6-0 No. 44738 is approaching Holywell Junction station as it heads an excursion from Manchester to Llandudno on 10 August 1953. The road overbridge, which replaced the level crossing here, is seen with the train passing under. (H. Casserley)

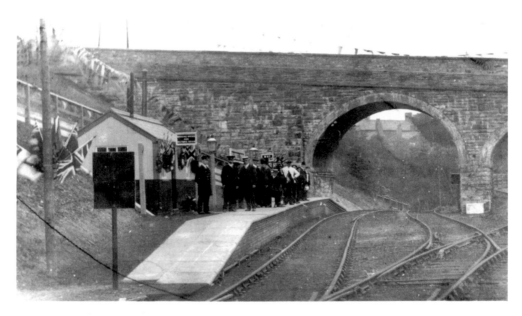

Opened in 1912, the Holywell Juction to Holywell Town branch was a little over a mile long and was on a gradient of 1 in 27, which made it one of the steepest gradients worked by locomotives in Great Britain. There was only one intermediate station on the line, at St Winefride's situated some distance from the famous well. Holywell itself was situated in a narrow valley that was packed with lead mines, had copper-smelting facilities and was involved in paper and flannel making. A 3-foot narrow gauge railway had been operating between Holywell and the River Dee at Greenfield to carry mined lead and limestone from the hills above the town. It was soon apparent that something better was required and, in 1864, the Holywell Railway Company proposed a line that connected with the C&HR, a working agreement being reached with the LNWR. The scheme was, however, abandoned after four years. In 1906, the LNWR obtained authority to build the Holywell branch, but appeared to forget about it for a while. However, once opened, the branch did much for the local economy. Trains started from a bay next to the side wall of the main building at the Chester end of Holywell Junction station, all trains being 'push-pull' fitted, the loco always at the main-line end of the formation. Here, on the first day of services, passengers are waiting at Holywell Town for the train from Holywell Junction. (Author's Collection)

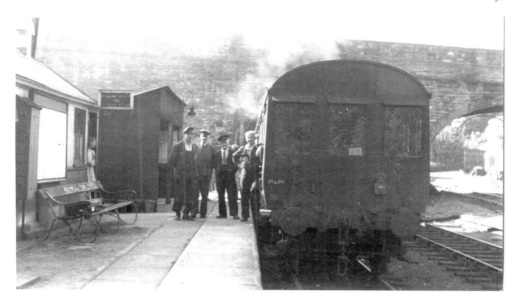

Holywell Town station on 10 August 1953, only a year before the line closed to passengers, with the train about to depart back to the junction. Train and station staff are posing before the train leaves. Despite high hopes for the branch, passenger services declined rather quickly, the situation not being helped by the fact that the LNWR operated a bus service to Holywell. Freight services survived until 1957, after which the junction was removed in 1958 and little now remains of Holywell Town station apart from a section of the platform under the overbridge. (H. Casserley)

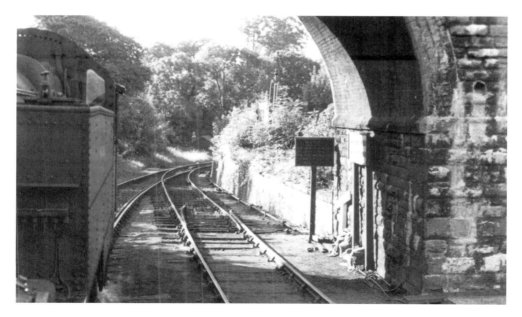

Departing from Holywell Town station on 10 August 1953, the little train is headed by ex-LMS Ivatt 2-6-2 tank No. 41324. Over the years, several tank locos operated the service between Holywell Junction and Holywell Town. In the early years, LNWR 2-4-2 tanks were used until replaced by LNWR 0-6-2 Coal Tanks. In BR days, Ivatt tanks operated the service until closure. All engines used on the branch were motor-fitted to save running round at the termini. (H. Casserley)

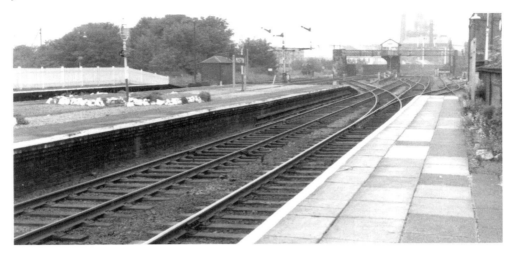

Back on the main line and the next station after Holywell Junction was at Mostyn, seen here looking towards Chester in the 1950s. Opened in 1848, goods facilities were provided from the early days with a goods shed being provided at the Holywell end of the station and livestock facilities at the other end. There were three exchange sidings on the Up side to serve the Darwen and Mostyn Iron Company, whose foundry can be seen in the background, and Mostyn Docks. The main station building was another of Francis Thompson's built in a 'grand' style, Mostyn Estates having wanted a 'first class' station here. The railway here was quadrupled, the work being completed on 22 June 1902, and an island platform was added to the station. Closed to passengers in 1966, nothing now remains of Mostyn station. (Author's Collection)

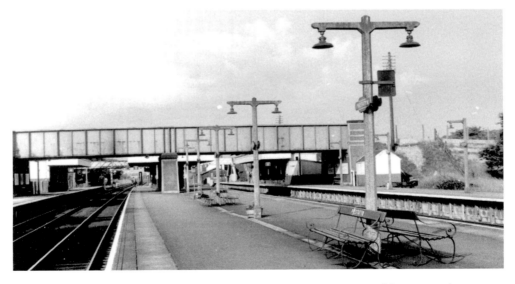

Prestatyn station as it appeared on 25 June 1966. Between Mostyn and Prestatyn, there was a small station at Talacre, which was opened in 1903 after quadrupling, closing in 1966. Talacre marked the end of industrial north-east Wales and, as the line curves gently west, the world of the holidaymaker now encroaches as rows of caravans can be seen on each side of the railway right through to the outskirts of Colwyn Bay. Tourism is a large part of the economy all the way through the remainder of North Wales, the railway being responsible for the growth of the holiday industry. (H. Casserley)

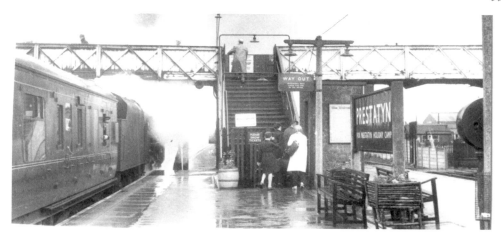

Departing from Prestatyn station on 25 June 1966 is ex-LMS Black Five 4-6-0 with the 11.00 Rhyl–Manchester train; the day appears to be a typical wet early summer day. Prestatyn was opened with the C&HR in 1848 and became the first of the holidaymaking destinations. There was another level crossing here until replaced by a road overbridge in 1897. The line between here and Rhyl was quadrupled by 1901 just as Prestatyn was becoming popular as a holiday destination. After the Grouping, the LMS went into partnership with Thomas Cook to develop a holiday camp at Prestatyn as a way of generating extra traffic. The camp opened in June 1939, just before the Second World War broke out. Containing hundreds of chalets, a week's holiday cost £3 13s 6d. The camp was taken over by the military during the war and never returned to the LMS. Pontins operated the camp as a holiday centre at Prestatyn in the post-war years. (H. Casserley)

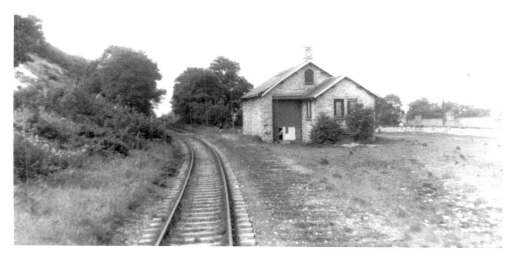

Meliden station on the Dyserth branch as it appeared on 18 July 1963. Constructed to tap lead and haematite in the Prestatyn Valley, the LNWR opened a 3-mile single-track branch between Prestatyn and Dyserth in 1869. From 1905 a passenger service was operated from a bay at the western end of Prestatyn station to Dyserth using steam railmotor cars. By 1928, three intermediate halts had been added. The steam railmotors continued to operate the passenger service until replaced by loco-hauled stock. Just before closure to passengers in 1930, buses operated by the Crosville bus company, of which 50 per cent was owned by the LMS, ran passenger services up the Prestatyn Valley. Freight continued to use the line until 1964, and the line then became a private siding until 1973. (R. Casserley)

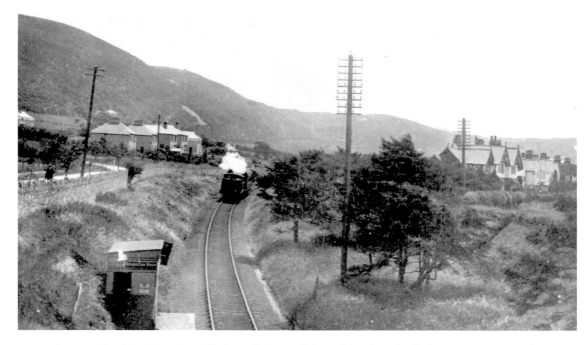

Approaching Rhuddlan Road Halt on the Dyserth branch is a loco-hauled passenger train in the final year of services on the line. The halt here looks totally deserted, buses, no doubt, having taken the passengers away from the railway. (Author's Collection)

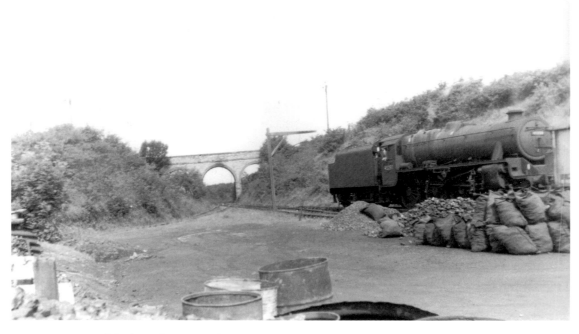

Terminus of the branch at Dyserth on 18 July 1963 with ex-LMS Black Five 4-6-0 resting as it awaits its turn of duty. (R. Casserley)

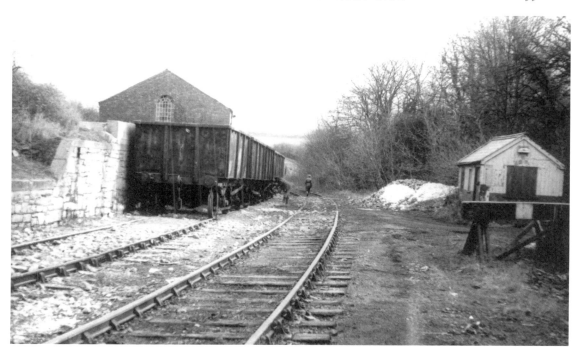

Dyserth station in the 1950s with wagons sitting on the goods siding awaiting collection. (Author's Collection)

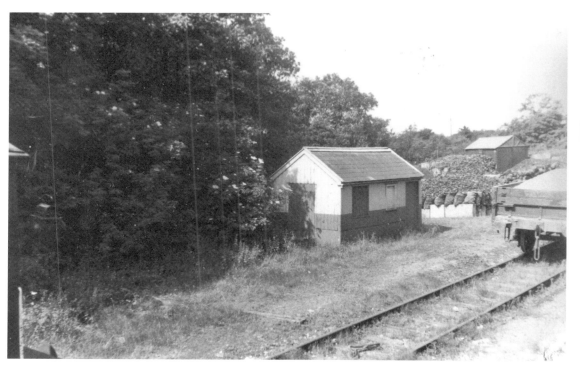

The simple booking office, long since out of use, at Dyserth on 18 July 1963. (R. Casserley)

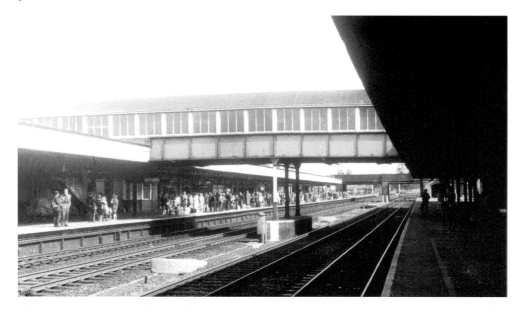

The important station of Rhyl lies 3¾ miles west of Prestatyn. It is still one of the big four revenue earners for the railway along the coast. In 1938, 750,000 passengers arrived at Rhyl; 639,000 between May and September. Even today, there are always plenty of people waiting to board trains at Rhyl. Here, on 19 August 1964, there are plenty of passengers waiting to board trains after spending a summer holiday in the town. Rhyl was also provided with a three-road loco shed, which provided motive power for local traffic and shunting in the goods yard. (H. Casserley)

Coded 6K, its allocation in January 1960 was as follows:

Ex-LMS 3F 0-6-0	43618
Ex-LMS 4F 0-6-0	43981, 44367
Ex-LMS 3F 0-6-0T	47350
Ex-L&Y 3F 0-6-0	52119, 52162, 52438
Ex-MR 2F 0-6-0	58287
BR Class 2 2-6-0	78031, 78055, 78056
	Total: 11

The shed also had an allocation of BR Class 4 4-6-0s between 1957 and 1959, and from June 1960 to September 1962. The shed was finally closed in February 1963, its last allocation was:

Ex-LMS 3F 0-6-0T	47350, 47507, 47669
BR Class 2 2-6-2T	84003

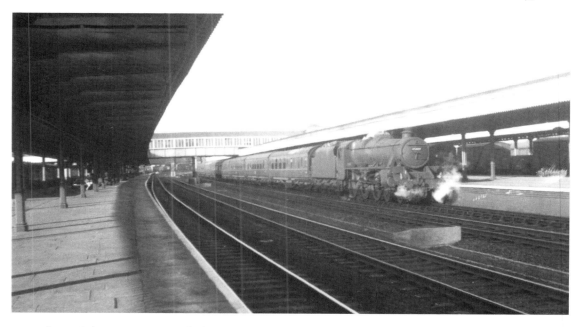

On 20 July 1963, ex-LMS Black Five 4-6-0 No. 45327 arrives at Rhyl station with a westbound train. The covered footbridge that connects the platforms is visible in the background. The main station building, along with the footbridge, was built by the LNWR in 1900 as part of the quadrupling of the line. An overbridge was also provided to eliminate level crossings here, which is visible on the previous photograph. (R. Casserley)

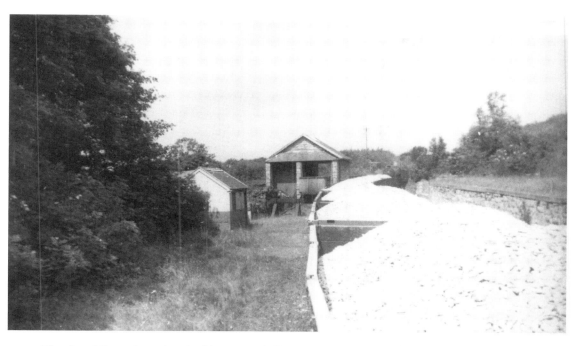

The site of Dyserth station, looking towards Prestatyn, as it appeared in 1963. (R. Casserley)

RHYL, LLANDUDNO JUNCTION, an

Down.

Miles			mrn	mrn	mrn	mrn	mrn		mrn	mrn	mrn	mrn	aft	mrn
—	Rhyl	dep.	3 35	7 12	....	m	9 7	....	m	1020	10 50	m	....	1157
	Llandudno Junc.	,,	6 40	8 15	8 30	9 15	10 0	....	1020	1115	11 27	1145	1215	1230
1¼	Deganwy		6 43	8 18	8 33	9 18	10 3	....	1023	1118	11 30	1148	1218	1233
3¼	Llandudno	arr.	6 50	8 25	8 40	9 25	1010	....	1030	1125	11 37	1155	1225	1240

Down.   **Week Days**—*Continued.*

			aft	aft	aft	aft	aft	aft	aft						
Rhyl		dep.	6 1	6 22	....	6 59	m	....	9 28	....	....	....	....	....	1
Llandudno Junc.		,,	6 35	....	6 55	7 50	8 0	9 35	1015	....	....	....	....	....	1
Deganwy			6 38	6 49	6 58	7 53	8 3	9 28	1018	....	....	....	....	....	1
Llandudno		arr.	6 45	6 55	7 5	8 0	8 10	9 45	1025	....	....	....	....	....	1

Up.   **W**

Miles			mrn	mrn	mrn	mrn	mrn	Mons.	mrn	mrn	mrn	mrn	mrn	mrn
	Llandudno	dep.	6 30	7 50	8 0	8 10	8 15		8 55	9 35	9 45	1040	11 5	1150
2	Deganwy [474		6 35	7 55	8 5	....	....		....	9 40	9 50	1045	1110	1155
3¼	Llandudno J.472,	arr	6 40	8 0	8 10	8 17	8 22		9 3	9 45	9 55	1050	1115	12 0
17¼	Rhyl	,,	7 25	....	....	8 43	8 48		9 38	m	1026	m	....	1246

Up.   **Week Days**—*Continued.*

			aft	aft	aft	aft	aft	aft						
Llandudno		dep	7 25	7 35	8 30	9 15	9 50	1035	....	....	....	....	....	2
Deganwy [474			7 30	7 40	8 35	9 20	9 55	1040	....	....	....	....	....	2
Llandudno Junc. 472,		arr.	7 35	7 48	8 40	9 25	10 0	1045	....	....	....	....	....	2
Rhyl		,,	....	8 37	m	10 0	....								2

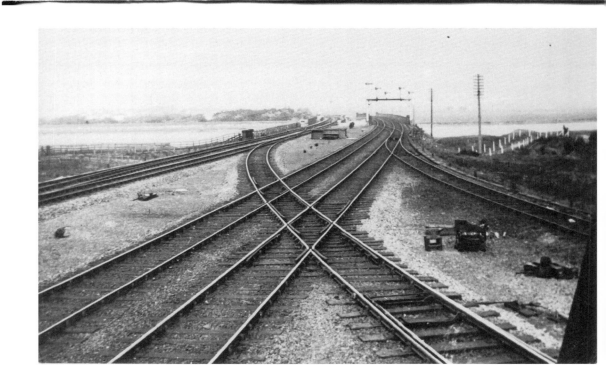

DUDNO.—London and North Western.

ays.

aft		aft		aft	aft	aft	aft			aft	aft	aft	aft
53	....	2 17	Sats.	m	2 53	3 23	3.28	Sats.		m	4 28	5 21	m
35	....	....		3 10	3 30	3 55	3 55			4 25	5 30	5 47	6 5
38	....	....		3 13	3 33	3 58	3 58			4 28	5 33	5 50	6 8
45	....	2 50		3 20	3 40	4 5	4 5			4 35	5 40	5 57	6 15

Sundays.

ft													
10	....	....	....	....	....	....	....	....	....	....	....	....	....
50	..	....	....	....	....	....	....	....	....	....	....	....	....
..	....	....	....	....	....	....	....	....	....	....	....	....	....
0	....	....	....	....	....	....	....	....	....	....	....	....	....

ys.

ft	aft	aft	aft	aft	aft	aft	aft	aft	aft	aft	aft	aft
30	1 45	2 15	2 30	2 55	3 25	3 45	4 45	4 55	5 10	5 45	6 10	6 35
35	1 50	2 20	2 35	3 0	3 30	3 50	4 50	5 0	5 15	5 50	....	6 40
40	1 55	2 25	2 40	3 5	3 33	3 55	4 55	5 5	5 20	5 55	6 17	6 45
..	2 38	3 0	m	3 46	4 3	m	m	....	6 10	....	6 46	m

Sundays.

ft													
15	....	....	....	....	....	....	....	....	....	....	....	....	....
..	....	....	....	....	....	....	....	....	....	....	....	....	....
25	....	....	....	....	....	....	....	....	....	....	....	....	....
0	....	....	....	....	....	....	....	....	....	....	....	....	....

NOTES.

———

m Motor Car, one class only.

Above: A 1910 LNWR timetable for local train services between Rhyl, Llandudno Junction (to connect with trains to Blaenau Ffestiniog) and Llandudno. (Author's Collection)

Opposite below: Foryd Junction just west of Rhyl station. The junction here was incorporated on the opening of the Vale of Clwyd line to Denbigh on 5 October 1858. A simple double-track layout facing Rhyl was reduced to a single track at the original Foryd station, which was closed in 1885 following opening of another Foryd station on the main line. Quadrupling brought facing connections from both fast and slow Down lines to the branch, whereas the connection from the Denbigh branch trailed directly onto the Up fast line, with a facing crossover to regain the Up slow line. A holding siding for the branch was provided on the south side of the junction. The main-line Foryd station was taken out of use as a wartime measure in July 1917 and reopened in July 1919. Although in use for military activities in the area, the LMS decided to close Foryd station in 1931 as an economy measure during the Great Depression. (Author's Collection)

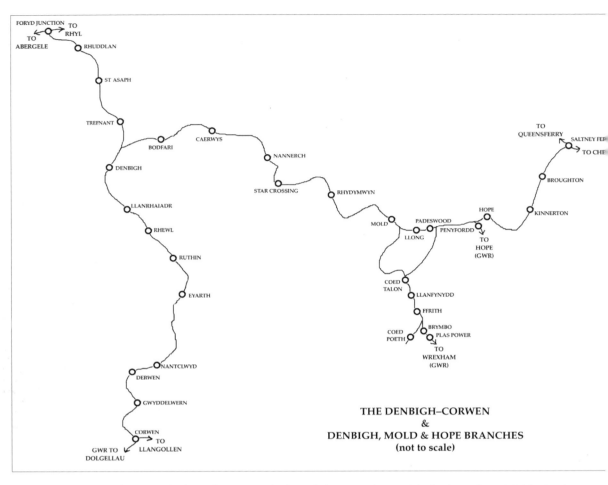

A map showing the branches to Denbigh and Corwen along with the branch to Mold, Coed Talon, Hope and Saltney Ferry where it joined the C&HR for access to Chester. (Author's Collection)

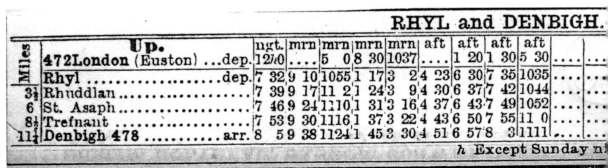

Miles	Up.	ngt.	mrn	mrn	mrn	mrn	aft	aft	aft	aft		
	472 London (Euston) ...dep.	12 0	....	5 0	8 30	1037	....	1 20	1 30	5 30	....	....
	Rhyl ....dep.	7 32	9 10	1055	1 17	3 2	4 23	6 30	7 35	1035	....	....
3½	**Rhuddlan**	7 39	9 17	11 2	1 24	3 9	4 30	6 37	7 42	1044	....	....
6	**St. Asaph**	7 46	9 24	1110	1 31	3 16	4 37	6 43	7 49	1052	....	....
8½	**Trefnant**	7 53	9 30	1116	1 37	3 22	4 43	6 50	7 55	11 0	....	....
11½	**Denbigh 478** ....arr.	8 5	9 38	1124	1 45	3 30	4 51	6 57	8 3	1111	....	....

h Except Sunday n[...]

A 1910 LNWR timetable for local services between Rhyl and Denbigh. (Author's Collection)

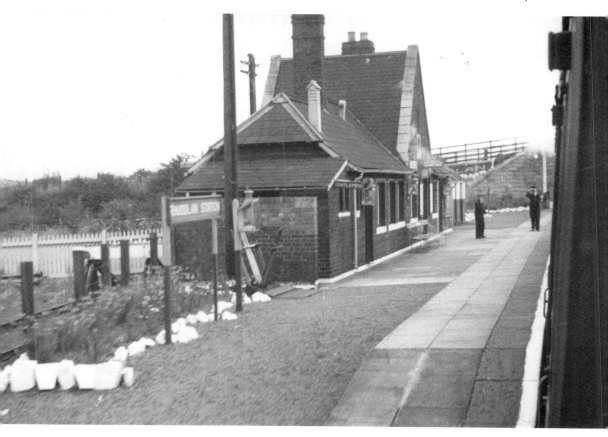

The line from Foryd Junction to Denbigh was opened by the Vale of Clwyd Railway on 5 October 1858 and was absorbed into the LNWR in 1867. At one time, the GWR had aspirations to gain access to potentially lucrative traffic on the North Wales coast by bringing a line up from Corwen to Rhyl. They were, however, thwarted by the LNWR whose line from Denbigh to Corwen, where it met the GWR Ruabon–Barmouth line, was opened on 1 March 1862. The first station on the section between Foryd and Denbigh was at Rhuddlan; its substantial main building is seen in this view of 27 August 1954. A small goods yard was also situated here and can be seen on the left of the picture. (H. Casserley)

and North Western.

DOWN.		mrn	mrn	mrn	mrn	aft	aft	aft	aft	aft		
Denbigh ....dep.		6 30	8 5	9 55	11 40	2 8	3 30	5 3	7 12	8 9	....	....
Trefnant		6 37	8 12	10 1	11 47	2 14	3 37	5 9	7 19	8 15	....	....
St. Asaph		6 43	8 18	10 7	11 53	2 20	3 43	5 15	7 25	8 21	....	....
Rhuddlan		6 50	8 25	10 14	12 0	2 28	3 50	5 23	7 32	8 28	....	....
Rhyl 472, 474 ....arr.		6 57	8 32	10 22	12 7	2 35	3 58	5 32	7 38	8 36	....	....
474 London (Euston)....arr.		....	1 40	3 15	5 40	8 10	9 5	....	....	3 r 50	....	....

1st and 3rd class.

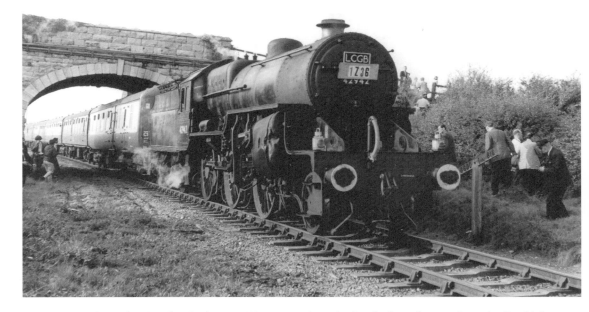

Ex-LMS Hughes-Fowler Crab 2-6-0 No. 42942 is at the head of a rail tour along the Denbigh branch, organised by the Locomotive Club of Great Britain on 24 September 1966, the line having closed to passengers in 1962. The train is seen just south of the station and passengers are leaving the train to take their pictures before the line disappears forever. (R. Carpenter)

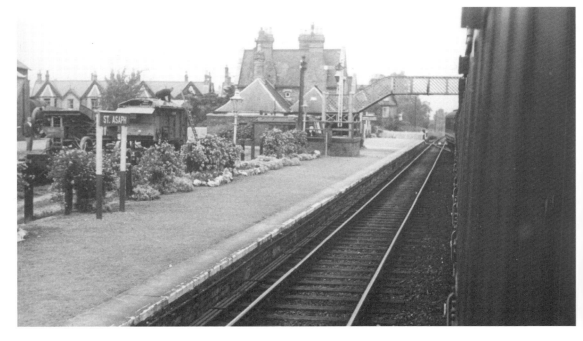

The next station along the branch was at St Asaph, recently given city status, which suffered severe flooding in early December 2012. The station can be seen here, looking towards Rhyl on 27 August 1954. The platform has a good display of flowers, common practice at stations in those days. (R. Casserley)

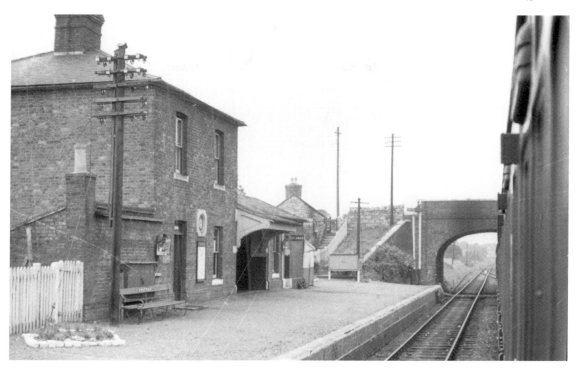

Between St Asaph and Denbigh lay the station at Trefnant, seen here in August 1954. The little station's booking office appears to be at the roadside. (R. Casserley)

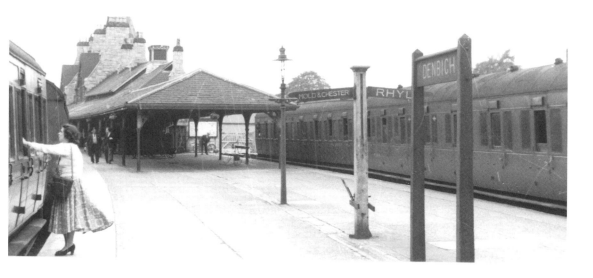

The junction station at Denbigh, looking towards Corwen, as it appeared in August 1954. Denbigh was once a busy railway junction for lines from Rhyl in the north and Mold to the east, with the line to Corwen continuing south. At one time Denbigh could offer a direct service, although rather slow, to Chester, which would avoid a change of trains at Rhyl. The handsome main station building can be seen on the island platform. The train on the right has just brought in a local service from Mold. (H. Casserley)

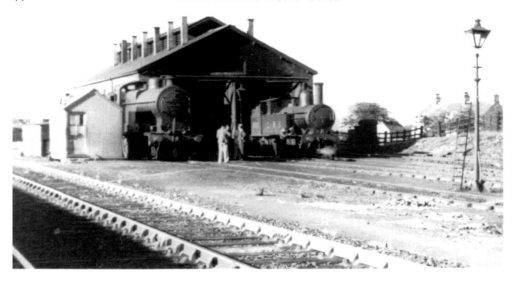

Denbigh was considered important enough to be provided with a small loco shed, supplying engines for local freight and passenger services to Mold, Corwen and Rhyl. The shed was actually a sub-shed of Rhyl (BR code 6K), its engines being supplied by the parent shed. The little shed is seen here on 6 July 1935, an ex-LNWR 2-4-2 tank and LMS 4F 0-6-0 tender engine are in view. The shed was closed in 1957, but still survives as a factory unit. (A. G. Ellis)

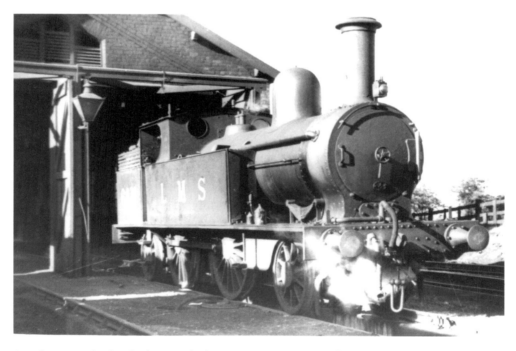

Standing outside the shed at Denbigh is ex-LNWR 2-4-2 tank, as LMS No. 6611, on 6 July 1935. (A. G. Ellis)

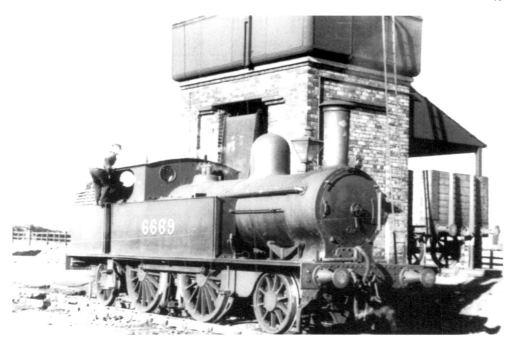

On the same day, another ex-LNWR 2-4-2 tank No. 6669, still in early LMS livery – the crest on the bunker and number on the tank side, is standing at the coaling stage and water tower as it is prepared for its next turn of duty. The difference in the liveries can be seen when compared with the previous picture. (A. G. Ellis)

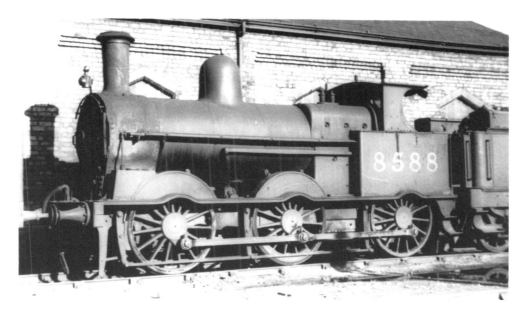

An ex-LNWR Coal Engine LMS No. 8588 is resting at the side of the shed on the same day. The engine may well have found itself on local services as well as freight traffic on occasions. (A. G. Ellis)

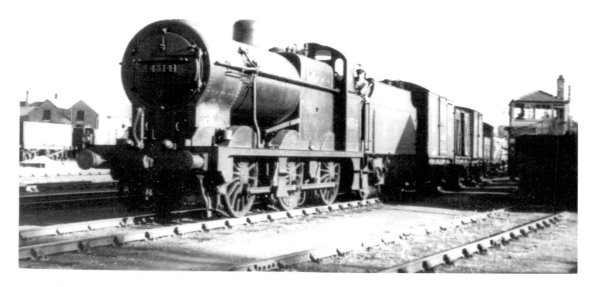

On 6 July 1935, LMS 4F 0-6-0 No. 4514 is seen passing Denbigh shed with a local freight train. (A. G. Ellis)

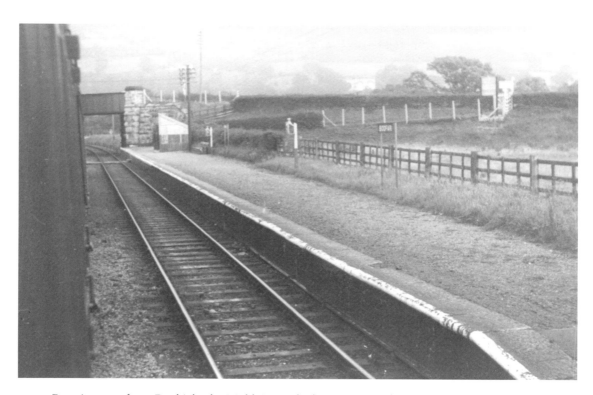

Running east from Denbigh, the Mold & Denbigh Junction Railway opened its line in 1869, being worked by the LNWR from the beginning, operating for nearly a century until closure on 30 April 1962. From Denbigh, the line was single to Bodfari, seen here on 27 August 1953 and looking towards Chester, but the rest of the line was double-track throughout. (R. Casserley)

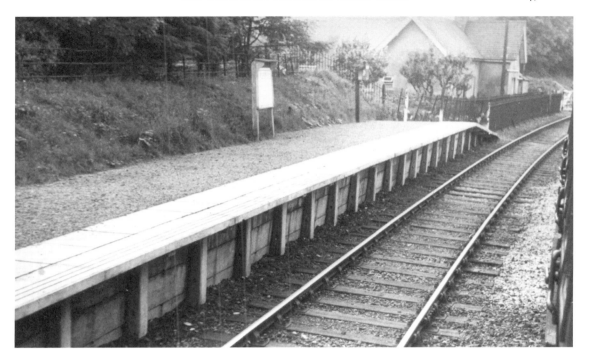

After leaving Bodfari, the line passed through Caerwys and Nannerch before reaching Star Crossing Halt, seen here looking towards Denbigh in August 1954. (R. Casserley)

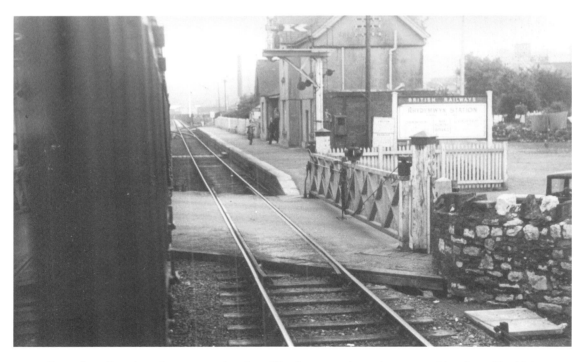

From Star Crossing, the next station is at Rhydymwyn, the train approaching from Denbigh and over the level crossing in August 1954. (R. Casserley)

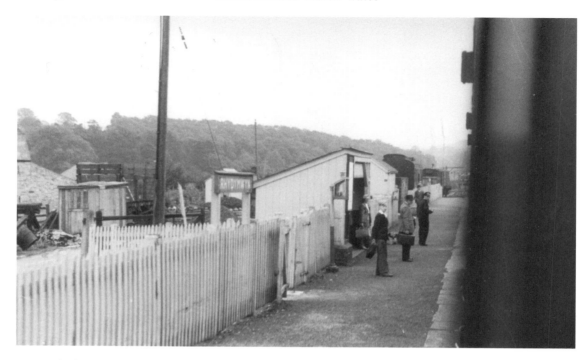

The little waiting shelter at Rhydymwyn station, a very primitive affair, as a train for Mold is about to depart. A scrapyard appears to be situated next to the station. (R. Casserley)

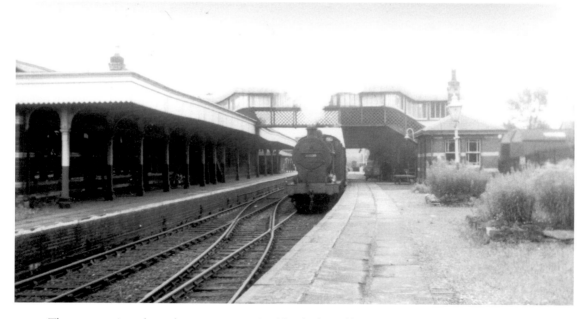

The next station along the route was at Mold, which itself was a junction for the line to Coed Talon, which connected with the joint GWR and LNWR line to Brymbo, home of a famous steelworks, and then the GWR line to Wrexham General. Here at Mold is ex-LMS 4F 0-6-0 No. 44595 at the head of the 9.30 a.m. train from Coed Talon. (R. Casserley)

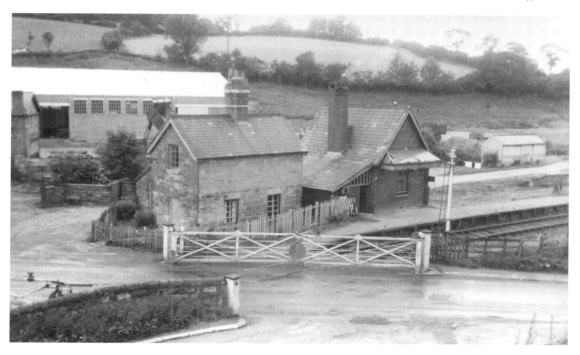

The little station on the single-line loop from Mold at Coed Talon, seen from above on a wet 15 July 1963. (R. Casserley)

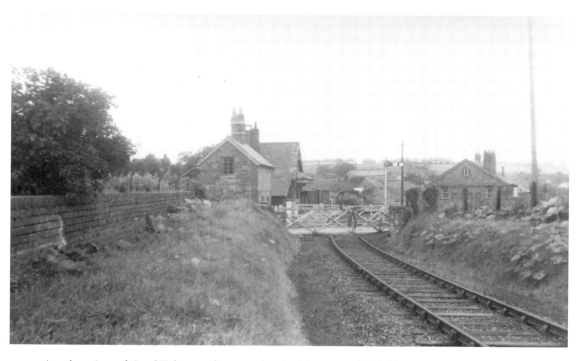

Another view of Coed Talon on the same day, looking towards Mold. Its smart station building looks more important than the little branch would deserve. (R. Casserley)

MOLD, COED TALON, and BRYMBO (One clas

Miles		Week Days.								
		mrn	mrn	aft	aft	Weds. & Sats.	aft			
	Mold ....dep.	8 22	11 39	3 30	6 22		8 36	....	..
4½	Coed Talon	8 32	11 49	3 40	6 32		8 46	....	..
6	Llanfynydd	8 38	11 55	3 48	6 40		8 52	....	..
7	Firith.................	8 42	11 59	3 52	6 44		8 56	....	..
8½	Brymbo 106, 671 ..arr.	8 48	12 5	3 58	6 50		9 2	....	..

A LNWR timetable for local, one-class-only, services between Mold, Coed Talon and Brymbo. (Author's Collection)

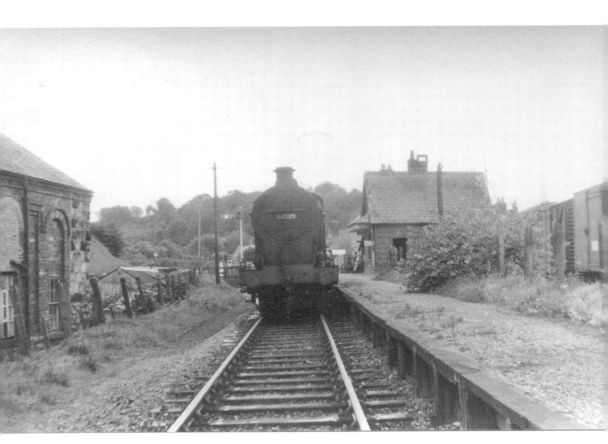

A shabby-looking Coed Talon station on 15 July 1963 with a local train for Mold, headed by ex-LMS 4F 0-6-0 No. 44595, about to depart at 9.30 a.m. Heading east, the loop will rejoin the line from Mold just east of Padeswood station. (R. Casserley)

nly).—London & North Western & Great Western.

			Week Days.					
		mrn	mrn	aft	aft	aft		aft
Brymbo ....dep.	....		10 0	2 10	5 25	7 43		9 10	....
1¼ Ffrith..............	....		10 6	2 16	5 31	7 49	Weds. only	9 16	....
2¼ Llanfynydd	....		1010	2 20	5 35	7 53		9 20	....
4 Coed Talon	8 40	1015	2 25	5 40	7 58		9 25	....
8½ Mold 478 ...... arr.	8 50	1026	2 36	5 51	8 9		9 36	....

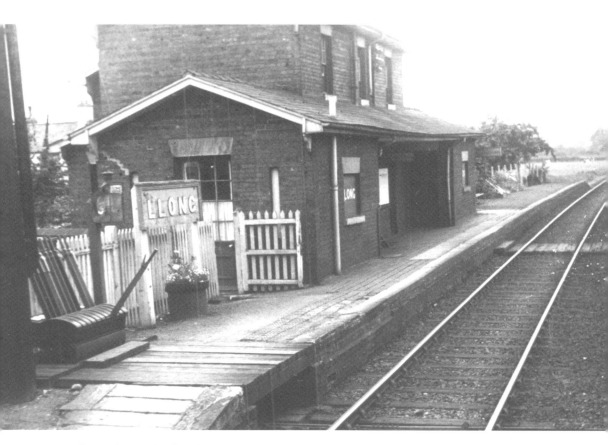

Just a few miles south of Mold, and between the loop to Coed Talon, lay the station at Llong, seen here looking towards Denbigh on 27 August 1953. Although the trains have long gone, the station building still exists and is in private use. (R. Casserley)

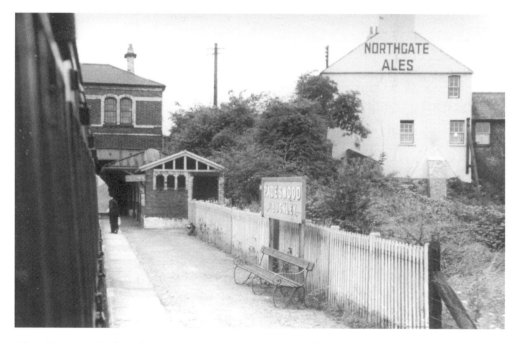

After Llong and before the loop from Coed Talon rejoined the line to Saltney Ferry, the station at Padeswood stood, seen here looking towards Denbigh in 1954. This rather substantial station was closed with the line in 1962. (H. Casserley)

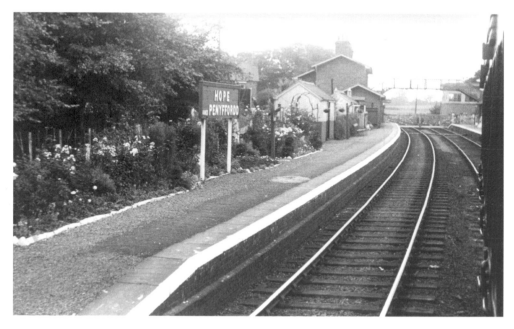

The next station along the line was Hope & Penyffordd, seen here in August 1954. Just before reaching the station, there was a junction to the GWR station of Hope. From Hope and Penyffordd, the line passed through stations at Kinnerton and Broughton before joining the C&HR main line at Mold Junction for access to Chester. (R. Casserley)

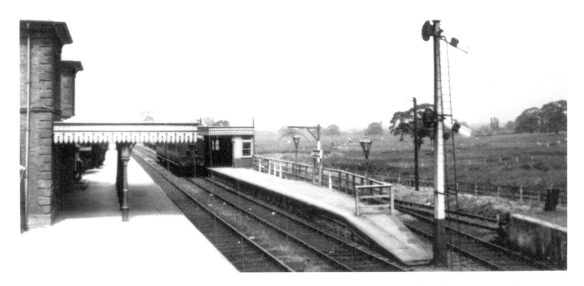

Back on the line to Corwen, stations were passed at Llanrhaiadr and Rhewl before reaching Ruthin, seen here in LNWR days. The substantial main building and waiting shelter can be seen in this view. The canopy that covered the full width of the platform was cut back in later years. A signal box was placed opposite the main building and a goods shed was also provided here. The line was double-track throughout to Corwen. (Author's Collection)

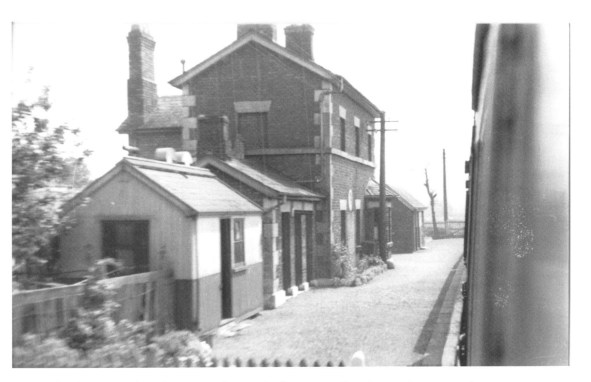

After leaving Ruthin, the next station on the line was at Eyarth, seen here on 13 August 1953. (H. Casserley)

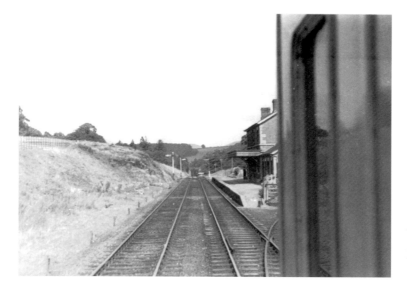

Following Eyarth, the next station on the line was at Nantclwyd, seen here in 1953 looking towards Rhyl. (H. Casserley)

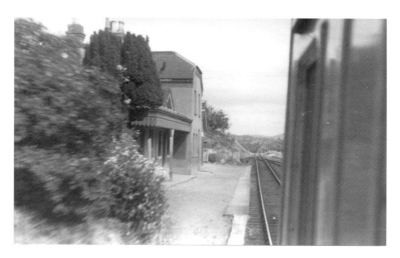

From Nantclwyd the line curved round to Derwen, seen here facing Rhyl in August 1953. The main station building seems to be in the 'Dutch' style. (H. Casserley)

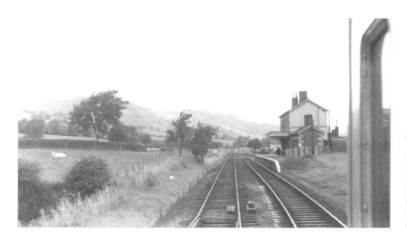

The final station before reaching Corwen was at Gwyddelwern. Its single-platformed building is seen as the train leaves for Corwen itself. (H. Casserley)

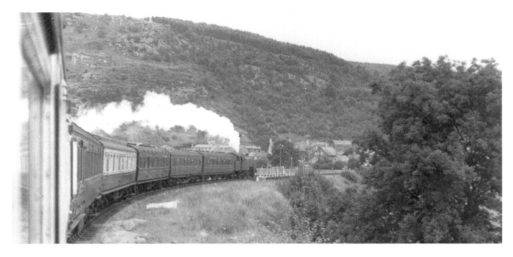

Approaching Corwen after leaving Gwyddelwern station on 13 August 1953 is ex-LMS Stanier 2-6-4 tank loco No. 42595 with the North Wales Land Cruise, which had left Rhyl at 2.05 p.m. The North Wales Land Cruise was a popular railway circular tour that started from Rhyl, ran down the Denbigh branch to Corwen, then joined the GWR line to run via Bala and Dolgellau to join the Cambrian Coast line to Pwllheli; then it ran up the line from Afonwen via Caernarfon to Bangor and rejoined the C&HR to return to Rhyl. When the branches were closed in the 1960s, the North Wales Land Cruise ceased to exist. Several engines were used on the train, and it would be no surprise to see, perhaps, a GWR Collet Goods 0-6-0 at Rhyl, having taken control of the train at Pwllheli. (H. Casserley)

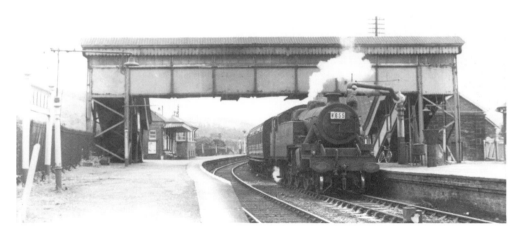

Arriving at Corwen with the North Wales Land Cruise in August 1953, 42595 will run down to Barmouth Junction to join the Cambrian Coast line for the journey to Pwllheli. Within a couple of years, from 1864, three small companies would arrive at Corwen, the first being the Denbigh & Corwen Railway in 1864, which thwarted any attempt by the GWR to invade the North Wales Coast as the LNWR operated the line; the Llangollen & Corwen Railway in 1865 and the Corwen & Bala Railway in 1866. The latter two lines were taken over by the GWR to form the Ruabon–Dolgellau line. Until 1927, the GWR had its own loco shed here as well as goods and carriage sidings. The demise of the railway at Corwen was as rapid as its arrival. The line to Denbigh closed in April 1962, but there had been no regular passenger service since 1953 with total closure of the GWR route following in December, after flood damage at Dolgellau. (H. Casserley)

CHESTER, MOLD, DENBIGH, RUTHIN, and CORWEN.—London and North Western.

Miles from Chester.	Down.	Week Days.															
	Euston Station,	ngt.	ngt.	mrn	mrn	mrn	mrn	mrn	aft	aft	aft	aft	aft	aft	aft	aft	
	404London ....dep.	1240	1240	....	....	5 0	8 30	1037	1210	....	1 20	1 30	....	....	2 40	5 30	....
	404Birmingham (N. St.) "	2g50	3a10	....	6 0	7 20	9 55	1210	....	....	2 55	3 30	....	....	....	6 50	....
	492Manchester (Ex.)... "	mrn	6 45	....	7 40	8 5	1045	1 5	....	2 40	3 55	4 55	....	....	5 10	7 15	....
	482Liverpool (Lime St.) "	....	7 25	....	....	8 35	1110	1225	s	....	4 0	5 5	....	....	6 20	7 20	....
	Chester (General).......dep.	6 45	8 45	Mondays only; also 1st Tuesday.	9 25	1020	1245	2 25	3 55	4 20	5 35	6 15	....	....	7 30	9 30	....
3¾	Saltney Ferry (Mold Junc.)	....	....		9 32	....	1252	2 34	....	4 27	5 42	....	....	....	7 37	9 37	....
4¾	Broughton and Bretton.....	6 53	....		9 36	1028	1256	2 38	....	4 31	5 46	....	....	....	7 41	9 41	....
6¼	Kinnerton..........	6 58	....		9 41	1033	1 1	2 43	....	4 36	5 51	....	....	....	7 46	9 46	....
9	Hope..........	7 7	9 5		9 52	1044	1 12	2 54	....	4 47	6 2	....	....	....	7 57	9 57	....
9¼	Hope (Exchange) 670, 671..	7 10	9 8		9 55	1047	1 15	2 57	....	4 50	6 5	....	....	....	8 0	10 3	....
10¾	Padeswood and Buckley....	7 13	....		9 58	1050	1 18	3 0	....	4 53	6 8	....	....	....	8 3	10 6	....
11½	Llong	7 16	....		10 1	1053	1 21	3 3	....	4 56	6 11	....	....	....	8 6	10 9	....
13¾	Mold 479 .... arr.	7 20	9 13		10 5	1057	1 25	3 7	4 18	5 0	6 15	6 38	....	....	8 11	1013	....
	Mold 479 .... dep.	7 22	9 15		....	11 2	1 27	3 9	4 21	....	6 17	6 40	6 50	....	....	1015	....
16½	Rhydymwyn	7 29	9 21		....	11 8	1 33	3 15	....	....	6 23	....	6 56	....	....	1021	....
19½	Nannerch..........	7 37	9 28		....	1115	1 40	3 22	....	....	6 30	....	7 3	....	....	1028	....
23	Caerwys..........	7 43	9 34		....	1121	1 46	3 28	....	....	6 36	....	7 9	....	....	1034	....
25¼	Bodfari..........	7 47	9 38		....	1125	1 50	3 32	....	....	6 40	....	7 13	....	....	1038	....
29¼	Denbigh 476......... arr.	7 57	9 48		....	1135	2 0	3 42	4 45	....	6 50	7 5	7 25	....	....	1048	....
	Denbigh 476......... dep.	8 30	....	9 52	....	1140	2 5	4 10	4 55	....	....	7 8	7 29	8 8	....	....	....
32¼	Llanrhaiadr..........	8 37	....	9 59	....	1147	2 12	4 17	b	....	....	....	7 36	8 15	....	....	....
34¼	Rhewl..........	8 42	....	10 4	....	1152	2 17	4 22	c	....	....	....	7 41	8 20	....	....	....
37	Ruthin..........	8 53	....	10 8	....	1156	2 21	4 30	5 7	....	....	7 20	7 45	8 24	....	....	....
37¾	Eyarth..........	8 57	....	....	....	12 6	2 28	4 35	....	....	....	....	7 52	....	....	....	....
40¼	Nantclwyd..........	9 4	....	....	....	1211	2 36	4 43	....	....	....	....	8 0	....	....	....	....
42¾	Derwen..........	9 8	....	....	....	1216	2 41	4 48	....	....	....	....	8 5	....	....	....	....
45½	Gwyddelwern..........	9 14	....	....	....	1223	2 48	4 53	....	....	....	....	8 11	....	....	....	....
48	Corwen 104, 105 ......arr.	9 21	....	....	....	1231	2 56	5 3	....	....	....	....	8 20	....	....	....	....

Miles.	Up.	Week Days.															
		mrn	mrn	mrn	mrn	mrn	aft	aft	aft	aft	aft	aft	aft	aft	aft		
	Corwen ....dep	....	7 10	....	....	1035	1 15	....	4 0	....	....	6 10	....	....	....	....	....
2¼	Gwyddelwern..........	....	7 17	....	....	1042	1 22	....	4 7	....	....	6 17	....	....	....	....	....
5¼	Derwen..........	....	7 23	....	....	1048	1 28	....	4 13	....	....	6 23	....	....	....	....	....
7¾	Nantclwyd..........	....	7 27	....	....	1052	1 32	....	4 17	....	....	6 27	....	....	....	....	....
10¼	Eyarth..........	....	7 33	....	....	1058	1 38	....	4 23	....	....	6 33	....	....	....	....	....
11	Ruthin..........	....	7 38	....	9 25	11 3	1 45	....	4 35	5 25	....	6 42	7 50	....	8 30	....	....
13¾	Rhewl..........	....	7 43	....	9 29	11 9	1 49	....	4 39	5 32	....	6 46	7 54	....	Sat.	....	....
15½	Llanrhaiadr..........	....	7 47	....	9 33	1113	1 53	....	4 43	5 38	....	6 50	7 58	....	n	....	....
18¾	Denbigh 476 .... arr.	....	7 55	....	9 41	1121	2 3	....	4 51	5 49	....	6 58	8 6	....	8 46	....	....
	Denbigh 476 .... dep.	7 0	8 12	8 25	9 51	1135	2 10	3 35	5 0	....	....	7 5	....	....	8 50	....	....
22¾	Bodfari..........	7 8	d	8 33	9 59	1143	2 18	3 43	5 8	....	....	7 13	....	....	8 58	....	....
25	Caerwys..........	7 14	n	8 39	10 5	1149	2 24	3 49	5 14	....	....	7 19	....	....	9 4	....	....
28¼	Nannerch..........	7 22	....	8 47	1013	1157	2 32	3 57	5 22	....	....	7 27	....	....	9 12	....	....
31¼	Rhydymwyn..........	7 30	....	8 55	1021	12 5	2 40	4 5	5 30	....	....	7 35	....	....	9 20	....	....
34¼	Mold 479 .... arr.	7 36	8 39	9 1	1027	1211	2 46	4 11	5 36	....	....	7 41	....	....	9 26	....	....
	Mold 479 .... dep.	7 40	8 41	9 3	1029	1213	2 48	4 13	5 38	....	5 45	7 43	....	8 30	9 28	....	....
36½	Llong	7 44	....	9 7	1033	1217	....	4 17	....	....	5 49	7 47	....	8 34	9 32	....	....
37¾	Padeswood and Buckley	7 47	....	9 10	1037	1220	2 53	4 20	....	....	5 52	7 50	....	8 37	9 35	....	....
38¾	Hope (Exchange) 670, 671..	7 52	8 46	9 15	1041	1225	2 57	4 25	5 43	....	5 57	7 55	....	8 42	9 40	....	....
39	Hope..........	7 54	....	9 17	1043	1227	3 2	4 27	....	....	5 59	7 57	....	8 44	9 42	....	....
41¾	Kinnerton	8 0	....	9 23	1049	1233	....	4 33	....	....	6 5	8 3	....	8 50	9 48	....	....
43¾	Broughton and Bretton	8 5	d	9 28	1054	1238	....	4 38	....	....	6 10	8 8	....	8 55	9 53	....	....
44¼	Saltney Ferry (Mold Junction)	8 8	....	9 31	....	1241	....	4 41	....	....	6 13	8 11	....	8 58	9 56	....	....
48	Chester * 480, 482, 493 arr.	8 17	9 4	9 41	11 2	1250	3 19	4 50	6 3	....	6 21	8 20	....	9 7	10 5	....	....
75	480Liverpool (Lime St.) arr.	9 50	10o5	1055	1245	2 50	4 32	5 55	....	....	8 5	....	....	....	1157	....	....
88	493Manchester (Ex.)... "	9 56	....	1120	1253	3 8	5 12	6 27	....	....	8 12	1010	....	....	3 23	....	....
122	413Birmingham (N. St.) "	a	1124	1217	1 57	4 18	6 41	7 24	....	....	9 34	....	....	....	2 33	....	....
227½	413London (Euston).... "	....	1 40	2 10	3 15	5 40	8 10	9 5	1045	r	11 0	....	....	....	3r50	....	....

NOTES.

a Stops to take up for beyond Chester on giving notice at the Station.

a Mondays only.

b Stops to set down from Chester and beyond on notice being given to the Guard.

c Stops to set down from Rhyl, or from Chester and beyond on notice being given to the Guard.

d Stop to take up for Liverpool or Manchester on notice being given at the Station.

g Except Mondays.

h No connection on Sunday night.

n Stops on Mondays and Saturdays.

o Arrives at 10 10 mrn. on Mondays.

q Sunday midnight only.

r 1st and 3rd class.

s Saturdays only.

* General Station; about ¾ mile to Northgate Station (Cheshire Lines).

A 1910 timetable for LNWR services along the Denbigh–Corwen branch and from Chester, through Mold, to Denbigh. (Author's Collection)

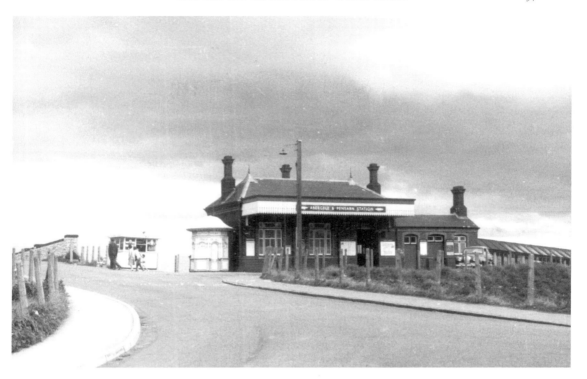

Back on the C&HR and the next station from Rhyl is at Abergele & Pensarn, the exterior of which is seen here next to the road overbridge. Access to the station was by a covered bridge and ramps leading from the back of the building. The enquiry kiosk to the left of the station was one of many provided by the LMS at seaside resorts. (H. Casserley)

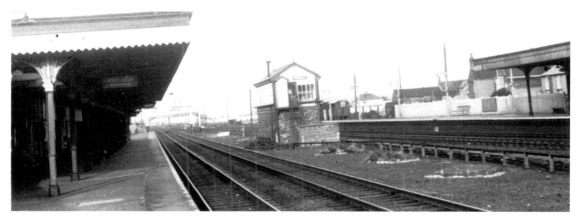

The platforms at Abergele on 28 August 1964 from the Up platform. The station was opened with the railway in 1848, its main building being another of Francis Thompson's. Platforms and sidings were extended in 1883 and a footbridge was constructed at the same time. When the line was quadrupled, many of the buildings on the Down side were swept away and a new station was brought into use in July 1902. The goods yard had to be removed when the line was widened, being relocated a few yards inland on a spur. A new timber goods shed was provided, which was replaced by a concrete type by the LMS to extend capacity. (H. Casserley)

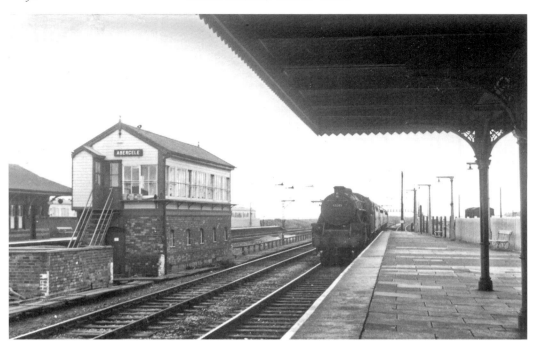

Abergele station on 28 August 1964 with the 4.32 p.m. Chester–Colwyn Bay train calling, headed by ex-LMS Black Five 4-6-0 No. 45285. A little west of Abergele is Llanddulas, with its quarries and sidings. There was a major accident at Llanddulas in August 1868 which resulted in the loss of thirty-seven lives. On the 20th of that month, a pick-up goods train arrived at Llanddulas sidings at 12.24 p.m. with forty-three wagons, two of which contained paraffin casks collected at Saltney. Unfortunately, all of the goods train could not be accommodated in the sidings, but by dividing the train there was room for it to shunt clear. While a shunting operation was being prepared, the Down Irish Mail was due to pass through. Rules stated that all shunting on the main line had to be completed at least ten minutes before a train was due. In breach of these rules, the Llanddulas stationmaster insisted that shunting was carried out. While shunting was in progress, the rear six wagons were left on the main line on a gradient of 1 in 147 and 1 in 100 falling towards Abergele. None of the wagon brakes had been pinned down, except that on the brake van. Three timber wagons were drawn out of the sidings and fly-shunted back onto the standing vehicles, with the brakesman running beside and attempting to apply the brakes. This he failed to do and they hit the wagons on the main line, causing the brake cog on the brake van to fracture and all the wagons, including those carrying paraffin, to run away. At 12.39, the Irish Mail ran through Abergele some five minutes late. Only 1¾ miles west of Abergele, the driver saw the runaway wagons approaching. When he realised what was happening, the wagons were almost upon the train. The driver jumped but the fireman, who was trying to apply the brakes, was not so fortunate. On impact, the front of the express was engulfed in paraffin. Spilt coal from the firebox ignited the paraffin, and the fire consumed the first four coaches, all of which were locked, a common practice on the LNWR at that time. The fireman and thirty-six passengers were killed. The fire was so intense that only two of the victims could be identified. The inquiry that followed blamed the LNWR for the accident, stating that many rules had been ignored. All of the victims of the accident now lie in Abergele churchyard. Llanddulas station itself was to survive until closure in December 1952. (H. Casserley)

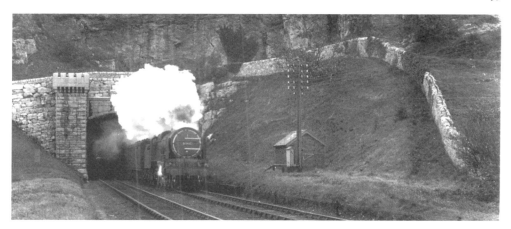

Just east of Llanddulas, the C&HR enters the castellated Penmaenrhos Tunnel, seen here in the 1930s with LMS Royal Scot Class 4-6-0 No. 6162 *Queen's Westminster Rifleman* at the head of the Down Irish Mail as it heads for Holyhead. Immediately after leaving Penmaenrhos Tunnel and heading towards Colwyn Bay, the railway now passes under the 1983-built Tan-y-Lan viaduct, which carries the new A55 Expressway into Colwyn Bay. The new road, which reflects the decline in railway travel, closely follows the railway through to the outskirts of Llandudno Junction. (D. Ibbotson)

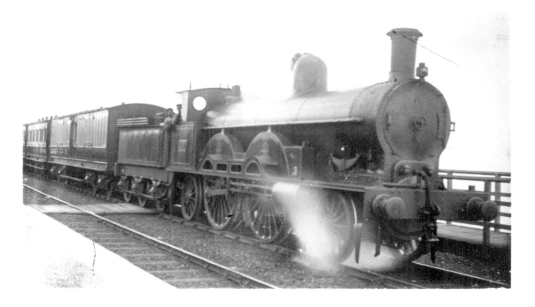

Shortly after leaving the 486-yard Penmaenrhos Tunnel, the C&HR entered Old Colwyn station. The station opened as Colwyn in 1884 with financial support from local residents, the name being changed to Old Colwyn a year later. The railway at this point is carried over an embankment after crossing a viaduct above the locality so the offices were built at road level with ramps leading to the platforms. Apart from extra siding capacity, to accommodate some twenty-six wagons, the track layout changed little despite proposals, in 1913, to widen the line from Penmaenrhos Tunnel through to Colwyn Bay, the war preventing such building. Passenger services at the station were withdrawn in 1952, but goods traffic still used the station until final closure in 1964. Back in 1905 and LNWR Greater Britain Class 2-2-2-2 compound No. 2051 *George Findlay* is seen entering Old Colwyn station with a stopping train for Chester. (R. Carpenter)

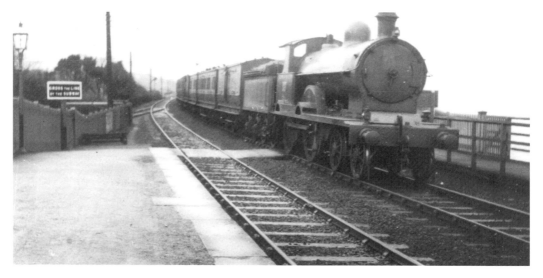

Just before the outbreak of the First World War, a LNWR Precursor Class 4-4-0 is approaching Old Colwyn station with a Chester-bound train. The entrance to the goods yard can be seen on the left, at the Colwyn Bay end of the station. (R. Carpenter Collection)

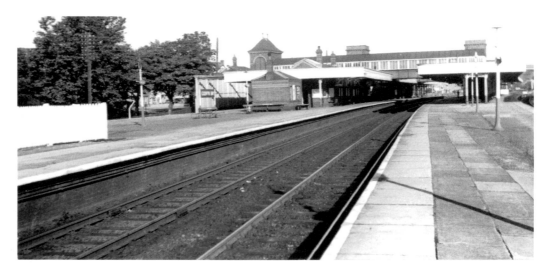

Colwyn Bay station on 20 July 1963, looking towards Llandudno Junction. Thought to be a suitable place to site a railway station, an agreement was reached between Lady Erskine and the C&HR to build a station in return for allowing the railway to cross her land. The station first appeared in timetables as 'Colwyn' in 1849, although it was thought to be a primitive affair. The presence of a station here encouraged local growth and the hamlet of 'Colwyn Bay' began to develop. Improvements to the station were authorised in in 1857 and again in 1881, but work was not completed until 1885. Widening of the railway between Colwyn Bay and Llandudno Junction was brought into use in 1904 and plans were made to enlarge the station and provide a goods yard. Work on the new station was completed by March 1908, platforms being lengthened in 1910. The title 'Colwyn Bay' was adopted for the station as early as 1876. (R. Casserley)

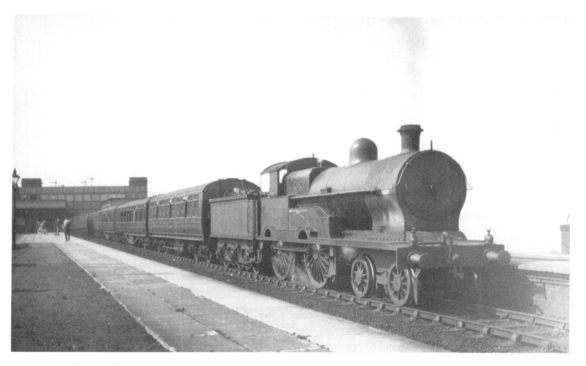

Standing with an express in early LMS days is ex-LNWR Precursor Class 4-4-0 No. 5335, awaiting departure from Colwyn Bay with a train for Chester and Crewe. (Author's Collection)

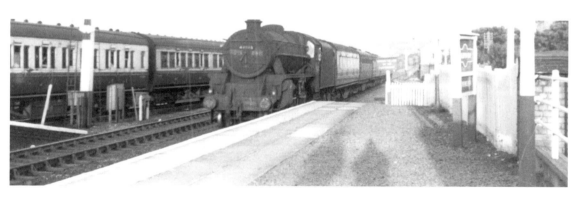

Approaching Colwyn Bay station on 10 August 1953, ex-LMS Black Five 4-6-0 heads the 5.25 p.m. Manchester–Llandudno express. (H. Casserley)

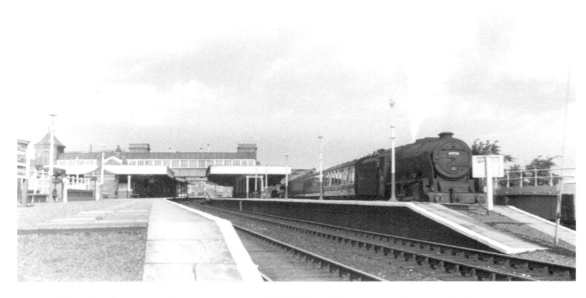

A few days later, on 14 August 1953, ex-LMS Jubilee Class 4-6-0, with larger boiler and rebuilt Royal Scot smoke deflectors, No. 45735 *Comet* prepares to leave Colwyn Bay station with the 9.10 a.m. express from Llandudno to Euston. (H. Casserley)

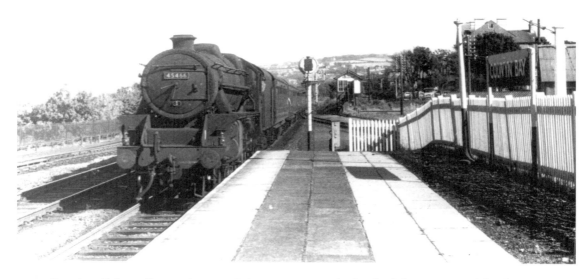

Entering Colwyn Bay station on 28 August 1964 at the head of the 1.40 p.m. Manchester–Bangor train is ex-LMS Black Five 4-6-0 No. 45466. The signal box on the right controls the entrance to the substantial goods yard here. (H. Casserley)

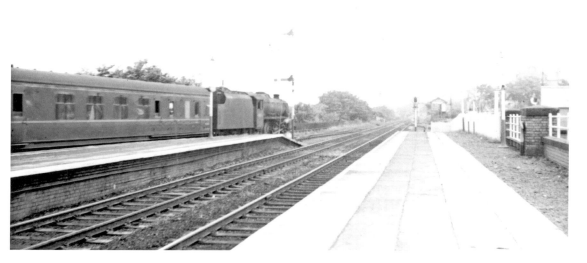

About to depart from Colwyn Bay station on 13 August 1966, ex-LMS Black Five 4-6-0 No. 45369 is seen at the head of the 1.15 p.m. Llandudno–Manchester train. (R. Casserley)

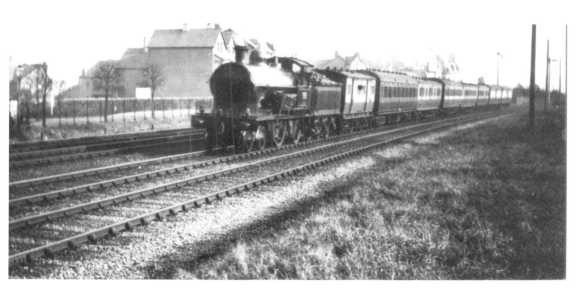

West of Colwyn Bay and into the four-track section, a LNWR George V Class 4-4-0 heads a Down express for Holyhead early in 1914. (R. Casserley)

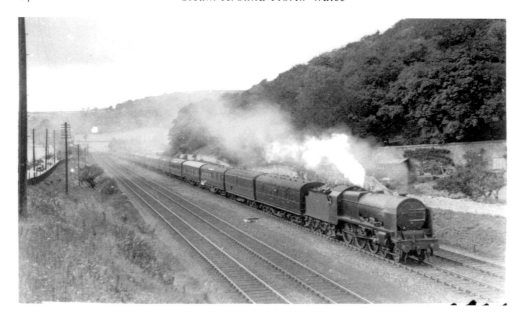

Approaching Colwyn Bay, LMS un-rebuilt Royal Scot Class 4-6-0 No. 6113 *Cameronian* is at the head of the Up Irish Mail around 1935. The railway between Llandudno Junction and Colwyn Bay was rationalised and returned to a two-track formation in the 1980s to make way for the new A55 Expressway, which runs alongside the railway just west of Colwyn Bay to just east of Llandudno Junction. (A. G. Ellis)

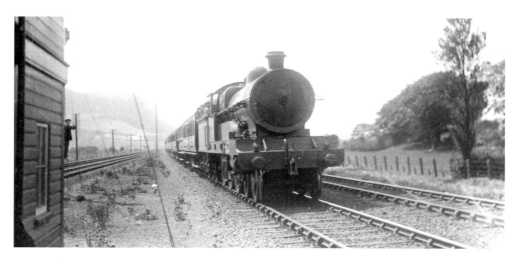

Approaching Mochdre & Pabo station, just east of Llandudno Junction, is ex-LNWR Claughton Class 4-6-0 No. 5994 at the head of an express to Holyhead in the 1920s. The station here was not opened until 1889, although it was authorised seven years earlier. Its simple wooden platforms, with signal box in the centre, only lasted until 1931. Even before a station was opened here, the first water troughs in the world, built to a design by LNWR CME, Charles Ramsbottom, were built here in 1860, the idea being to improve journey times for Irish Mail services, taking water from Mochdre stream under an agreement with Lord Mostyn, the local landowner. Scarcity of water prompted removal of the troughs to Aber in 1871, Lord Penrhyn agreeing a forty-year lease, which was renewed regularly until steam ceased in 1968. (Author's Collection)

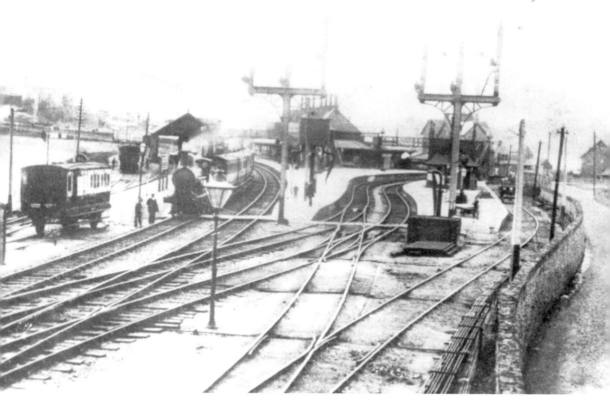

When the C&HR was opened in 1848, all trains, including the Irish Mail, were dealt with at Conwy. Opening of the Llandudno branch made train handling at Conwy station rather inconvenient. Further, plans were in hand to build a branch to Llanrwst, later to become the Conwy Valley Branch. In order to deal with this prospective new traffic, a new station was opened east of Conwy at the junction of the Llandudno branch in 1860. Being situated at the junction made the station 'V'-shaped, with the Llandudno branch being served by a curved platform, and the main line by a straight platform on the island side. By 1883, a bay was constructed on the Up platform for the Conwy Valley Branch, which terminated virtually opposite the Llandudno Branch. Also, by this time the branch connection had been remodelled and the ticket platform had been taken out of use. Seen here is the original Llandudno Junction station, around 1895, showing the curved platform for Llandudno on the right, and a now-curved platform on the left with an LNWR train heading east leaving the station. A small goods shed is visible on the left and the castle at Conwy can be seen in the background. (Author's Collection)

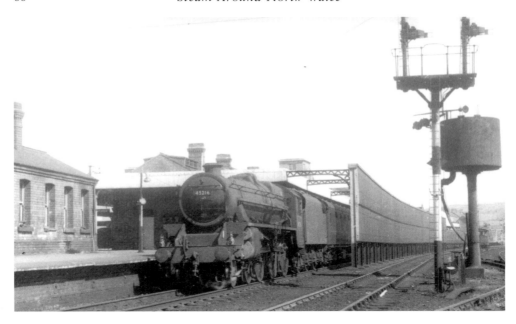

The original station at Llandudno Junction remained in use for several years until the LNWR decided that a new, larger station was required, which would be situated a few yards east of the original. This new station was completed in 1897 with four through platforms and a bay at the western end for Llandudno trains and a further bay at the eastern end for Conwy Valley trains. The island platforms were connected to the main entrance by a stairway and covered footbridge, which still exists with facilities for both passengers and luggage. The buildings were slightly better than the standard LNWR types and were built of brick with deep, flat awning over the platforms. Resiting of the station meant that the Conwy Valley branch connection had to be moved to the east. Extensive use was made of the old branch as carriage sidings. These sidings later found use for storage of engines during the winter months and, from the mid-1950s, to store withdrawn locos while awaiting their fate. Along with carriage sidings, the station was also provided with freight facilities. The station was controlled by two signal boxes, the 101 levered No. 1 box on the Down line at the east end of the station, while No. 2 box was west of the station on the Up line. Another signal box was placed at the start of the Llandudno branch that controlled a level crossing here. The level crossing became redundant when a road flyover was built in the late 1950s; the signal box then became redundant. The rebuilt station can be seen here on 26 August 1964 with an ex-LMS Black Five 4-6-0 No. 45216 in charge of the 1.55 a.m. Manchester–Holyhead express. (H. Casserley)

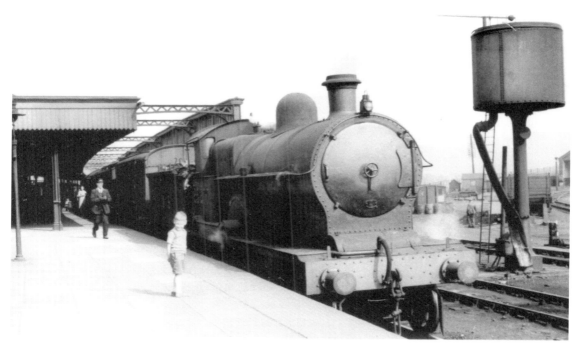

Llandudno Junction station during the Second World War with ex-LNWR 4-4-0 No. 25277 with a westbound train on 12 July 1941. The loco shed is just visible to the right. (H. Casserley)

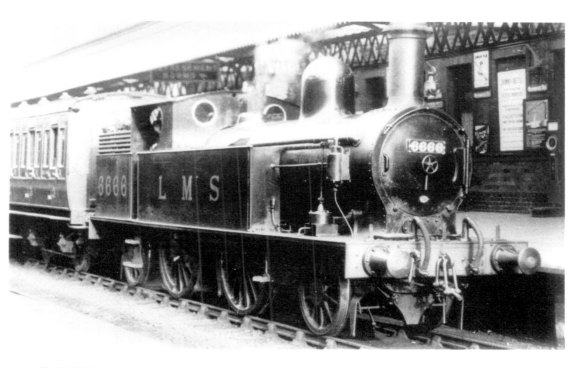

Ex-LNWR 2-4-2 tank engine No. 6666 at Llandudno Junction station on 3 June 1932 with a local train for Llandudno. (Author's Collection)

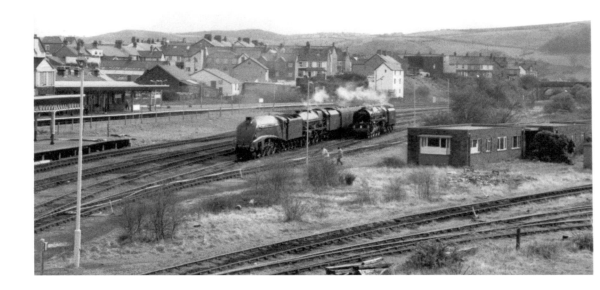

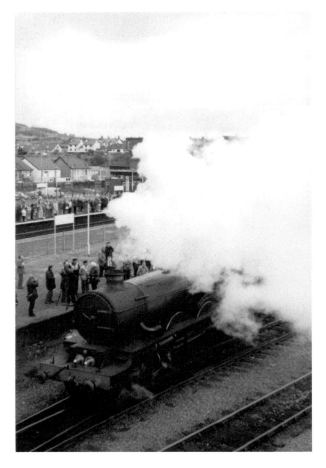

Above: Since the late 1980s, the C&HR line has been licensed to operate steam trains between Crewe and Holyhead, which allowed running of special trains to run on the day that British Rail ceased to exist when privatisation was introduced on 1 April 1994. To mark the end of the nationalised railway, steam locomotives from the four 'post-grouping' companies and British Railways were displayed on the old sidings at Llandudno Junction on that day, special trains having been brought in from Crewe. In this view are the first three locos to arrive: ex-LNER A4 Pacific No. 4498 *Sir Nigel Gresley* sits in front of ex-LMS Princess Royal Pacific No. 46203 *Princess Margaret Rose* and ex-BR 8P Pacific No. 71000 *Duke of Gloucester* is standing alongside; all are waiting to be shunted into place. (Author's Collection)

Left: Just arrived with its special train on the same day and shunting into position is ex-GWR Castle Class 4-6-0 No. 5029 *Nunney Castle*. The LMS and GWR engines represent locos that worked trains between Chester, Holyhead and Wrexham. (Author's Collection)

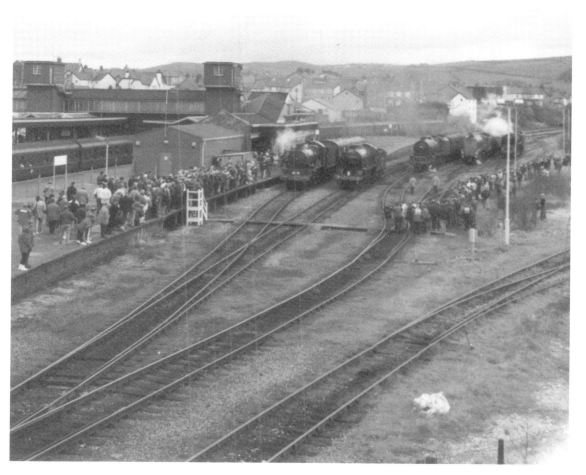

While awaiting arrival of the representative from the Southern Railway, which would be a Bulleid Pacific, the four locos already arrived are being shunted into position, watched by large crowds on the platform and in the old goods yard. (Author's Collection)

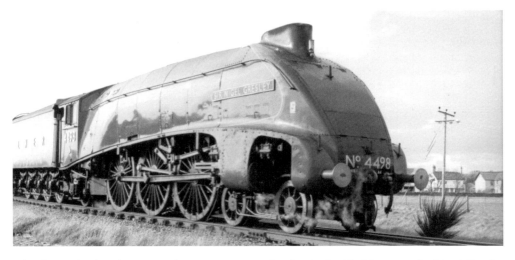

After being displayed on 1 April 1994, ex-LNER Gresley A4 Pacific No. 4498 *Sir Nigel Gresley* is seen leaving Llandudno Junction and continuing its excursion to Holyhead. The other four locos in the display returned light engines to Crewe. (Author's Collection)

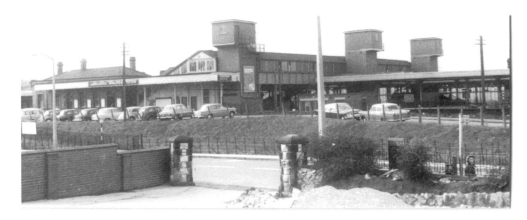

Exterior of Llandudno Junction station as it appeared on 29 August 1964. The covered footbridge is clearly seen in this view and several cars are in the small car park, virtually all British-built. A look at the same car park today would show that very few are still built in this country. (H. Casserley)

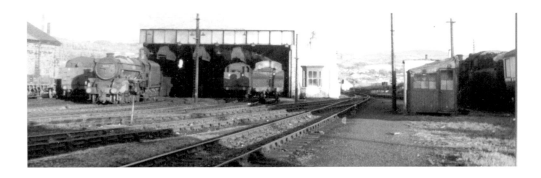

Opposite bottom: The loco shed at Llandudno Junction on 25 June 1966 with a Black Five in view, along with tank engines inside the shed. At around the same time as the original Llandudno Junction station was opened, a loco shed for twelve engines was provided here, opened on the eastern side of the Conwy Valley Branch, coinciding with the extension from Betws-y-Coed to Blaenau Ffestiniog. The shed's capacity was increased to twenty-four in 1898. (H. Casserley)

Examples of allocations at Llandudno Junction shed are provided below from BR days when it was coded 6G:

January 1954

Ex-LMS Stanier 2-6-2T	40083, 40086, 40095, 40123, 40130, 40133, 40208
Ex-MR 2P 4-4-0	40548
Ex-LMS 2P 4-4-0	40559
Ex-LMS 4P 4-4-0	40925, 41086, 41093, 41111, 41114, 41119, 41123, 41124, 41150
Ex-LMS Ivatt 2-6-2T	41236, 41237, 41238
Ex-LMS 3F 0-6-0	43887
Ex-LMS 4F 0-6-0	44389, 44738, 44739, 44740
Ex-LMS Black-Five 4-6-0	45331
Ex-LMS 3F 0-6-0T	47394
BR Standard Class 4 4-6-0	75010, 75011, 75012, 75013, 75014
	Total: 33

December 1960

Ex-LMS Stanier 2-6-2T	40077, 40093, 4095, 40123, 40128, 40130, 40133, 40185
Ex-LMS Ivatt 2-6-2T	41227, 41235, 41236, 41238
Ex-LMS 4F 0-6-0	44389, 44525
Ex-LMS Black-Five 4-6-0	44686, 44687, 44738, 44739, 44740, 44741, 44742, 44749, 44750
Ex-LMS Jubilee Class 4-6-0	45553 *Canada*, 45583 *Assam*, 45638 *Zanzibar*, 45655 *Keith*, 45671 *Prince Rupert*, 45740 *Munster*
Ex-LMS Royal Scot Class 4-6-0	46138 *The London Irish Rifleman*, 46163 *Civil Service Rifleman*
Ex-LMS 3F 0-6-0T	47361, 4758, 47631
Ex-LMS 8F 2-8-0	48046, 48253, 48667
BR Standard Class 4 4-6-0	75010, 75011, 75012
	Total: 40

The loco shed closed on 3 October 1966, its final allocation was:

Ex-LMS Black-Five 0-6-0	44766, 44875, 45042, 45064, 45277, 45282, 45298, 45345
	Total: 8

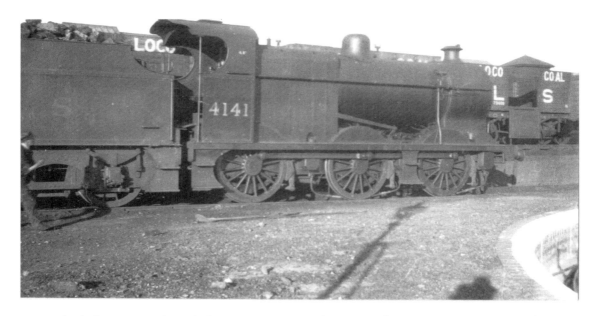

Llandudno Junction loco shed on 12 June 1935 with LMS Fowler 4F 0-6-0 No. 4141 near the turntable and wagons full of locomotive coal in the background. (LOSA)

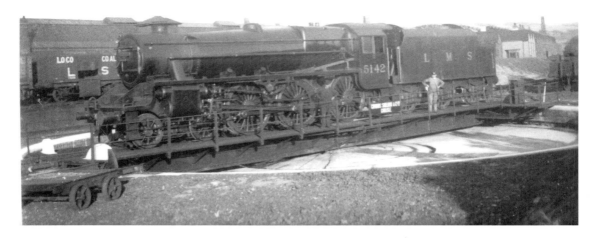

Sitting on the turntable at Llandudno Junction shed on 12 June 1935 is LMS Stanier Black Five 4-6-0 No. 5142, which would have been virtually new when seen here. (LOSA)

Opposite above: Leaving Llandudno Junction station behind ex-LNWR 4-4-0 No. 25277 as it heads towards Bangor with the 4.15 p.m. train. On the right is the start of the Llandudno branch with the level-crossing gates closed. The train will climb up to the tubular bridge over the river before it enters Conwy station. (H. Casserley)

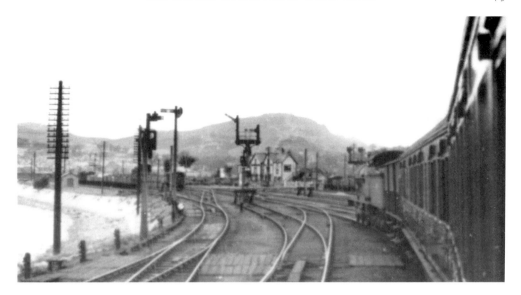

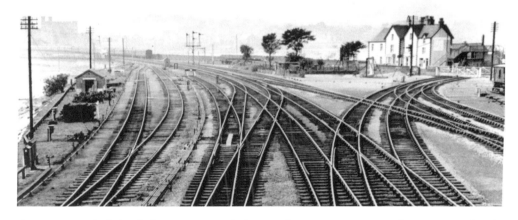

The western end of Llandudno Junction with the main line running up towards Conwy Castle. The branch to Llandudno can be seen going off to the right with the level-crossing gates closed and the footbridge over the line in view. Although the St George's Harbour and Railway Company were thwarted in their attempt to establish an Irish Sea packet port in what was to become Llandudno, the company tried again with a much simpler proposal and an Act was passed for a line to Llandudno in 1853. This proposal was for a single-line railway from Llandudno to a junction with the C&HR, which was opened on 1 October 1858 and was worked by a tank engine and coaches hired from the LNWR, trains running from a very limited Llandudno Junction station. This arrangement did not last long and trains ran through to Conwy because the C&HR found that their trains were being delayed at the junction by these branch workings, although the Board of Trade had not authorised use of Conwy station by Llandudno branch trains. An accident involving a Llandudno train at Conwy brought these unauthorised movements to the attention of the Board of Trade. In October 1859, a Llandudno train was crossing from the Down to the Up line at Conwy when it was hit by an Up main-line train. The Board of Trade was not pleased and pointed out that Conwy station did not have enough capacity to deal with Llandudno branch trains. Urgent talks between the interested companies took place with a view to improve facilities at Conwy, but it was decided that better interchange facilities could be offered by improving the rudimentary station at Llandudno Junction. (Author's Collection)

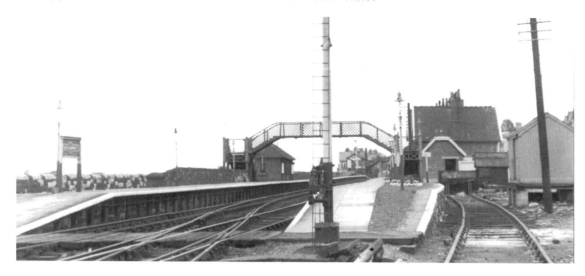

Deganwy station, looking towards Llandudno, as it appeared on 13 August 1953. The station was opened in 1866 and the main building opened at the same time. Before the station here was built, the LNWR withdrew its engine in the winter of 1860 and no services were worked until the following spring. The branch itself was in poor condition, not least because the St George's Company was without funds and the LNWR often had to pursue the company for hire charges. The LNWR took possession of the line through a lease in 1862, and carried out essential repairs. In the summer, when services were back to normal, the LNWR decided to use a pair of privately owned carriages that were not fit for normal services on a horse-drawn service for the following winter. One Thomas Page was hired to 'horse the branch' for £3 per week. The branch passed into LNWR ownership in 1873 and several improvements were made, including doubling the line over a period of three years in the 1870s due to large increases in passenger traffic to the newly popular resort at Llandudno. In October 1863, the sharp curve from the junction to the branch was flattened out and the Llandudno service was worked continuously and locomotives hauled throughout the year. From February 1877, new connections were put in at Llandudno Junction which allowed through running between Llandudno and Betws-y-Coed. When the line was doubled, a new platform was built at Deganwy and connected with the main building by a standard LNWR-type footbridge with rolled columns. (H. Casserley)

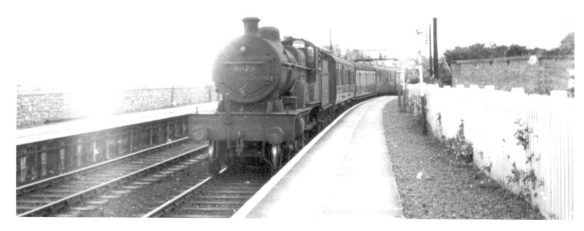

Arriving at Deganwy on 14 August 1953 is the 7.45 p.m. Llandudno–Chester train, headed by ex-LMS 4P Compound 4-4-0 No. 41123 (H. Casserley)

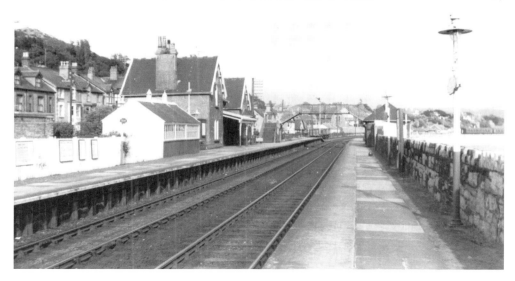

Deganwy station, facing Llandudno Junction, on 11 July 1960. Between here and Llandudno Junction, a slate quay was developed for seagoing vessels in 1882, using spoil from the opening out of Belmont Tunnel, Bangor. The LNWR had helped to centralise all seagoing traffic at Deganwy and sent prospectuses to slate quarry owners at Blaenau Ffestiniog, Bethesda and Llanberis. Opening of the Conwy Valley line allowed easy access from Blaenau Ffestiniog to Deganwy, and the main C&HR could transport slate from other quarries, all of which, the LNWR hoped, would increase traffic revenues. Narrow gauge tracks and wagons were utilised in the slate quarries and on the quay at Deganwy; these wagons could be transported between quarries and quays on specially adapted standard gauge goods wagons. This traffic commenced in 1885 and died out between the wars. The quay stood out in the Conwy Estuary, giving two faces to load ships. The area has now been developed into a marina and private housing. (R. Casserley)

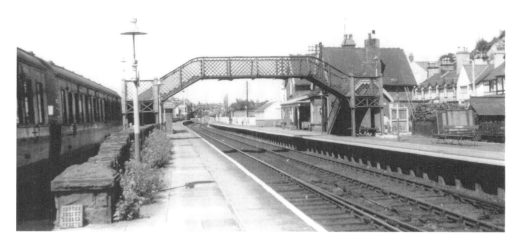

Another view of Deganwy station, facing Llandudno on 20 July 1963, showing the standard LNWR footbridge, the main building and the village on the right. Deganwy was supplied with two signal boxes. Number 1 controlled workings on the quay and into the quay, while Number 2 controlled a level crossing at the Llandudno end, just visible in this view, which gives road access to the beach. Pedestrians were provided with a footbridge that could be used when the gates were closed. (R. Casserley)

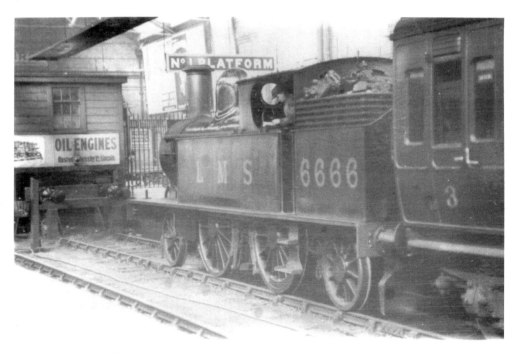

Standing at the buffer stops at Llandudno station in 1932 is ex-LNWR 2-4-2 tank loco No. 6666 after bringing in a local service from Llandudno Junction. Llandudno, in the shelter of the Great Orme, very quickly became a fashionable resort and the small station platform, which opened with the branch, was lengthened by the LNWR in 1863. A level crossing was abolished and some new sidings put in. Between 1869 and 1872, the platform was further extended, a run-round loop was put in and a waiting shed was built. When the branch was brought into LNWR ownership, the town was rapidly expanding with visitors pouring in. Another extension to the platform was ordered in 1876, along with a new warehouse and engine shed. The plan for an engine shed here was dropped in favour extending that at Llandudno Junction. All of this work did not relieve congestion at Llandudno and excursion trains were hurriedly unloaded and backing into increasing numbers of sidings – nearly 2 miles were laid between 1876 and 1894. Many complaints were made by locals about the facilities at Llandudno station and, in October 1890, contracts were let for a new station in red brick, with five platforms and a centre carriage drive, all enclosed under a 'Euston'-style station roof. This new station opened in the summer of 1892, a grand terminus, which befitted a highly successful branch line, as it had become by this time. (Author's Collection)

Opposite above: Standing at Llandudno station in the summer of 1954 is ex-LMS 4P 'Compound' 4-4-0 No. 41158 with a train for Chester. The 'Euston' roof at the station can be seen here, but has since been cut right back in the 1980s and 90s, leaving the now-rationalised station opened to the elements. However, the elegant exterior remains intact, giving an idea of what the station was like in its heyday. (LOSA)

Opposite below: A map showing the western section of the C&HR with its long branch from Menai Bridge to Afonwen, via Caernarfon. This branch had its own branches, mostly to serve local slate quarries in the locality. The main C&HR will cross the 1850-built Britannia Bridge, which suffered a massive fire in 1972; this extended the life of the line as far as Caernarfon until the bridge could be repaired, and gained access to the Isle of Anglesey and the seaport at Holyhead. (Author's Collection)

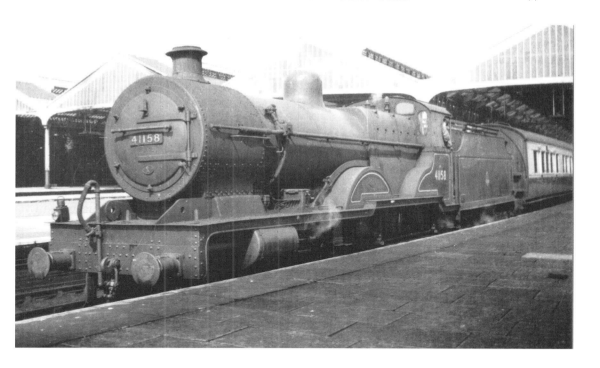

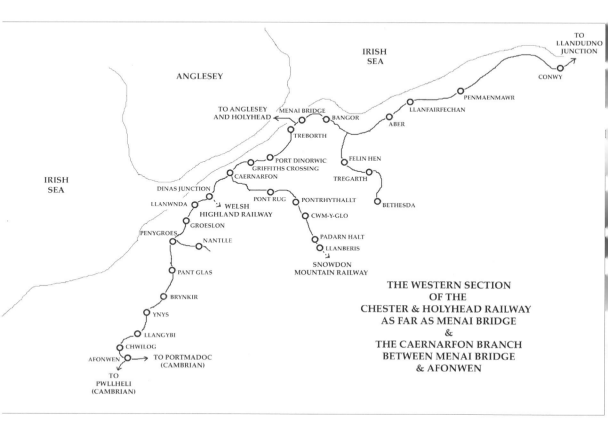

THE WESTERN SECTION
OF THE
CHESTER & HOLYHEAD RAILWAY
AS FAR AS MENAI BRIDGE
&
THE CAERNARFON BRANCH
BETWEEN MENAI BRIDGE
& AFONWEN

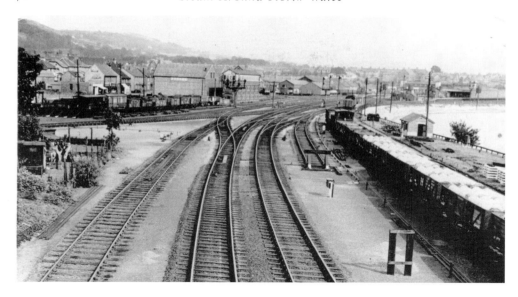

Looking back towards Llandudno Junction station as the C&HR climbs away to the tubular bridge at Conwy. The station, loco shed and signal box are in view, along with the village on the left. The Fyffes banana warehouse is situated just in front of the signal box and has since become an antiques store. (Author's Collection)

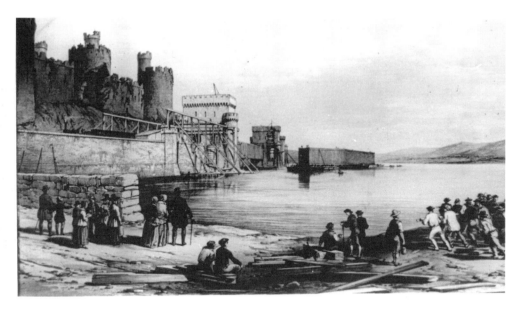

In order to cross the River Conwy, Robert Stephenson proposed a tubular bridge that would carry the C&HR into Conwy itself. Here, before the line was opened in 1848, the second of the iron tubes, to carry the Down line, is being prepared to be put into place. The tube carrying the Up line is already *in situ*. The portals were designed to blend with the castle, which can be seen on the left. The procedure is being watched by interested locals who would not have seen anything like it before. The bridge here was also the model on which the more ambitious Britannia Bridge was based, although the latter bridge would have to be longer and higher to cross the Menai Strait into Anglesey. (Author's Collection)

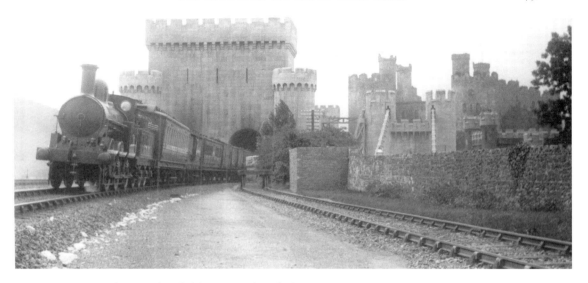

An Up parcels train, headed by an unidentified LNWR 0-6-0 loco, is seen leaving the tubular bridge as it heads towards Llandudno Junction at around 1900. On the right is Thomas Telford's Conwy suspension bridge, a smaller version of the one that crosses the Menai Strait, built as part of his coast road with the castle in the background. As can be seen, the portals for the tubular bridge blend well with the castle in the background. (Author's Collection)

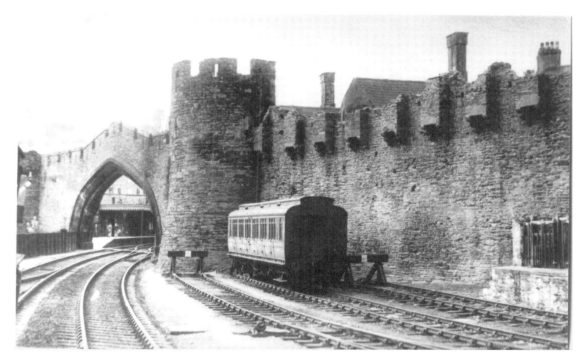

The approach to Conwy station after leaving the tubular bridge as it appeared on 20 July 1941. The castle wall is on the right with an old clerestory coach in the siding. In order to gain access to Conwy, the railway had to pass through the castle wall, achieved by creating an arch. (H. Casserley)

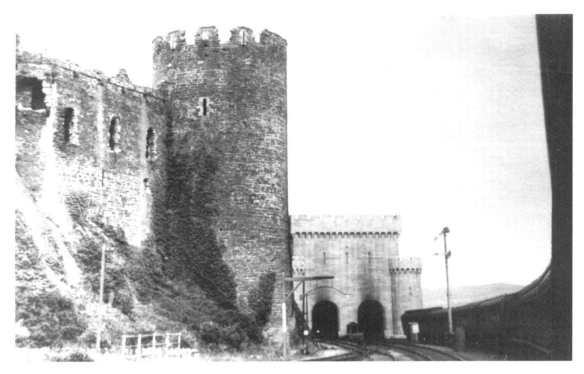

Looking in the opposite direction and the exit from the tubular bridge is in view, with the castle on the left. (H. Casserley)

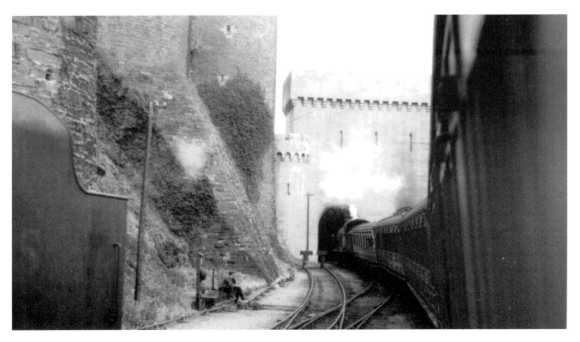

Ex-LNWR 4-4-0 loco No. 25277 is entering the tubular bridge on 21 July 1941 with the Up 2.15 p.m. Caernarfon–Llandudno Junction train. (H. Casserley)

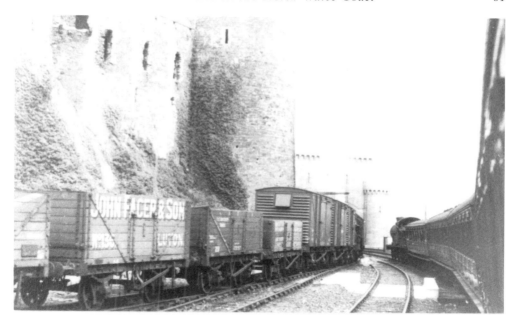

The same train is seen leaving Conwy station past the goods yard, busy with wagons waiting to proceed to Llandudno Junction when this passenger train passes through the tunnel. (H. Casserley)

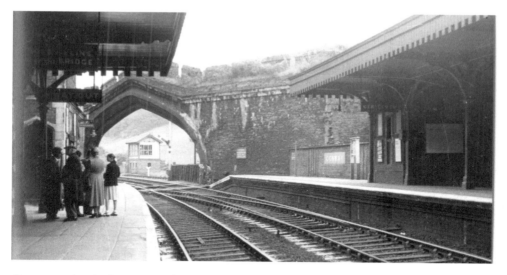

Conwy station looking towards Llandudno Junction with the signal box visible through the arch. The station at Conwy was built in the Gothic style, which was designed to blend with the castle, but only modest facilities were provided when the station was opened in 1848, although it was the main station and even dealt with trains from the Llandudno branch until Llandudno Junction station was opened. A number of improvements were made over the years, including widening of the platforms in 1857 and again as far as the tunnel on the west side of the station in 1873, but they were not raised to the full height until the 1890s. At this time, a new footbridge was put in and deeper LNWR awnings replaced the smaller Thompson ones. Better accommodation was also put in on the Down platform. (H. Casserley)

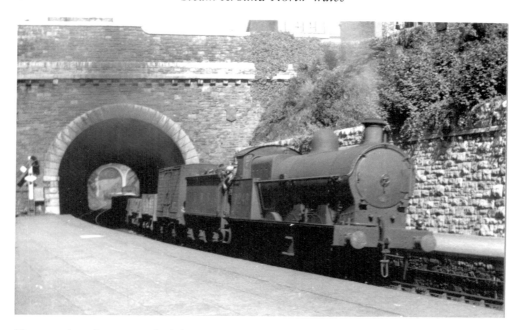

The tunnel at the west end of the station and, as can be seen, the platforms meet the tunnel entrance. Here, in August 1936, ex-LNWR 7F 0-8-0 No. 9248 is seen entering Conwy station after leaving the tunnel with an Up freight. (Author's Collection)

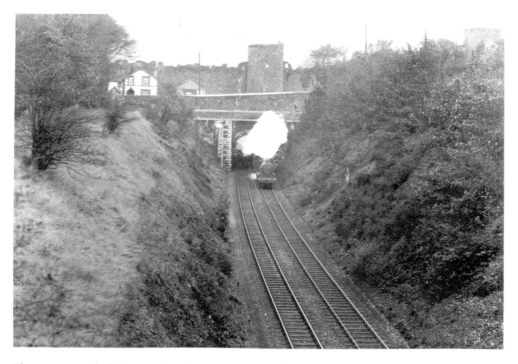

The western end of the tunnel at Conwy station, with the castle and town behind, is the setting as a rebuilt Caprotti valve-geared, large-boilered LNWR Claughton Class 4-6-0 heads the Down Irish Mail bound for Holyhead. (D. Ibbotson)

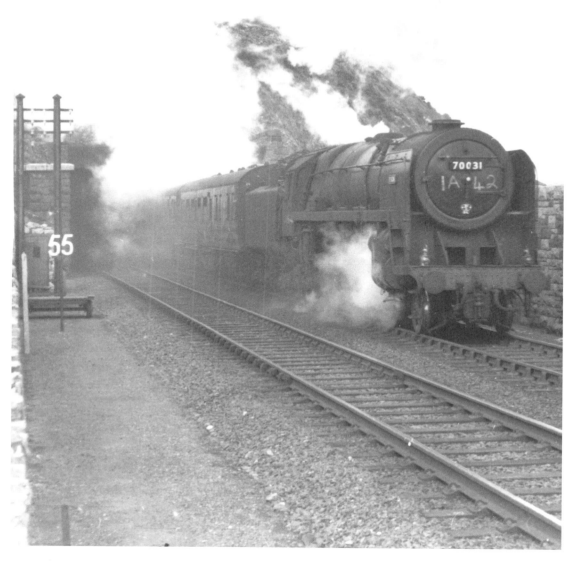

The second obstacle facing Stephenson as he planned the C&HR was the mountains at Penmaenbach and Penmaenmawr. He decided to tunnel through them rather than taking the railway around the difficult and dangerous headlands. Here, after leaving Penmaenbach tunnel with a Down express, is BR Britannia Pacific No. 70031 *Byron* on 21 July 1962. (P. Owen)

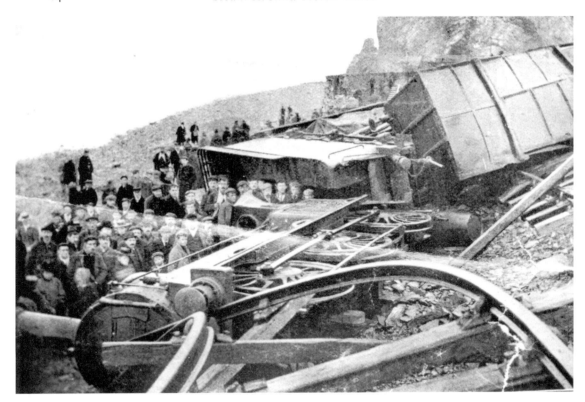

Stormy seas and high winds have often created problems in the Penmaenmawr area and the LNWR were aware of this and, in such conditions, watchmen were placed at Penmaenbach Tunnel to monitor the situation. On the night of 12 January 1899, storms coincided with a very high tide and at around 10.00 p.m. the sea became very rough and washed over the track, water entering the carriages of the Up Irish Mail as it passed. At around 10.45, watchmen noticed that the railway was completely covered by seawater, caused by a breach in the sea wall, although it was some 20 feet high and 6 feet thick at the base. The noise of falling masonry was lost in the noise of the gale, the sea having washed away the ballast and ground underneath to leave the rails suspended over a gaping hole. At the same time, a goods train was expected and one of the watchmen immediately entered Penmaenbach Tunnel with a warning lamp, but was too late to prevent the accident. The line curved through the tunnel and the train was almost upon the watchman as he waved his lamp. The engine whistled as it passed and the watchman assumed that the driver had seen his light. Indeed, he had as he was applying the brakes and reversing gear as he approached the damaged track. The train, headed by an LNWR Ramsbottom DX 0-6-0 tender loco with twelve wagons and a brake van went over the damaged track, which immediately collapsed, sending the engine, with driver and fireman, and eight wagons into the pit created by the sea; it immediately submerged them, killing both the driver and fireman. The guard and a passenger in the brake van were unaware of what had happened, assuming that the train had broken in half. Thus, he sent the passenger to warn staff at Penmaenmawr station. When the tide abated the following morning, the engine was found on its side with a length of rail twisted underneath. The tender had come down on top of the loco, with the wagons and their contents smashed in a heap and scattered around the immediate area, as can be seen in this view taken the morning after the accident. The body of the driver was found on Conwy Morfa, about 4 miles away, the following morning, but the fireman was never found. The wreckage took a week to remove, but train services were restarted some thirty hours after the accident. A new, much stronger wall was also built and there have been no further incidents since that fateful night. (Author's Collection)

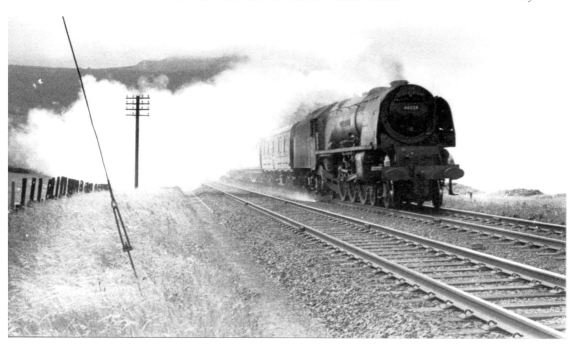

Ex-LMS Princess Coronation Pacific No. 46238 *City of Carlisle* is at the head of the Up Irish Mail as it approaches Penmaenbach Tunnel on a windy day in the early 1960s. These locos had been transferred from the West Coast main line after modern traction had replaced steam on Euston–Glasgow services but were rarely used on the Irish Mail, making this view quite rare. (P. Owen)

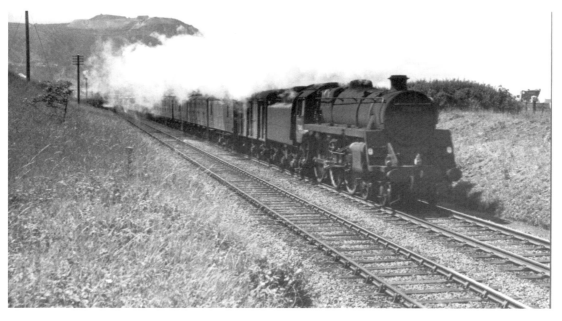

In the early 1960s, a BR Standard Class 4-6-0 is east of Penmaenmawr station with an Up goods train. (P. Owen)

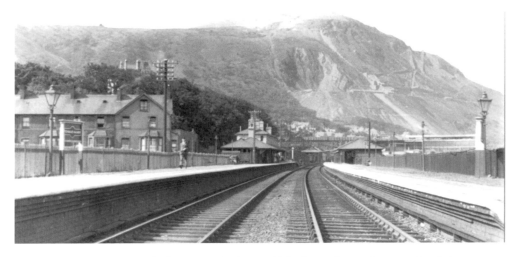

Penmaenmawr station, with the mountain from which the station and town take their name, as it appeared on 12 August 1953 looking west. When the railway first opened, a railway station did not exist here despite the fact that Penmaenmawr mountain was the site of two granite quarries, although a jetty existed in the town, which dealt with stone traffic from the quarries. A station was opened here in 1849, the railway company adopting the name of Penmaenmawr, although the then village was actually in the parish of Dwygyfylchi, which the C&HR felt would be unpronounceable by visitors, though the name of the mountain would be suitably Welsh and acceptable. The original station here was rather basic and, despite later extensions, the platforms were not properly paved until August 1888 at a cost of £106. (H. Casserley)

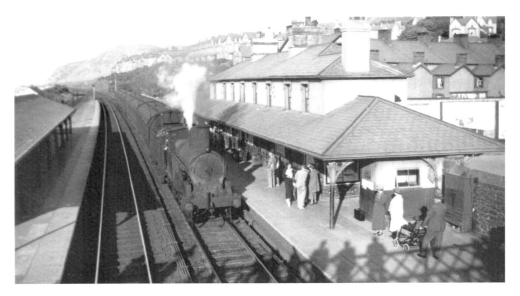

Penmaenmawr station on 24 August 1937 with ex-LNWR Cauliflower 0-6-0 No. 8485 on a local train to Bangor. The town, and its substantial houses, was built by wealthy newcomers after the station had been opened. At the end of the Up platform is the entrance to quarry sidings, which were developed from the late 1870s. The town became popular with wealthy visitors thanks to patronage by William Gladstone, a friend of the Darbishire family who owned the granite quarry here. (Author's Collection)

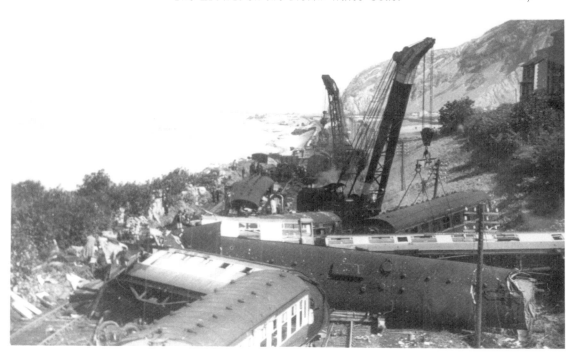

On 27 August 1950, an accident occurred in the vicinity of Penmaenmawr station when, at 3.05 a.m., the Up Irish Mail hit a light engine, which caused six deaths and thirty-seven injuries. At 2.52 a.m., ex-LMS Crab 2-6-0 No. 42885 arrived tender first at the Down platform from Llandudno Junction to collect a stone train from the sidings. The loco stopped at the signal box, which was beyond the Down platform and footbridge on the Down side, before crossing over to the Up line in order to enter the sidings to collect its train for Mold Junction. The Up Irish Mail, running around thirty minutes late, had been accepted by the signalman at 2.50 a.m., just before the light engine arrived. After crossing to the Up line, No. 42885 whistled and waited for the points to be changed so that it could enter the sidings. From this point, confusion arose and the light engine did not set back into the sidings as expected. At the same time, the signals were cleared for the Irish Mail. The driver misunderstood the signal and thought he was to head back to Llandudno Junction and he waited for his fireman to join him as he had gone to the sidings to prepare the wagons. As the fireman was walking back to the engine, he heard the sound of the mail train and waved his red lamp to warn the signalman that the light engine was still on the main line. The signalman immediately reset the signal to danger, but it was too late, although the driver of the light engine realised what was happening and had started to move forward. The express was travelling at about 70 mph, in order to make up time, when the driver saw the signal change and immediately applied the brakes but was unable to prevent a collision. The loco *Lancashire Fusilier* smashed halfway into the tender of the Crab, derailing two rear wheels and all wheels of the express engine, but kept on a straight course. The first two vehicles telescoped together and this is where most of the fatalities occurred, while other coaches remained upright. At the same time, a heavy goods train was due from Llandudno Junction and the signalman set all signals to danger while the fireman put detonators on the track to warn the oncoming train. The driver of the freight train heard the explosions and braked hard just before a collision would have occurred. The heavy goods train contained explosives and could have caused substantial damage had it crashed. Local people helped victims at the station and a subsequent inquiry felt that the signal box was at the wrong end of the station, so it was moved opposite the sidings and track circuiting was also put in as recommended at the inquiry. The aftermath of the accident can be seen here with cranes and heavy-lifting gear in use to clear the wreckage. (Author's Collection)

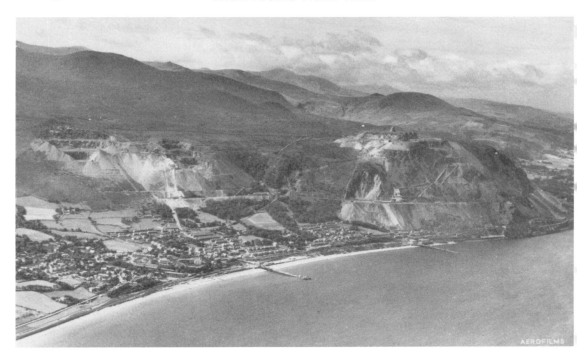

Granite quarrying was a major part of the economy at Penmaenmawr and brought a great deal of revenue for the LNWR over the years. The quarries here also introduced granite railway ballast when stone-crushing equipment was introduced in 1888. Such was the quality of granite ballast that the LNWR Permanent Way Engineers felt, when reporting to the Board on 19 June 1889, that 'ballasting with crushed granite is economical and advantageous to the preservation of rails, chairs and sleepers'. The LNWR was already using granite ballast by then, spending some £1,400 per month on such material. As well as crushed stone for ballast and road macadam, the quarries were producing stone setts for use on city tramways; the LNWR, and later LMS and BR, were moving most of this material on their railways. Even today, thousands of tons of stone are moved by rail from Penmaenmawr sidings. The extent of quarry workings can be seen in this 1930s view, with jetties in view which allowed seagoing vessels to load stone as required. The railway here is running along the coastline. (Author's Collection)

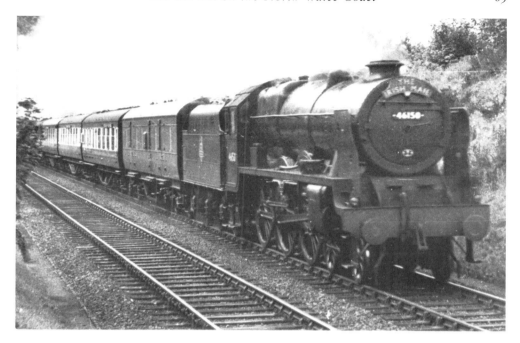

The Up Irish Mail heads east through Penmaenmawr headed by ex-LMS rebuilt Royal Scot Class 4-6-0 No. 46150 *The Life Guardsman* in the 1950s. It was a member of this class that was involved in the 1950 accident. (Author's Collection)

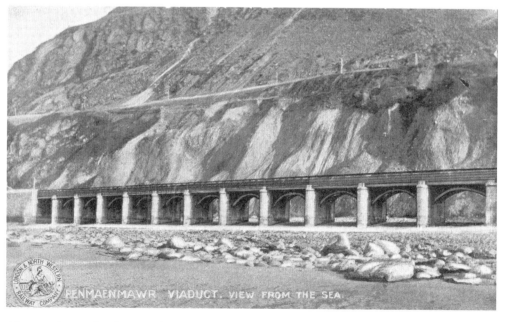

After passing under the quarries over Penmaenmawr Tunnel, the C&HR enters Llanfairfechan over a low viaduct, seen here in LNWR days. When the C&HR opened, the line here was on an embankment but it was frequently washed away by the action of the sea. To solve this problem the low viaduct was built and has never been threatened since. (Author's Collection)

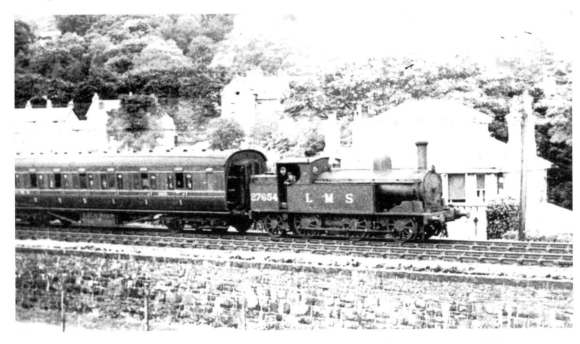

Approaching Llanfairfechan station from Penmaenmawr on 14 July 1941 is ex-LNWR 0-6-2 Coal Tank No. 27654, seen at the head of a local train. (H. Casserley)

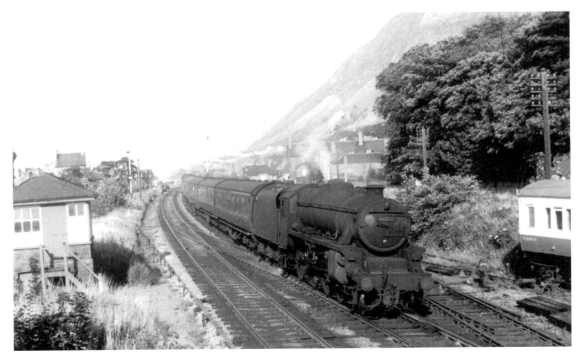

Crossing over a bridge that takes a road down from Llanfairfechan village to the seashore just before entering the station is ex-LMS Black Five 4-6-0 No. 44770 with the 5.02 p.m. Llandudno Junction–Holyhead train. (H. Casserley)

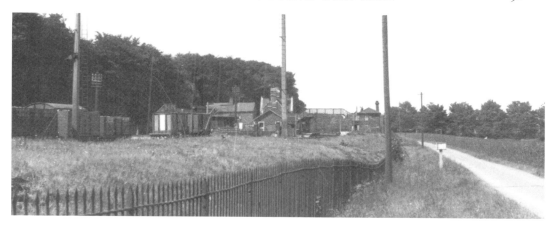

The exterior of Llanfairfechan station during wartime on 17 July 1941. (H. Casserley)

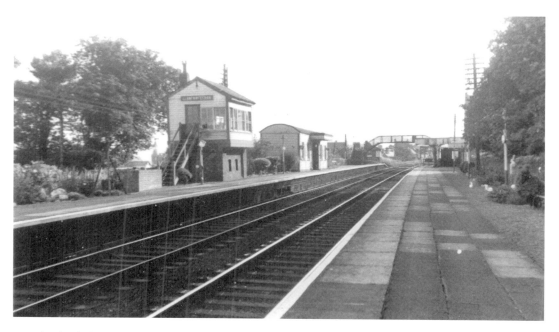

Llanfairfechan station, looking east, on 19 July 1963. The station here opened in May 1860 and its buildings were unlike others on the C&HR, having been constructed by the LNWR. The Up platform here has an unusual waiting shelter and the signal box is of the standard LNWR type, having replaced the original Saxby and Farmer box in 1889. A small goods yard for thirty-one wagons was on the Down side, while a lay-by for forty-four wagons was on the Up side. These goods facilities were removed in 1964. (R. Casserley)

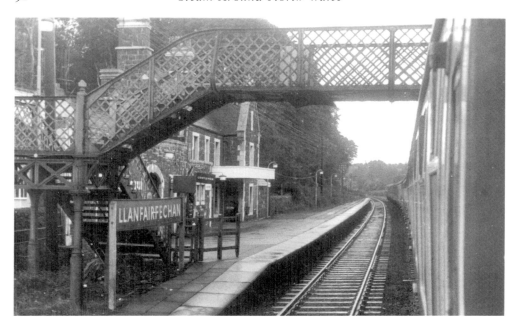

The main station building at Llanfairfechan, which was demolished in 1987 to make way for the A55 Expressway at this point. A simple waiting shelter was provided at the station in 1989. (H. Casserley)

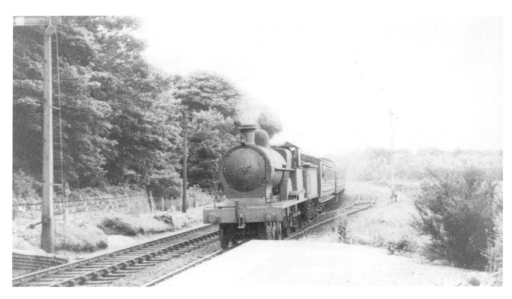

Approaching the western end of the station at Llanfairfechan in 1941 is ex-LNWR Precursor Class 4-4-0 No. 25277 with a train for Llandudno Junction. (H. Casserley)

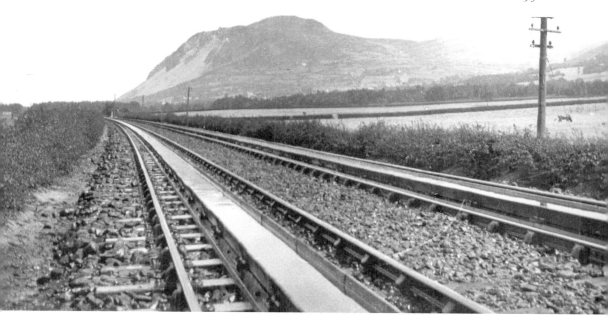

The water troughs at Aber, some 2 miles west of Llanfairfechan, which were built to replace those at Mochdre. The troughs allowed the Irish Mail to pick up water without stopping. Penmaenmawr mountain can be seen in the background. (Author's Collection)

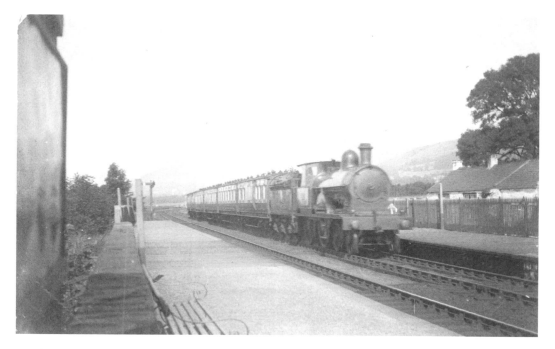

The little station at Aber, around 1900, with a train for Bangor headed by an unidentified LNWR 4-4-0. Aber was the only station opened between Conwy and Bangor when the C&HR was opened, but was also the only one to close, in 1960, due to the rural nature of the location and a lack of passengers. (Author's Collection)

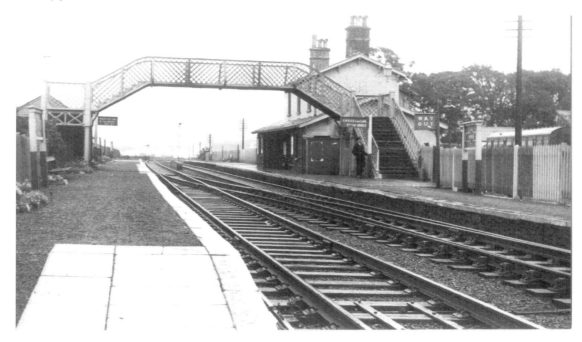

Aber station looking east on 24 August 1954, showing the original Thompson main building, which remains *in situ* and has been privately owned since the station was closed. (R. Casserley)

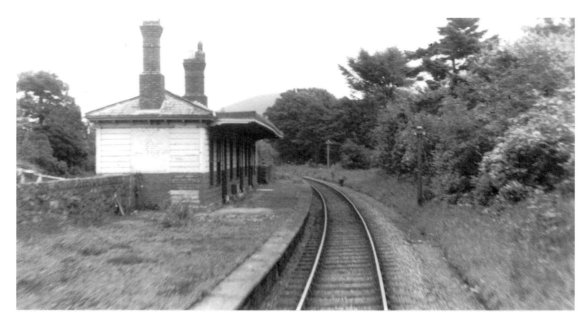

Just east of Bangor Tunnel and a couple of miles west of Aber was the 4½-mile branch to Bethesda, built to tap slate traffic at the vast quarries in the town. The branch had stations at Felin Hen, Tregarth and Bethesda itself. The branch was opened in July 1884 and closed in 1963. Just before closure is the little timber-built station at Tregarth, facing Bethesda, on 19 July 1963. (R. Casserley)

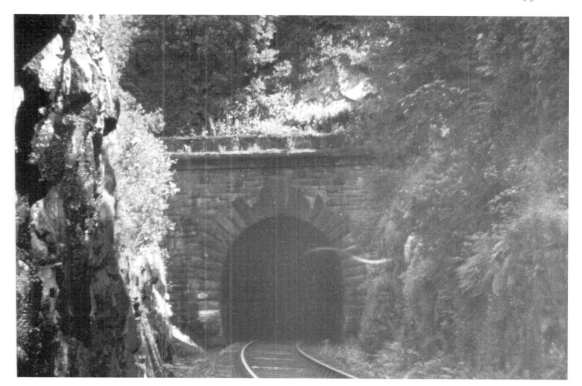

Before entering the station, the branch ran through Bethesda Tunnel, seen here in 1952. (D. Ibbotson)

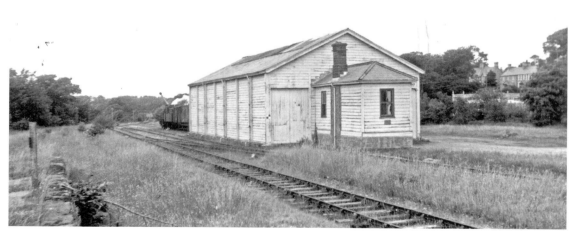

The remains of the goods shed at Bethesda on 19 July 1963 with an ex-LMS tank loco shunting in the yard. (R. Casserley)

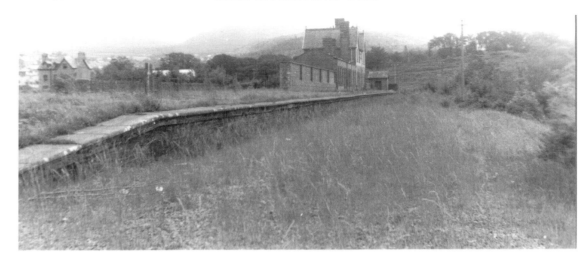

The main station building at Bethesda station on the same day and facing the dead end. All track has been removed at the station and the mountains from which slate has been extracted can be seen in the background. From here, the C&HR enters the heart of Snowdonia. (R. Casserley)

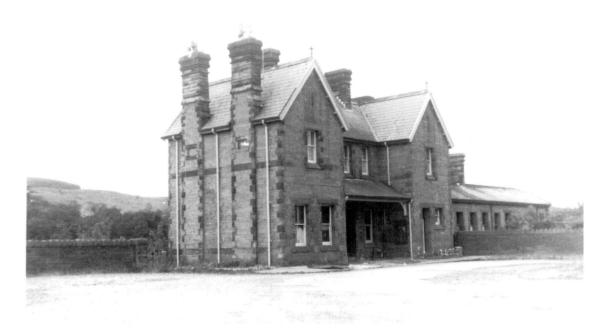

Exterior of the main station building at Bethesda in 1963, an imposing structure worthy of such an important location for the LNWR. (R. Casserley)

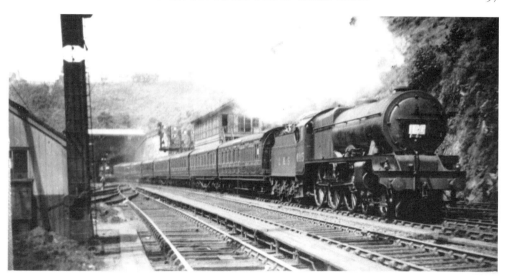

Back on the main line and LMS Royal Scot 4-6-0 No. 6115 *Scots Guardsman* enters Bangor station with the Up Irish Mail and past North signal box. For the first two years of its existence, Bangor was the terminus of the C&HR until the Britannia Bridge was opened. Passengers were then carried by stagecoach across Telford's suspension bridge over the Menai Strait to join another train for the journey over Anglesey for the packet port at Holyhead and the onward journey to Ireland. (Author's Collection)

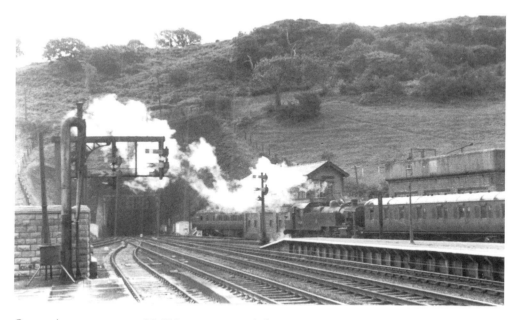

On 14 August 1953, ex-LMS Ivatt 2-6-2 tank loco No. 41287 departs from Bangor with a local service to Caernarfon and will enter Bangor Tunnel before reaching Menai Bridge station and then taking the branch to Caernarfon. As an important station, substantial buildings were provided here, designed by Francis Thompson, isolated on an island platform as many improvements were made to the station here. The LMS built new main buildings in 1927 but the Thompson building was retained on the Up island platform. (H. Casserley)

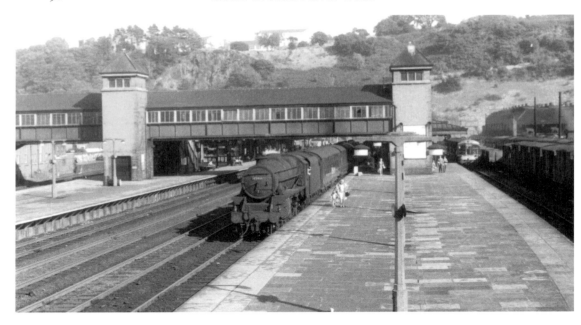

Bangor station on 26 August 1964 with ex-LMS Black Five 4-6-0 No. 45466 in view having brought in the 1.50 p.m. train from Manchester. The footbridge was built as part of the 1927 improvements. The train will have passed through Belmont Tunnel to gain access to Bangor station with its Egyptian-style architecture at the Bangor end. Belmont Tunnel is 135 yards long and, in 1881, permission was given to open out the tunnel at the eastern end to ease shunting movements, the spoil going to Deganwy for the quay there. (H. Casserley)

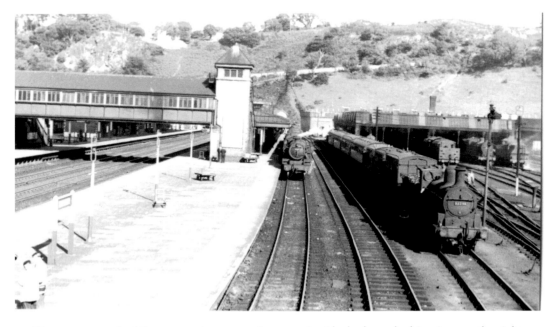

The western end of Bangor station on 25 June 1956 with the loco shed in view on the right. An ex-LMS tank engine waits to depart with a local train for Holyhead and ex-L&Y 0-6-0 No. 52238 shunts in the yard. (H. Casserley)

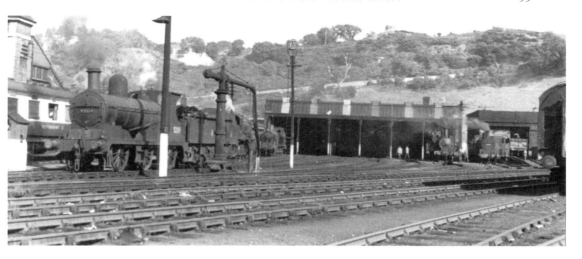

The loco shed at Bangor on 11 August 1953 before a new roof was built. In view is ex-L&Y 0-6-0 No. 52119, along with ex-LNWR and MR types. A loco shed has been provided here since the opening of the station, as it was the terminus of the C&HR until the Britannia Bridge was opened. (H. Casserley)

By the 1950s it had five roads and was coded 7B in BR days. Its allocation in 1950 was as follows:

Ex-MR 2P 4-4-0	40524
Ex-LMS 2MT 2-6-2T	41223, 41224, 41233
Ex-LMS 4MT 2-6-4T	42156, 42157, 42258, 42259, 42260, 42261, 42460, 42588, 42617, 42628, 42660
Ex-LMS 4F 0-6-0	44445
Ex-LMS Black Five 4-6-0	45144
Ex-LNWR 2P 0-6-2T	46899, 46906
Ex-L&Y 3F 0-6-0	52230, 52269, 52407
Ex-LNWR 2F 0-6-0	58375, 58381
	Total: 24

The shed was closed on 14 June 1965, its final allocation was:

Ex-LMS 2MT 2-6-2T	41200, 41233, 41234
Ex-LMS 4MT 2-6-4T	42074, 42251, 42267, 42283, 42606
Ex-LMS Black Five 4-6-0	44821, 45145, 45223, 45298, 45345
BR 2MT 2-6-0	78003, 78032, 78058, 78059
	Total: 17

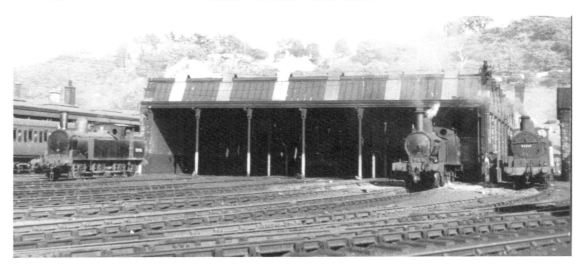

The loco shed at Bangor on 12 August 1953 with ex-LNWR 2F 0-6-2 Coal Tank No. 58903, ex-LNWR 1P 2-4-2 tank No. 46604 and ex-L&Y 0-6-0 No. 52269 standing outside on a sunny day. All of these engines would have disappeared by the end of the decade to be replaced by more modern traction. (H. Casserley)

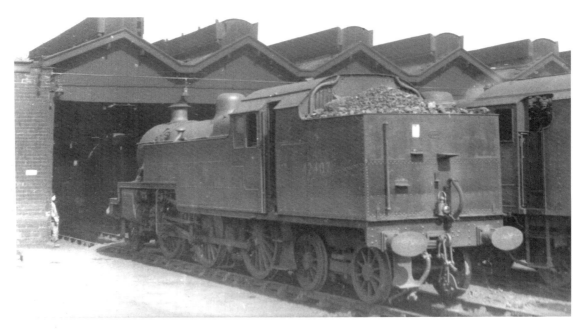

Standing outside the recently reroofed Bangor shed in 1962 is ex-LMS Fowler 2-6-4 tank No. 42407. (LOSA)

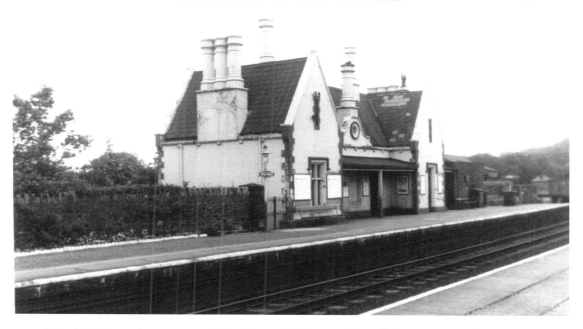

Menai Bridge station was opened in 1859, replacing a station called Britannia Bridge near the Caernarfonshire shore of the Menai Strait. The station served the main C&HR as well as the 1852-built Caernarfon branch. The attractive main building can be seen here on 19 July 1963 on the Down line. (R. Casserley)

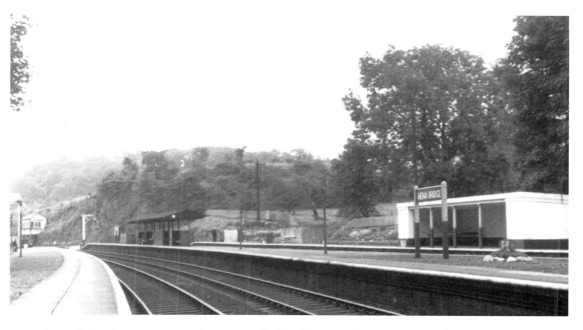

A much simpler structure can be seen on the Up side on 12 August 1953. In the 1880s, a small marshalling yard, capable of holding some 204 wagons, was opened and handled freight to and from Anglesey branches as well as traffic from Afonwen and the Nantlle and Llanberis branches and relieving traffic at Bangor. (H. Casserley)

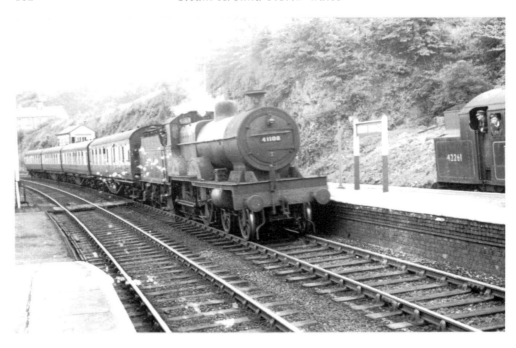

Ex-MR 4P Compound 4-4-0 No. 41108 enters Menai Bridge station on 12 August 1953 with the 7.35 p.m. Holyhead–Crewe train. On the right, ex-LMS Fairburn 2-6-4 tank No. 42261 waits to depart with a local train for Caernarfon and Afonwen. (H. Casserley)

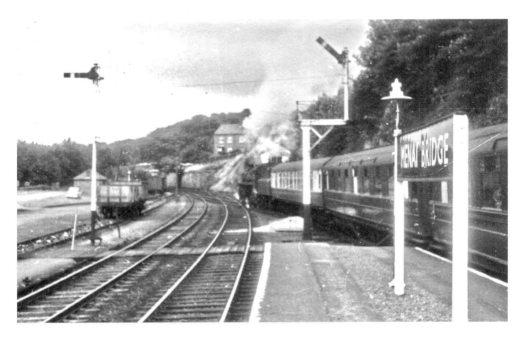

Leaving Menai Bridge station on 11 July 1960 is BR Standard Class 4-6-0 No. 75010 with the 3.10 p.m. Pwllheli–Llandudno train. This service will have run along the Cambrian Coast line from Pwllheli to Afonwen, then along the branch via Caernarfon to join the C&HR for Bangor to Llandudno Junction and then down the branch to Llandudno. (R. Casserley)

BANGOR, CARNARVON, PENYGROES, and AFONWEN.—London and North Western.

Down. — Week Days / Sundays

Miles	Station	mrn	mrn	mrn	mrn	aft	aft	aft	aft	aft	aft	aft	aft	aft	aft	aft	Sun mrn	Sun mrn	Sun aft
0	Bangor ....dep.	4 48	....	9 0	1037	12 51	1 10	2 29	4 5	4 37	6 10	....	7 30	8 30	9 5	1050	....	4 48	....	9 5
1¼	Menai Bridge ¶	....	....	9 4	1041	12 9	1 14	2 32	4 9	4 41	6 13	....	7 33	8 34	9 9	1054	....	....	....	9 9
2½	Treborth	....	....	9 12	1046	1214	1 23	2 37	4 15	4 47	6 18	....	7 38							
4½	Port Dinorwic	4 58	....	9 18	1051	1219	1 28	2 42	4 20	4 52	6 23	....	7 43	8 43	9 18	11 3	....	4 58	....	9 18
6¾	Griffith's Crossing	....	....	9 23	1056	1224	1 33	2 47	4 25	4 57	6 28	....	7 48							
8¾	Carnarvon 478 { arr.	5 5	....	9 27	11 0	1228	1 37	2 51	4 30	5 1	6 32	....	7 52	8 50	9 26	1111	....	5 5	....	9 26
	{ dep.	5 8	6 35	9 40	....	1235	....	2 57	....	5 10	....	6 45	7 57					....	7 55	
12	Dinas Junction 477	a	6 45	9 50	....	1245	....	3 7	....	5 20	....	6 55	8 7							
12½	Llanwnda	....	6 49	9 54	....	1249	....	3 11	....	5 24	....	6 59	8 11						8 8	
13½	Groeslon	5 22	6 53	9 58	....	1253	....	3 15	....	5 28	....	7 3	8 15						8 12	
15½	Penygroes 478 { arr.	5 27	6 58	10 3	....	1258	....	3 19	....	5 32	....	7 8	8 19						8 17	
	{ dep.	5 28	7 0	10 6	....	1259	....	3 22	....	5 33	....	....	8 20						8 18	
19¼	Pant Glas	....	7 9	1015	....	1 8	....	3 31	....	5 42	....	....	8 29							
21¼	Brynkir	5 40	7 14	1020	....	1 12	....	3 35	....	5 46	....	....	8 34						8 31	
23½	Ynys	....	7 20	1026	....	1 18	....	3 41	....	5 52	....	....	Sat.							
25	Llangybi	....	7 24	1030	....	1 22	....	3 45	....	5 56	....	....	8 44							
26	Chwilog †	5 50	7 27	1033	....	1 25	....	3 48	....	5 59	....	....	8 48						8 41	
27¼	Afonwen 469 ....arr.	5 56	7 32	1040	....	1 30	....	3 53	....	6 4	....	....	8 54						8 47	
31¼	469 Pwllheli ....arr.	6 10	8 10	1055	....	1 55	....	4 20	....	6 20	....	....	9 12						8 58	

(Some week-day columns are marked "Saturdays only".)

Up. — Week Days / Sundays

Miles	Station	mrn	mrn	mrn	mrn	mrn	mrn	mrn	aft	aft	aft	aft	aft	aft	aft	aft	Sun mrn	Sun aft
	469 Pwllheli ....dep.	....	6 15	....	7 40	....	....	11 0	....	1 25	....	4 0	....	7 0	8 50			....	6 40
—	Afonwen ....dep.	....	6 30	....	7 55	....	....	1120	....	1 50	....	4 15	....	7 20	9 10			....	7 0
1¼	Chwilog †	....	6 35	....	8 0	....	....	1125	....	1 55	....	4 20	....	7 25	9 15			....	7 5
2½	Llangybi	....	....	Sig.	8 4	....	....	1130	....	1 59	....	4 24	....	7 29				....	....
4	Ynys	....	....	b	8 8	....	....	1135	....	2 3	....	4 28	....	7 33				....	....
6¼	Brynkir	....	6 45	....	8 13	....	....	1140	....	2 7	....	4 32	....	7 37	9 25			....	7 15
8	Pant Glas	....	6 51	....	8 19	....	....	1146	....	2 12	....	4 38	....	7 43	Sig.			....	....
11¾	Penygroes 478 { arr.	....	7 0	....	8 28	....	....	1155	....	2 21	....	4 47	....	7 52	9 39			....	7 29
	{ dep.	....	7 1	....	8 29	1125	....	1157	1 55	2 22	....	4 48	....	7 53	9 40			....	7 30
13¾	Groeslon	....	7 5	....	8 34	1130	....	12 2	2 0	2 26	....	4 52	....	7 57	9 45			....	7 35
15	Llanwnda	....	7 8	....	8 37	1134	....	12 6	2 3	2 30	....	4 55	....	8 0	9 49			....	7 39
15½	Dinas Junction 477	....	7 11	....	8 40	1138	....	12 9	2 6	2 35	....	4 58	....	8 5				....	....
18½	Carnarvon 478 { arr.	....	7 21	....	8 50	1150	....	1221	2 18	2 45	....	5 8	....	8 18	10 2			....	7 52
	{ dep.	7 10	7 25	8 10	8 55	1055	....	1155	1250	2 10	....	2 55	4 5	5 13	6 30	8 22		6 15	8 20
20¼	Griffith's Crossing	Sig.	Sig.	....	11 2	....	Sig.	1255	2 15	....	3	4 10	....	6 37					
22¼	Port Dinorwic	7 18	7 33	8 20	9 3	11 8	....	12 3	1 2	21	....	3	6 4	15 5	21 6	43 8 30		6 23	8 28
25	Treborth	....	Sig.	....	1115	....	....	1 8	2 27	....	....	4 22	....	6 50				....	....
26	Menai Bridge ¶	....	7 24	7 39	8 27	9 10	1119	....	12 10	1 12	2 31	....	3 13	4 26	5 28	6 54	8 37	6 30	8 35
27¾	Bangor * ¶ 472, 474 ....arr.	7 31	7 46	8 32	9 15	1124	....	1215	1 19	2 36	....	3 18	4 32	5 33	6 59	8 44		6 37	8 42

a Stops to set down on informing the Guard. **b** Stops on Mondays and Saturdays to set down on notice being given to the Guard, and to take up on notice being given at the Station.

* Station for Beaumaris. † Station for Four Crosses (2¼ miles) and Nevin (8¾ miles).

¶ For **Omnibus Service** between Bangor and Beaumaris, see page 479.

A 1910 LNWR timetable for trains along the Caernarfon branch from Bangor to Afonwen, where it will meet the Cambrian Coast line for access to Pwllheli or to connect with trains for Barmouth. (Author's Collection)

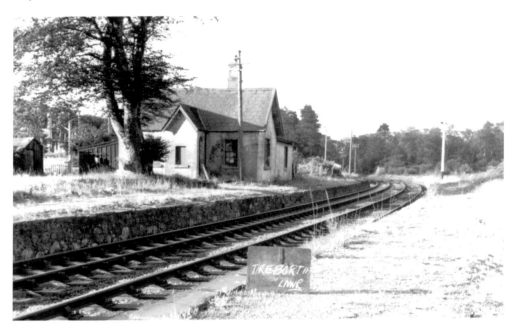

The first station on the branch to Afonwen was at Treborth, seen here in the early 1960s. The line as far as Caernarfon was singled in 1966, closed to goods traffic in 1969 and closed to passengers on 5 January 1970. However, a fire on the Britannia Bridge in May 1970 meant closure to freight traffic at Holyhead, and Caernarfon became a temporary container port. The line had new rail services from 15 June 1970 until 5 February 1972. (Author's Collection)

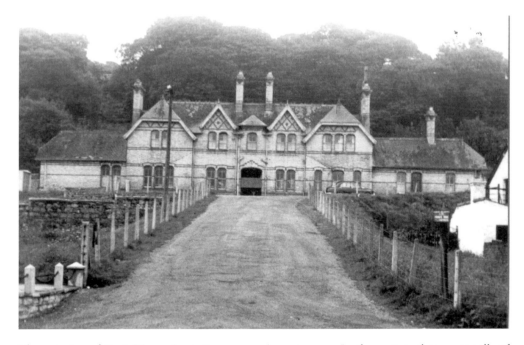

The exterior of Port Dinorwic station on 24 August 1954. In the 1980s, there was talk of reopening the branch to Caernarfon, but nothing came of it. (R. Casserley)

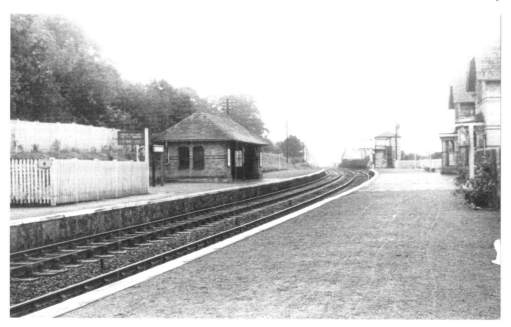

The platforms at Port Dinorwic station on the same day, looking towards Caernarfon. The village here has now taken the Welsh name of Y Felinheli. (R. Casserley)

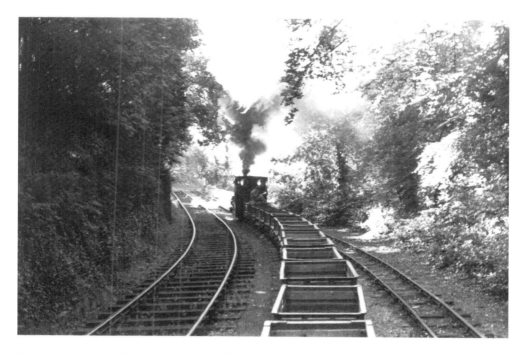

Port Penrhyn was the point where exchange sidings between the LNWR and the Penrhyn Quarries at Port Dinorwic and, in 1953, the narrow gauge quarry railway can be seen at the sidings with an empty slate train, headed by Penrhyn Quarries loco *Blanche*, making its way back to the quarry workings after transferring slate at the sidings. (H. Casserley)

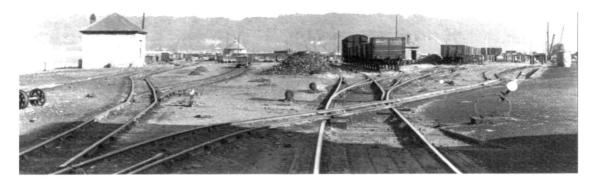

The sidings at Port Penrhyn, on 11 August 1953, showing the LNWR standard gauge line with open goods wagons and a van awaiting loading with slate. To the left are the narrow gauge tracks of the quarry company's railway. (H. Casserley)

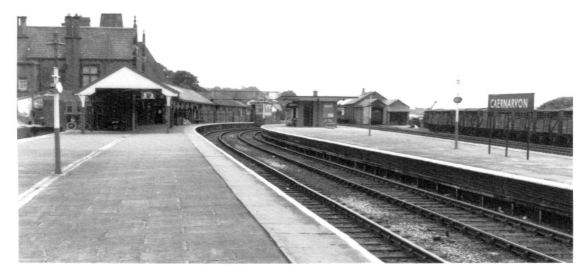

The handsome station at Caernarfon, built in 1870 to replace a simpler structure that had been in existence since the line had opened, which was necessary with the opening of the branch to Llanberis. Caernarfon became a terminus when the rest of the branch to Afonwen was closed in 1964 and the buildings here were fully repainted for the investiture of the Prince of Wales at Caernarfon in 1969, only for the demolition men to move in shortly afterwards. (Author's Collection)

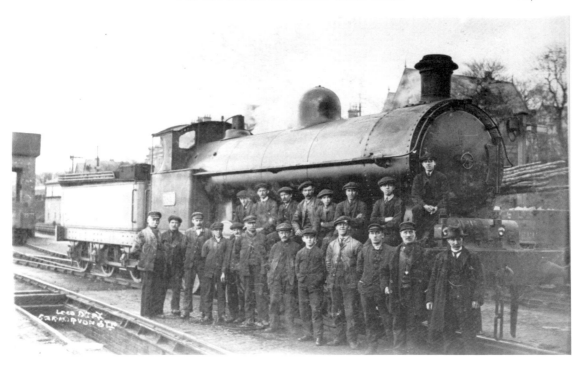

Back in LNWR days, Caernarfon was supplied with its own loco shed, supplying engines for services to Bangor and Afonwen as well as for traffic along the Llanberis and Nantlle branches. Standing outside the shed is a LNWR 0-8-0 mineral engine, such a loco being required for heavy slate trains, with shed staff posed in front. The gentleman in the bowler hat and waistcoat was the shed foreman. (Author's Collection)

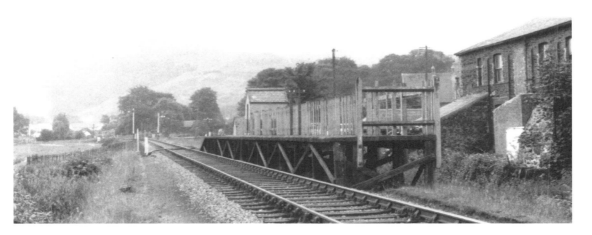

Llanberis West Halt, on the Llanberis branch on 27 June 1956. Although narrow gauge railways served the quarries in the area, with transfer facilities at Port Dinorwic, the LNWR successfully brought in a standard gauge line from Caernarfon to Llanberis in 1869, running through Pont Rug and Cwm-y-Glo. Passenger services on the branch lasted until 1930, although excursion trains, to connect with the Snowdon Mountain Railway, ran during the summer months. The only other traffic on the branch was freight traffic serving the quarry at Llanberis. (H. Casserley)

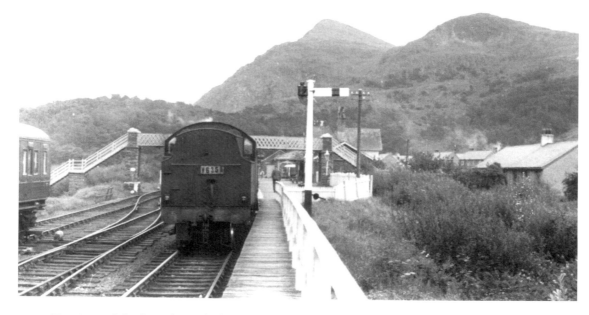

Terminus of the branch at Llanberis on 14 August 1953. An excursion train to Rhyl, which was due to leave at 5.20 p.m., is waiting to depart with ex-LMS 2-6-4 tank engine No. 42444 in charge. (H. Casserley)

CARNARVON and LLANBI

	DOWN.	Week Days
Miles.		mrn	aft	aft	aft	aft	aft
	Carnarvon ....dep.	9 35	1240	3 0	5 15	6 35	8 2
3¼	Pont Rug	9 46	1251	3 10	5 25	6 46	8 3
5¼	Pontrhythallt	9 54	1259	3 18	5 33	6 54	8 3
6¼	Cwm-y-Glo............[464	10 0	1 5	3 24	5 39	7 0	8 4
9-	Llanberis, for Snowdon. arr.	10 8	1 11	3 30	5 45	7 6	8 5

A 1910 timetable for passenger services along the Llanberis branch. (Author's Collection)

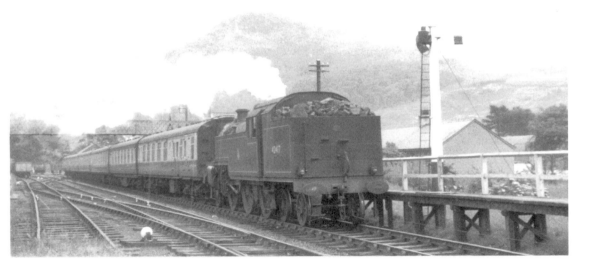

Two years later, on 26 June 1956, another train for Rhyl is standing at Llanberis station, headed by another ex-LMS 2-6-4 tank, No. 42417. The branch survived until 7 September 1964 when it was closed. The main station building has survived and is now a restaurant and craft centre. (H. Casserley)

London and North Western.

	Miles.	Up.	mrn	mrn	aft	aft	aft	aft	
...		**Llanberis** ......dep.	8 25	12 0	2 20	4 30	6 0	7 20	...
...	2¾	Cwm-y-Glo	8 30	12 5	2 25	4 35	6 5	7 25	...
...	3¼	Pontrhythallt......	8 34	12 9	2 29	4 39	6 9	7 29	...
...	5½	Pont Rug...........	8 42	1217	2 37	4 47	6 17	7 37	...
...	9	**Carnarvon 471**.arr.	8 50	1225	2 47	4 55	6 25	7 45	...

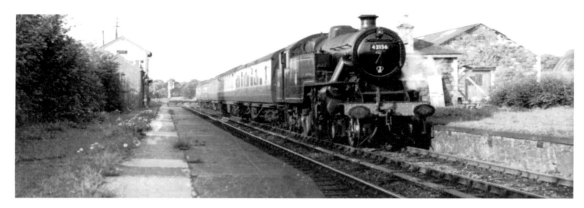

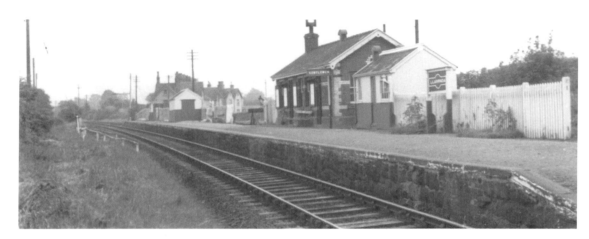

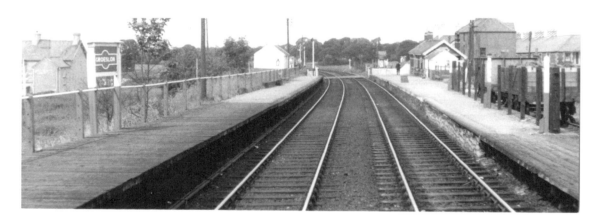

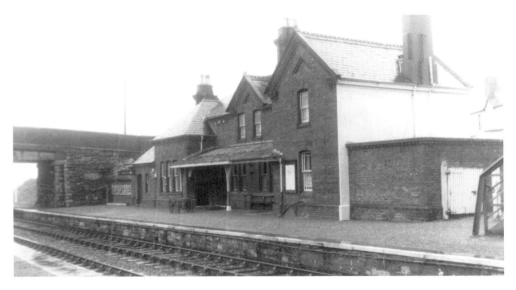

The important-looking station at Pen-y-Groes, facing Caernarfon, as it appeared on 17 July 1963. Pen-y-Groes was the junction for the little branch to Nantlle. (R. Casserley)

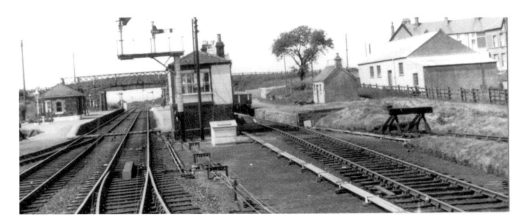

Pen-y-Groes station as it appeared on 27 June 1956. (H. Casserley)

Opposite top: The first station after leaving Caernarfon, on the Afonwen line, was at Dinas Junction, where it met the narrow gauge Welsh Highland Railway, which is under restoration at this time. Here, on 26 August 1954, ex-LMS Stanier 2-6-4 tank arrives at the station with the 5.39 p.m. Bangor–Afonwen service. (H. Casserley)

Opposite middle: The single-platform station at Llanwnda on 12 August 1953. The line from Caernarfon to Afonwen was single and relatively little-used by passengers when it was closed in 1964; the line is now a cycle path. (H. Casserley)

Opposite bottom: Groeslon station, facing Bangor and complete with passing loop, is seen here in 1956. (H. Casserley)

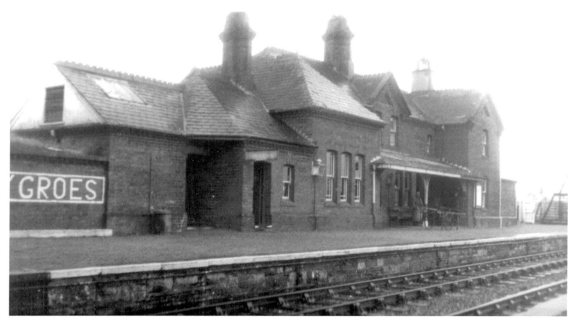

The main building at Pen-y-Groes station as it appeared in 1963. (R. Casserley)

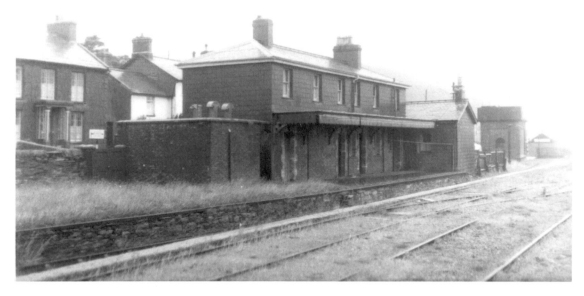

Terminus of the little branch from Pen-y-Groes to Nantlle looking overgrown on 17 July 1963. Nantlle was the terminus of the first railway in Caernarfonshire when opened in 1828 as a horse-drawn tramway on a 3-foot-6-inch-gauge track. The little line served the many quarries in the area, taking slate down to the quayside at Caernarfon. In 1872, the section from Pen-y-Groes to Nantlle was converted to standard gauge for use by LNWR trains. Exchange sidings were still needed at Nantlle because quarry railways were 2-foot gauge. The branch survived for freight traffic until December 1963. (R. Casserley)

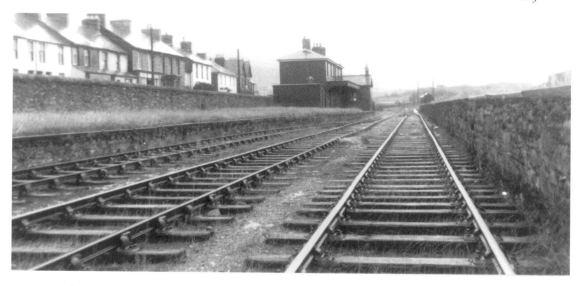

Another view of the dead end of the Nantlle branch on the same day. (R. Casserley)

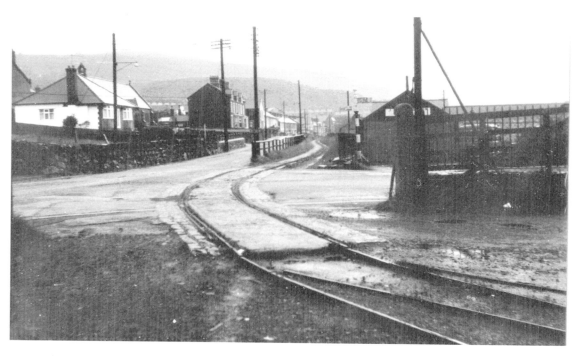

The Nantlle branch, looking toward Pen-y-Groes in 1963, with the village in view and the slate quarry in the background. (R. Casserley)

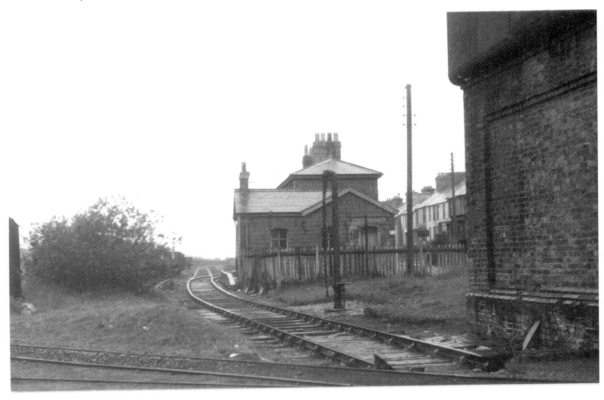

The Nantlle branch on 26 June 1956 with a narrow gauge line in the foreground. (H. Casserley)

	Miles	**Down.**		mrn	mrn	non	Sat.	aft	aft
		Penygroes ....dep.		7 5	1010	12e0		1230	1
1¼		Nantlle.................arr.		7 10	1015	12e5		12 35	1
		Up.		mrn	mrn	mrn	Sat.	mrn	m
		Nantlle..............dep.		6 50	8 20	9 55		1115	11e
1¼		Penygroes 471.........arr.		6 55	8 25	10 0		1120	11e

PENYGROES and NANTL.

e Exce

A 1910 timetable for the infrequent passenger services along the Nantlle branch. A petrol-driven railcar was often used on these trains. (Author's Collection)

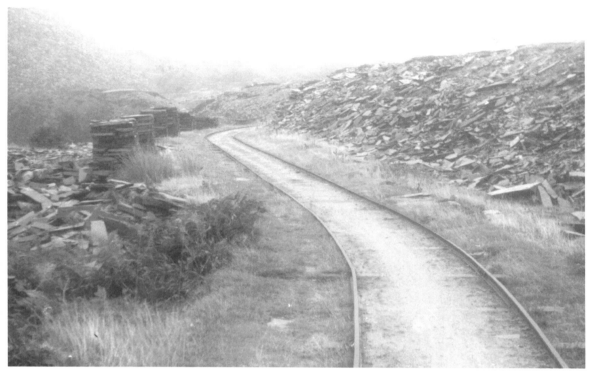

The 4-foot-gauge Nantlle tramway at the quarry face as it appeared on 23 September 1958 (R. Casserley)

London and North Western.

		aft	aft								
35	Sat. {	7 10	8 25	....	....	....	....	....	....	....	....
40		7 15	8 30	....	....	....	....	....	....	....	....

Days.

		aft	aft	aft	aft						
Sat. {		1 45	2 10	4 35	7 42	...	...	...	...	...	...
		1 50	2 15	4 40	7 47	...	...	...	...	...	...

urdays.

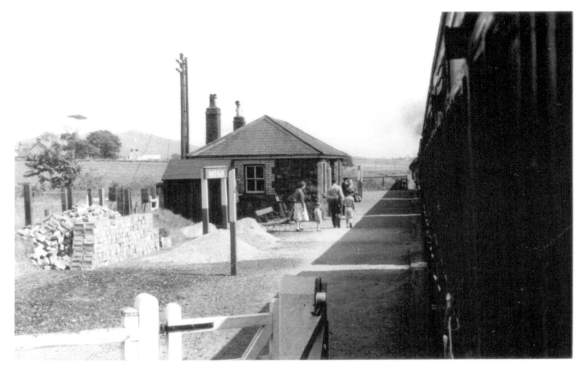

Back on the line to Afonwen and a train approaches Pant Glas station on 27 June 1956. Pant Glas was the summit of the line to Afonwen. (H. Casserley)

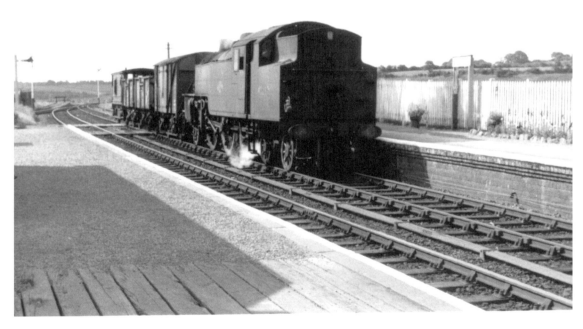

An unidentified ex-LMS 2-6-4 tank arrives at Brinkir station with a pick-up goods train in the 1950s. (Author's Collection)

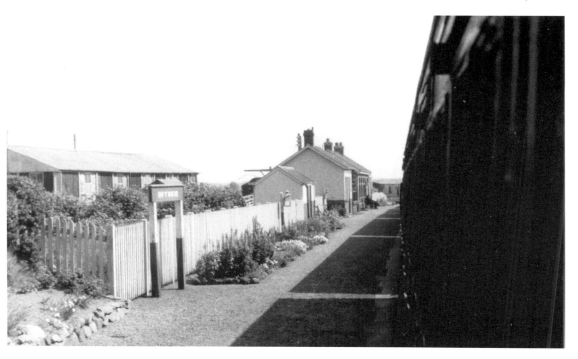

On 27 June 1956, a train from Caernarfon is approaching Brinkir station. (H. Casserley)

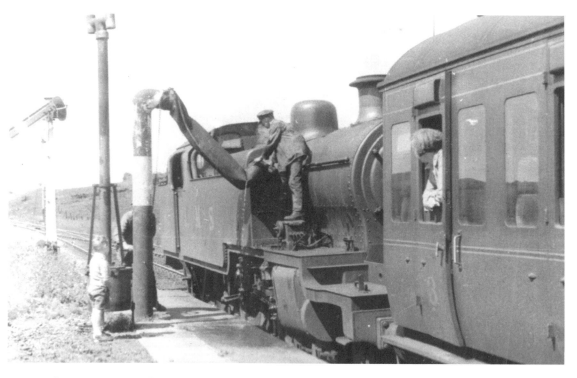

Taking water at Brinkir station on 18 July 1941 is LMS Fowler 2-6-2 tank loco No. 42 on the 3.50 p.m. Pwllheli–Bangor service. (H. Casserley)

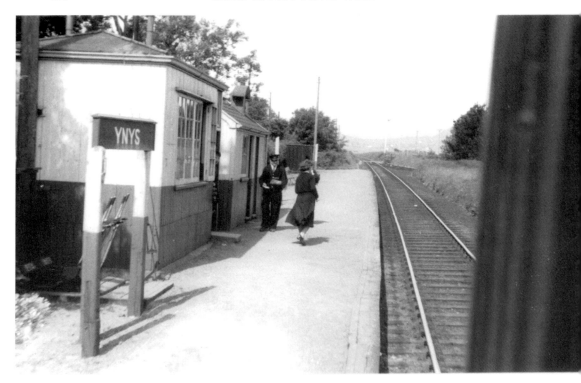

Leaving Ynys station on 27 June 1956 as the train heads for Afonwen. (H. Casserley)

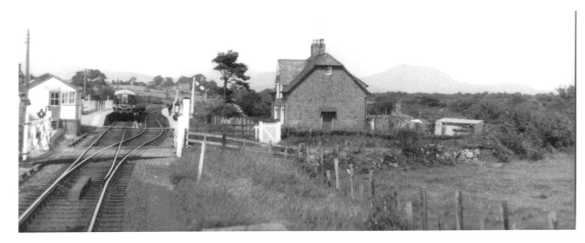

A new DMU, which would replace steam traction and, it was hoped, allow poorly performing branches to remain open, is seen with a train for Caernarfon at Llangybi on 27 June 1956. A train is expected from Afonwen shortly. (H. Casserley)

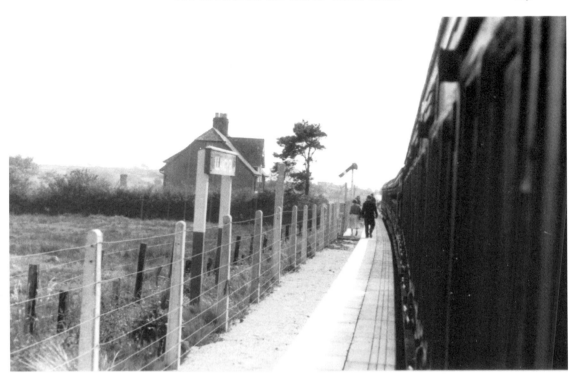

Llangybi station with a train for Caernarfon awaiting departure. (H. Casserley)

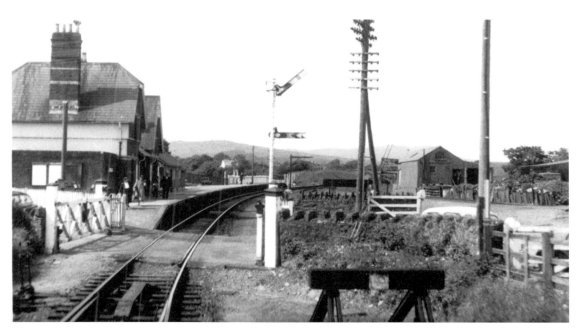

The rather substantial main building at Chwilog station on 27 June 1956, looking towards Caernarfon. A train for Afonwen is due and there are some passengers waiting. Chwilog was the last station on the line from Caernarfon before arriving at Afonwen. (H. Casserley)

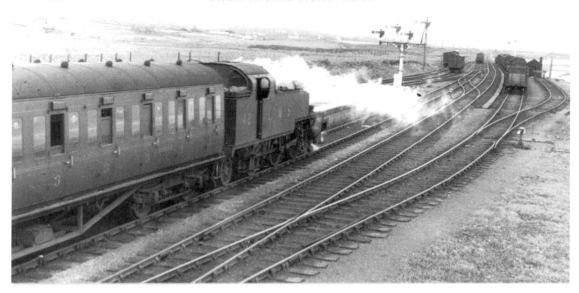

Arriving at Afonwen from Bangor on 18 July 1941 is LMS Fowler 2-6-2 tank No. 42. It was the Caernarfonshire railway that arrived at Afonwen first, the line, at that time, continuing over what would be Cambrian metals to Penrhyndeudraeth. These services commenced on 2 September 1867, only a month before the Cambrian line itself arrived at Afonwen with its services to Pwllheli, making it an important junction. The station itself was in a remote location with little habitation in the area, so Afonwen station could be a lonely place, particularly in winter. (H. Casserley)

TWO

RAILS TO BLAENAU FFESTINIOG

Substantial slate-quarry workings at Blaenau Ffestiniog attracted railway interest during the nineteenth century. The first railway to reach the town was the narrow gauge Ffestiniog Railway, which received royal assent in 1832. The line was built to transport slate products from the quarries to the harbour at Portmadoc for onward shipment. The line was originally horse-operated but was soon operated by steam. The double-ended Fairlie locomotives became famous on the line and still operate preserved trains there. Eventually, the Ffestiniog Railway had exchange sidings with the LNWR and GWR as well as the Cambrian, at Portmadoc. In an effort to tap slate traffic for itself, the LNWR built its branch from Llandudno Junction to Blaenau Ffestiniog in stages between 1863 and 1879 giving the Euston company a monopoly on slate traffic in the town for a short period as, in 1883, the GWR built its own line from Bala Junction to Blaenau Ffestiniog. However, the GWR line never made a profit because it arrived in the town later than that of the LNWR. Indeed, the two termini at Blaenau Ffestiniog were never physically connected, even though they were on the same alignment until a chord was built to serve the nuclear power station at Trawsfynydd, which was situated on the old GWR line, after it was closed. The LNWR line to Llandudno Junction remains open and still runs a passenger service.

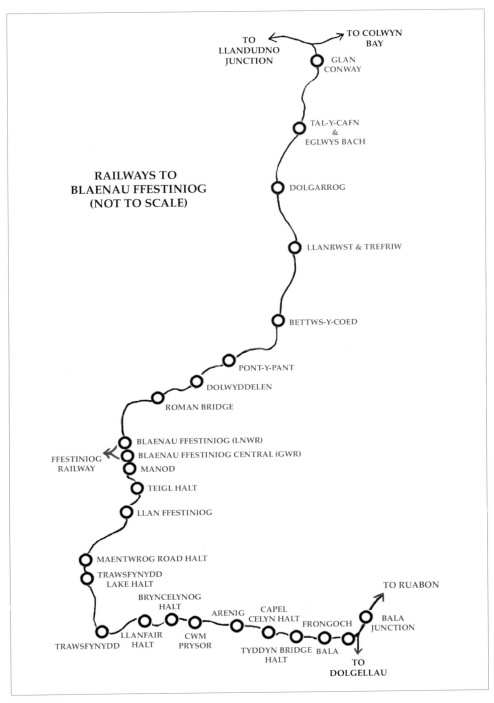

The railways that served the slate town of Blaenau Ffestiniog. The LNWR line left the C&HR just east of Llandudno Junction station, while the GWR branch left the Ruabon–Barmouth Junction route at Bala Junction. As can be seen, the two stations in the slate town were not connected although they lay on the same alignment. The other line into Blaenau Ffestiniog was the narrow gauge Ffestiniog Railway, which carried slate to the harbour at Portmadoc for onward shipment. (Author's Collection)

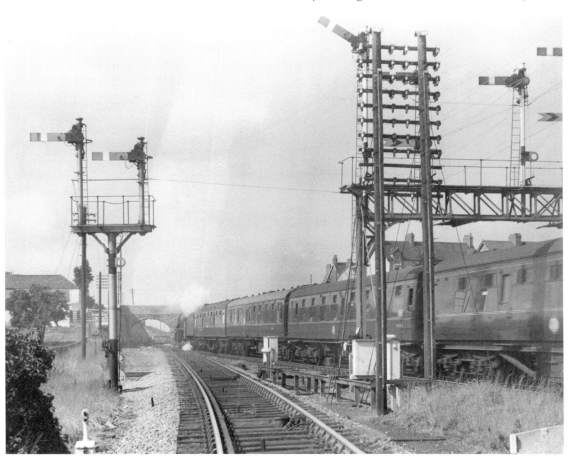

An express is seen passing the entrance to the Blaenau Ffestiniog branch in the early 1960s. Proposals to build a line in the Conwy Valley were first suggested as early as 1846, two years before the C&HR was opened. An early suggestion was that a line was to leave the coast from under the Conwy Castle walls and follow the Gyffin Valley to Llanrwst, then an important lead-mining area and market town, via Dolgarrog and Trefriw. In 1853 there was a further proposal, by the Conway & Llanrwst Railway Company, to build a line along the east bank of the Conwy River. This plan was eventually withdrawn in favour of a route along the west bank, the route preferred by the C&HR. Just to complicate matters further, one Edmund Sharp of Lancaster proposed a 3-foot-3-inch-gauge line along the west bank in 1858, but this was rejected by the C&HR in September of that year. Finally, on 23 July 1860, the Conway & Llanrwst Railway Bill received royal assent and the first sod was cut at Llanrwst Abbey on 25 August. Two months later, the LNWR, who had absorbed the C&HR in 1863, bought all the necessary land to complete the line and appointed Hedworth Lee as engineer. The new line was 11¼ miles long and single-track throughout, with sidings at Llanrwst. Stations were provided at Llansantffraid, later to become Glan Conway, perhaps because the Welsh name would be difficult for English tongues to pronounce, and Tal-y-Cafn. The new branch had its own separate line and platform at Llandudno Junction. On 9 June 1863, the line was inspected and approved for opening provided a turntable was installed at Llanrwst within six weeks. The station at Llanrwst included a goods station, yard and engine shed, constructed by J. Gibson & Son at a cost of £3,161. In 1881, the engine shed and tank house were demolished, the material being used in the rebuilding of Holyhead shed wall. The 42-foot-long turntable was also removed and installed at Llanberis, where it remained out of use from the 1920s to the 1950s. (P. Owen)

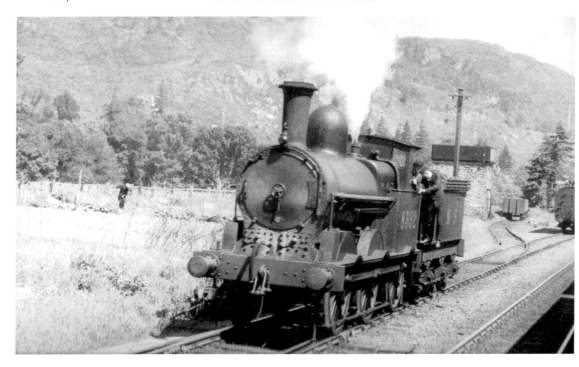

By 1867, the Conwy Valley line was extended to Betws-y-Coed, following an Act of 5 July 1865. The new 3¾-mile extension was from north of Llanrwst station, which was replaced by a new building. On 18 October 1867, the line opened to goods traffic and sidings were provided at Betws-y-Coed (then spelt Bettws-y-Coed; the second 't' was dropped in 1953). Much traffic emanating from the sidings was slate and those sidings can be seen in this view of ex-LNWR Cauliflower 0-6-0 No. 8392, which is shunting during working of the 10.35 a.m. 'pick-up' goods from Llandudno Junction to Blaenau Ffestiniog on 3 June 1932. Passenger services at Betws-y-Coed commenced on 6 April 1868 and refreshment rooms were opened at the station in the summer of that year. A single-road engine shed was built on the Up side, north of the station, but was never used and was demolished during the Second World War. The water tank, column and inspection pit between the tracks survived until the loop that existed there was removed in the 1960s. The first accident on the line occurred on 5 July 1904 when the 10.25 a.m. passenger train from Llandudno to Betws-y-Coed became derailed 2 miles south of Tal-y-Cafn. The train, headed by LNWR 2-4-2 tank No. 891, jumped the rails as it was being driven at the timetabled speed of 60 mph. The loco landed in marshy land and it took eight engines to drag it out some two weeks later. Subsequent inquiries discovered that the track was not suitable for such speeds and trains were not permitted to operate at 60 mph again until the track was improved. (H. Casserley)

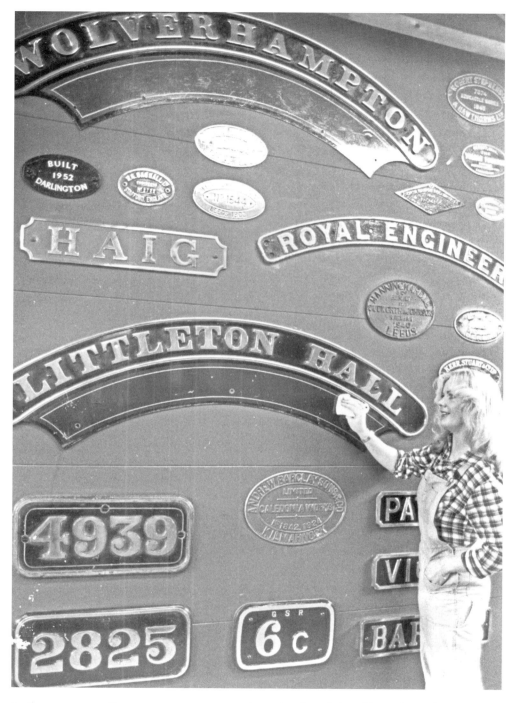

In the 1970s, a railway museum was opened on the site of the old goods yard at Betws-y-Coed station and contains a wide variety of exhibits and dioramas depicting the old LNWR. A collection of old standard gauge coaches are in the museum yard and are used as a café, and a miniature steam railway runs around the site. Here, a collection of ex-GWR and LMS nameplates can be seen, along with makers' plates and old narrow gauge plates, which are being cleaned by a member of staff. (G. Roberts)

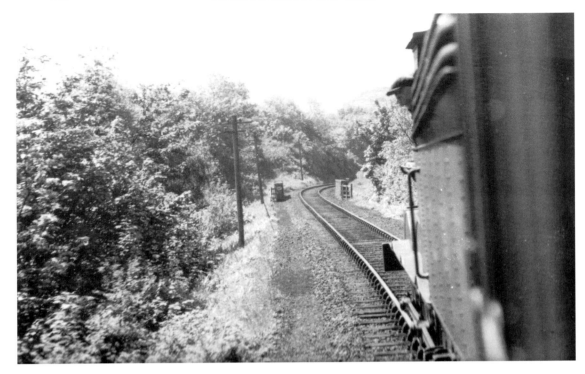

Ex-LNWR loco No. 8392 is seen close to Betws-y-Coed in June 1932. During construction of the Betws-y-Coed extension, quarry owners at Blaenau Ffestiniog approached the LNWR with a view to building a narrow gauge line that would connect with the Ffestiniog Railway; the latter company was still using horses at this time and quarry owners were concerned about delay in moving slate. While negotiations were underway, the Ffestiniog adopted steam power and quarry owners no longer guaranteed traffic to the LNWR. The Euston Company looked at other narrow gauge proposals in 1870, but a junction with the Ffestiniog was withdrawn from the LNWR Bill. A narrow gauge line was surveyed, terminating with the Ffestiniog Dinas branch. Royal assent for the Betws-y-Coed and Ffestiniog line, which specified a minimum gauge of 1 foot 11.58 inches up to a maximum of 4 feet 8.5 inches, was received on 18 July 1872. During construction, the LNWR decided to alter the line to standard gauge, which meant dispensing with the connection to the Ffestiniog. (H. Casserley)

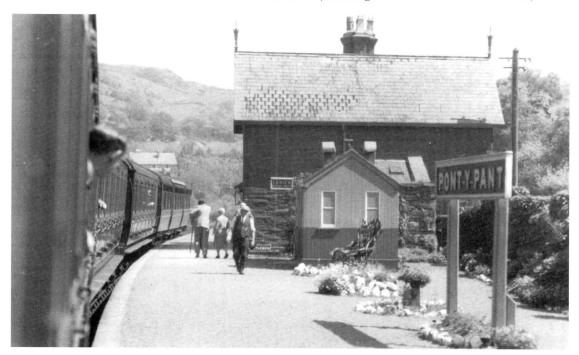

Pont-y-Pant station as it appeared on 3 June 1932. In January 1878, single-platform stations were situated at Roman Bridge and Pont-y-Pant, all constructed by D & E Jones of Betws-y-Coed, and a loop with an island platform was approved for Dolwyddelan. Second platforms and passing loops were provided at Llanrwst and Tal-y-Cafn. Betws-y-Coed remained as a single-platform station despite traffic demands brought about by increases in tourism in the town. (H. Casserley)

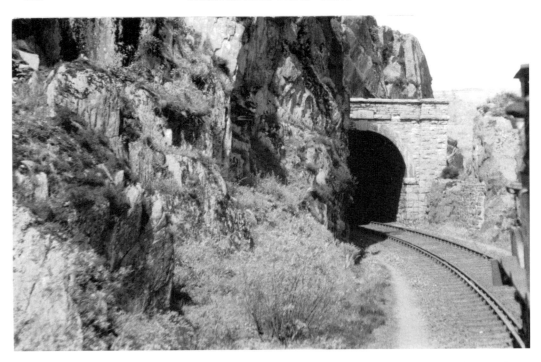

Approaching the tunnel at Roman Bridge on 3 June 1932. This is the tunnel that brings the railway into Blaenau Ffestiniog. To allow access to the slate town, a tunnel was required here to pass under the 1,712-foot-high Moel Drynogydd. This complete tunnel is 2 miles 340 yards long, the seventh-longest railway tunnel in Britain. Designed by Hedworth Lee, construction began on 6 December 1873, with contractor Gethin Jones starting work on the northernmost of three shafts used for excavation of the tunnel. Eight headings were used from the bases of the shafts and the portals. Extremely hard stone was encountered, causing Jones to abandon the work, the tunnel being completed by direct labour under the supervision of William Smith, who had succeeded Lee as district engineer at Bangor. The tunnel itself is 18 feet 6 inches high and 16 feet 6 inches wide. It is straight except for a short curved section at either end. Most of the tunnel is on an ascending gradient of 1 in 660, except for a short level section at the summit near the southern end, where the rail level is 673 feet above the level of Betws-y-Coed station. The tunnel was opened to traffic on 22 July 1879, completing the whole link between Llandudno, Llandudno Junction and Blaenau Ffestiniog. On arriving in the town, the lush green of the Conwy Valley line is replaced by the grey of the slate tips that greet trains as they emerge from the dark tunnel. (H. Casserley)

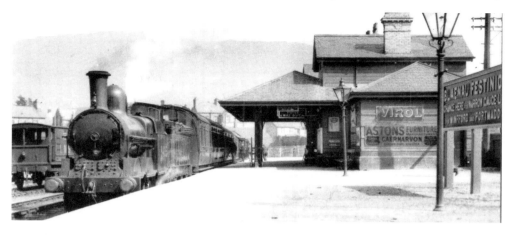

End of the line; the LNWR station at Blaenau Ffestiniog as seen with ex-LNWR Cauliflower o-6-o goods engine No. 8405 at the head of the 4.30 p.m. train for Llandudno Junction on 3 June 1932. The rail connection between the tunnel and the permanent station at Blaenau Ffestiniog was completed and opened on 1 April 1881; the temporary station was then closed and removed. As part of the new station complex, a combined locomotive and carriage shed, which contained one and three roads respectively, was built. The shed closed on 14 September 1931 and was demolished. The North Western Hotel was opened by the LNWR adjacent to the station in 1881. It was not a great success and was let privately and finally sold in 1906. (H. Casserley)

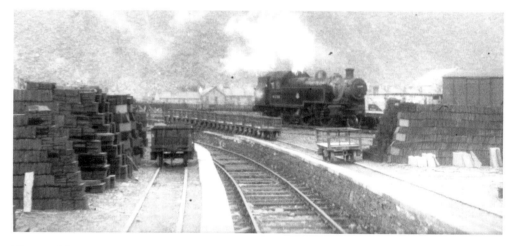

Blaenau Ffestiniog station on 20 March 1959 with ex-LMS Ivatt 2-6-2T No. 41258 simmering in the yard after bringing in a train from Llandudno. Incidents have been rare on the Conwy Valley line over the years, but there were two in the 1950s. The first occurred in 1952 when a driver sustained injury at Dolwyddelan goods shed as he leaned out of the cab of his ex-LMS Stanier 2-6-2T to observe the shunter's signal and collided with the door pillar of the shed. The incident was attributed to the fact that the driver had forgotten that the engine was wider than the one he usually drove, so had less clearance than he expected. The second incident occurred on 29 October 1958 when the 6.30 a.m. freight, headed by an Ivatt 2-6-2T, from Llandudno Junction to Blaenau Ffestiniog was derailed by a kitten that had become wedged in converging points at the south end of Blaenau Ffestiniog station. The body of the kitten prevented the point blades from making proper contact, causing the derailment. The incident caused some disruption as it took four hours to return the loco to the tracks. (R. Casserley)

LLANDUDNO, BETTWS-Y-COED, and BL

Miles	Down.	mrn	mrn	mrn	mrn	aft	a
	476 LLANDUDNO ....dep.	....	8*d*10	9 45	11 5	12*g*15	1
—	Llandudno Junction....dep.	4 25	8 35	1020	1130	12*g*35	2
1¼	Glan Conway...............	....	8 39	1024	1134	12*g*39	2
5½	Tal-y-Cafn and Eglwysbach..	4 39	8 47	1032	1142	12*g*47	2
11¼	Llanrwst and Trefriw	5*b*10	9 0	1045	1155	1 *g* 0	2
15	Bettws-y-Coed, for Capel Curig arr.	5 20	9 10	1055	12 4	1*g*10	2
	Bettws-y-Coed, for Capel Curig dep.	5 25	9 14	11 0	12 9	.....	..
19¼	Pont-y-pant	5 40	9 26	1112	1221	.....	..
20¾	Dolwyddelen.	5 50	9 30	1116	1225	.....	..
22½	Roman Bridge ....[477	5 57	9 36	1122	1234	.....	..
27½	Blaenau Festiniog 105, arr.	6 12	9 49	1137	1248	.....	..

Miles	Up.	mrn	mrn	mrn	aft	aft	aft
	Blaenau Festiniog......dep.	6 45	7 50	10 0	1210	....	1 5
5	Roman Bridge...............	6 57	8 2	1012	1222	....	2
6¾	Dolwyddelen	7 2	8 7	1017	1227	....	2 1
8¼	Pont-y-pant................	7 8	8 12	1023	1234	....	2 1
12½	Bettws-y-Coed, for Capel Curig arr.	7 20	8 24	1035	1246	....	2 3
	Bettws-y-Coed, for Capel Curig dep.	7 25	8 27	1039	1251	1*g*20	2 3
16¼	Llanrwst and Trefriw	7 32	8 34	1046	1258	1*g*27	2 4
22	Tal-y-Cafn and Eglwysbach..	7 48	8 47	11 1	1 14	1*g*40	2 5
26¼	Glan Conway ....[474	7 57	8 57	1111	1 24	1*g*50	3
27½	Llandudno Junction 472 arr.	8 1	9 2	1116	1 29	1*g*55	3 1
30¾	476 LLANDUDNO..........arr.	8 25	9 25	1137	2 2	2*g*15	3 4

b Arrives at 4 55 mrn.   *d* Leaves at 8 15 m

A 1910 timetable for LNWR passenger services between Llandudno and Blaenau Ffestiniog. In those days, most trains operated between the slate town and the seaside resort. (Author's Collection)

AU FESTINIOG.—London and North Western.

Days.								**Sundays.**				
aft	aft	aft	aft	aft				mrn				
....	3g45	5 45	6 35	7 35	....	....	....	....	....	....	....	..
....	4 0	6 2	7 0	8 10	....	....	....	5 10	..	....	....	..
....	4 4	6 6	7 4	8 14	....	....	....	....	....	....	....	..
....	4 12	6 14	7 12	8 24	....	....	....	5 21	....	....	....	..
....	4 25	6 27	7 25	8 43	....	....	....	5 35	....	....	....	..
....	4 34	6 37	7 35	8 56	....	....	....	5 44	....	....	....	..
2 52	4 38	....	....	9 0	....	....	....	5 49	....	....	....	..
3 4	4 50	....	....	9 12	....	....	....	....	....	....	....	..
3 8	4 54	....	....	9 16	....	....	....	6 4	....	....	....	..
3 15	5 1	....	....	9 23	....	....	....	....	....	....	....	..
3 29	5 14	....	....	9 37	....	....	....	6 22	....	....	....	..

Days.								**Sundays.**				
aft		aft	aft					aft				
10		8 0	....	....	....	....	....	6 20	....	....	....	..
22		8 12	....	....	....	....	....	....	....	....	....	..
27		8 17	....	....	....	....	....	6 36	....	....	....	..
33		8 22	....	....	....	....	....	....	....	....	....	..
45		8 34	....	....	....	....	....	6 53	....	....	....	..
50	....	8 39	....	....	....	....	....	6 58	....	....	....	..
57	....	8 45	....	....	....	....	....	7 5	....	....	....	..
12	....	8 59	....	....	....	....	....	7 19	....	....	....	..
22	....	9 8	....	....	....	....	....	7 29	....	....	....	..
27	....	9 13	....	....	....	....	....	7 35	....	....	....	..
0	....	9 45	....	....	....	....	....	8 0	....	....	....	..

Saturdays only.

Mondays.   *g* Rail Motor Car, one class only.

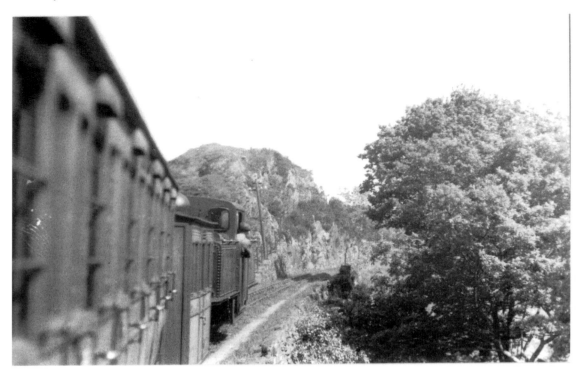

Like many nineteenth-century quarrying companies, the slate-quarry owners at Blaenau Ffestiniog had their own narrow gauge railway system to carry completed product to the harbour on the river estuary at Portmadoc. The Ffestiniog Railway received royal assent in 1832, and this 1-foot-11.5-inch-gauge line was opened in the same year as a horse-drawn tramway. It was converted to steam power in 1860, its most famous locomotives being double-ended Fairlie 0-4-0 0-4-0 machines, one of which, *Taliesin*, is seen here on 3 June 1932 leaving Tan-y-Bwlch with the 3.10 p.m. service from Portmadoc. The railway here was the first narrow gauge line to carry passengers when a free service was introduced in 1864. Once the main LNWR and GWR lines had been established, the Ffestiniog Railway built exchange sidings at their termini. They also built exchange sidings at the Cambrian Railways Minffordd station in 1871. Decline of the slate industry in the 1930s, and the need to repair much of the line, led to its complete closure in 1946. However, this was not the end as the section between Portmadoc and Tan-y-Bwlch was reopened privately a few years later. Flooding to create a new reservoir in the area around Moelwyn Tunnel meant that the line could not be reopened throughout until preservationists built a deviation line; the work was not completed until the early 1980s, the whole line being reopened in 1982 and connecting with the main line at Blaenau Ffestiniog. (H. Casserley)

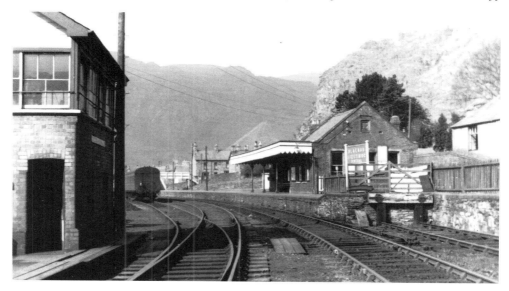

The GWR Blaenau Ffestiniog Central station, facing the dead end on 20 March 1959. Built to compete with the LNWR for slate traffic, the Bala & Ffestiniog Railway was opened between Bala Junction and Llan Ffestiniog, where it made a head-on connection with the narrow gauge Ffestiniog & Blaenau Railway, this line being the same gauge as the Ffestiniog Railway and directly connected with it (the GWR line opened in 1882). The narrow gauge line was brought up to standard gauge by the GWR to give direct access to the slate town and was opened on 10 September 1883, four years after the LNWR line entered the town. Thus, the GWR branch was never quite as successful as that of the LNWR in attracting slate traffic. The two stations at Blaenau Ffestiniog were not physically connected, perhaps due to old enmities between the LNWR and GWR that dated back to early railway days. (H. Casserley)

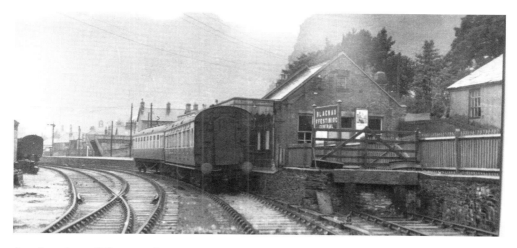

Another view of Blaenau Ffestiniog Central station as it appeared in 1953. The large slate tips and mountains can be seen in the background, the very reason why the line was here. The scene is rather damp and misty and it has often been said that it always seems to rain in the slate town, making it appear a rather grey and drab place. Although the line was not a great commercial success, it did run through some very spectacular Snowdonia scenery and was popular with tourists in the summer months. (H. Casserley)

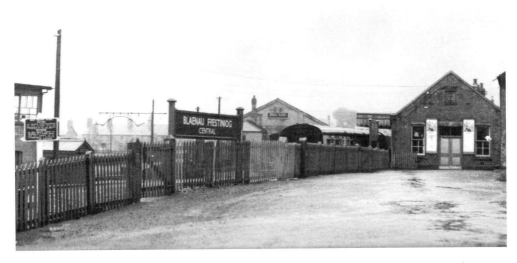

Entrance to Central station on 15 August 1953, yet another wet day in Blaenau Ffestiniog. The simple stone main building is visible and cottages can be seen in the background. The two stations were not physically connected until 1964, and the old GWR station in the town had the last laugh when the ex-LNWR station was closed in 1982 and the former GWR station was reopened because it made a direct connection with the newly restored Ffestiniog Railway. (H. Casserley)

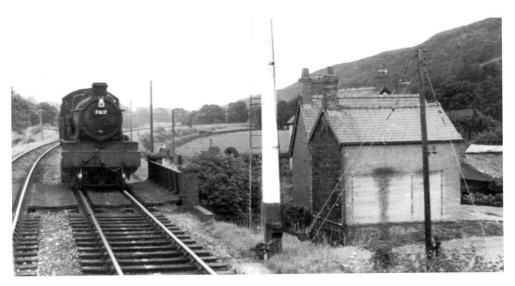

The first station on the GWR line from Blaenau Ffestiniog was at Manod, on the original narrow gauge section. An unusual feature of freight operations on this section was the carriage of narrow gauge slate wagons, which had been provided by the Paddington Company, on standard gauge transporter wagons between here and the sidings at Blaenau Ffestiniog; these wagons were then offloaded and the dressed slate was transferred to standard gauge wagons for onward transit to Bala via Manod. (H. Casserley)

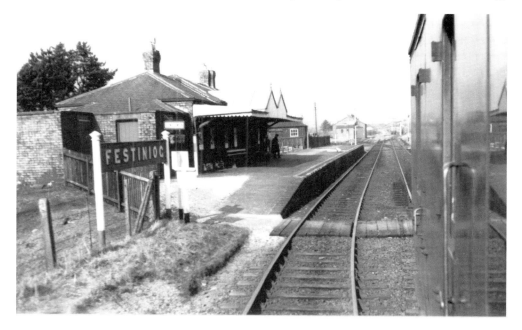

After leaving Manod, the line passed Cwm Teigl Halt before entering Llan Ffestiniog station, seen here with its fairly substantial main building in view in March 1959. This was the point where the GWR line from Bala met the narrow gauge section for access to Blaenau Ffestiniog. As can be seen, by this time, the 'Llan' had been removed from the station name. (R. Casserley)

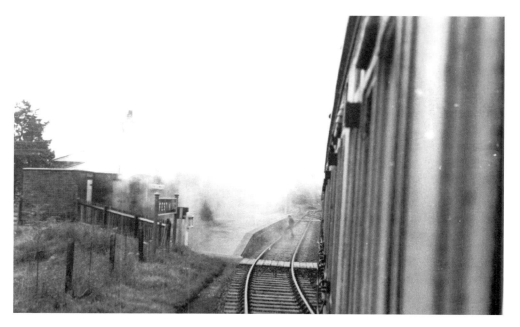

Another view of Llan Ffestiniog station, facing Blaenau Ffestiniog, on 15 August 1953. As can be seen, a passing loop was provided at the station, the line being single throughout. (H. Casserley)

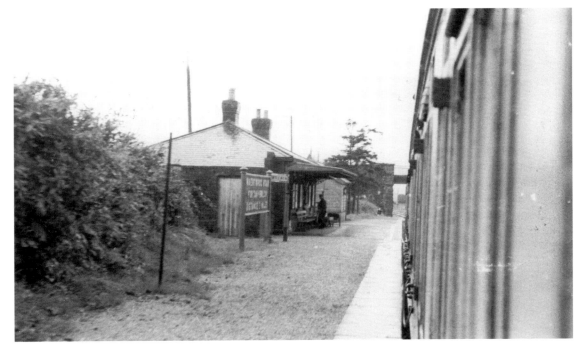

On the same day, a passenger train is seen leaving Maentwrog Road station with its neat little station building. (H. Casserley)

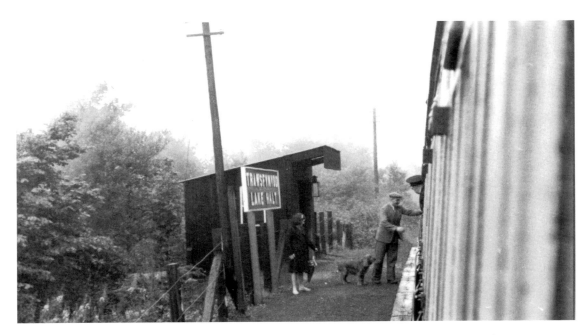

Trawsfynydd Lake Halt on 15 August 1953. The lake here was very popular with tourists and could be very busy during the summer months, trains often being double-headed from Bala, so heavy was traffic, and the halt was provided here just for visitors in the summer. (H. Casserley)

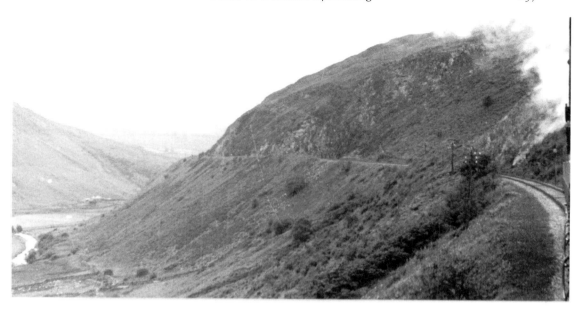

The GWR line ran through some of the wild Snowdonia country so popular with tourists, as can be seen in this view of 15 August 1953. (H. Casserley)

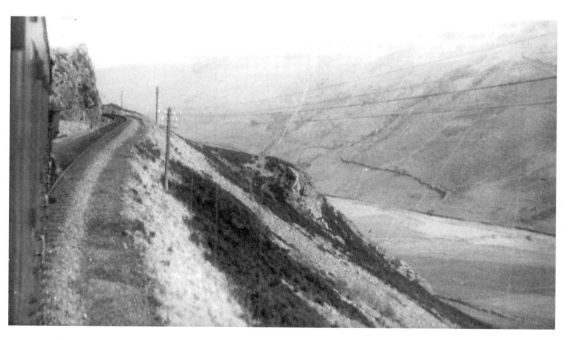

Ex-GWR 57xx 0-6-0 pannier tank No. 8727 is heading the 2.20 p.m. service from Blaenau Ffestiniog to Bala in August 1953 and is seen close to Trawsfynydd, with the lake in view below. Most traffic over the line was in the hands of 0-6-0 tank engines throughout the life of the line. As if to make the point, the last passenger train over the line, organised by the Stephenson Locomotive Society on 22 January 1961, was headed by a pair of pannier tanks. Normal passenger services on the branch had been discontinued on 2 January 1960. (R. Casserley)

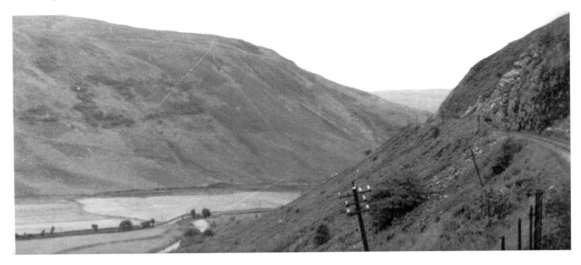

Another view of the line near Trawsfynydd on 15 August 1953. (H. Casserley)

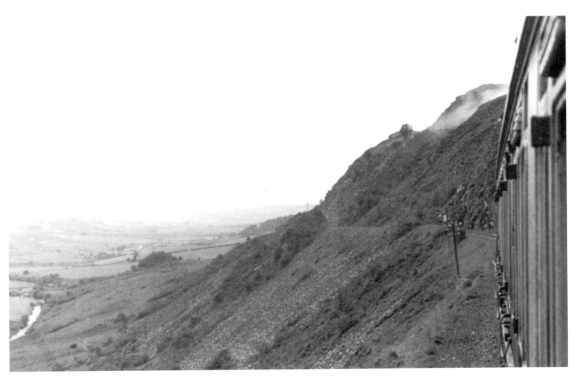

Closer to Trawsfynydd and through the mountains on the same day. (H. Casserley)

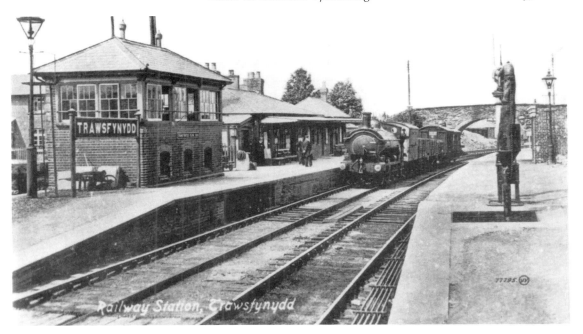

Trawsfynydd station at the end of the nineteenth century with a 0-6-0 saddle tank, probably built in Wolverhampton, at the head of a local goods train. The loco in this view would have been converted to the famous pannier tank in a few years' time. Along with the lake, Trawsfynydd was also the site of military camps that were established in 1903, soldiers coming to the firing ranges throughout the summer months. Military trains, which used Trawsfynydd Camp station just north of Trawsfynydd station itself, were often double-headed by pannier tanks as they became heavier but these were soon inadequate to deal with such traffic. Therefore, in 1935 the GWR decided to reconstruct thirty-four bridges between Bala Junction and Trawsfynydd, which would allow heavier tender engines to operate along the branch. When the work was completed, troop trains were handled by 43xx 2-6-0s operating in pairs or, on some occasions, single Manor Class 4-6-0s. As so much traffic was using the line at Trawsfynydd, a loco shed was provided, a sub-shed of Croes Newydd. Although the line closed to all traffic on 4 January 1961, it was not the end for the section between Blaenau Ffestiniog and Trawsfynydd as it was reopened in 1964 to serve a new nuclear power station, and was the reason why a chord linking the old LNWR and GWR lines was built. The LNWR branch was busy with freight traffic as the power station was being built and the line remained in use for carrying nuclear flask trains to Llandudno Junction for onward shipment to Cumbria. The power station was closed in 1998 and all traffic on the line ceased; the only section to remain open was the chord to the old Central station, although the track remains *in situ* and special excursions are run to Trawsfynydd. The station itself was closed on 4 May 1964 when construction of the power station was completed; the extensive remains of the station and goods yard are now in use as an agricultural supply depot. The military station still exists and remains largely intact. (Author's Collection)

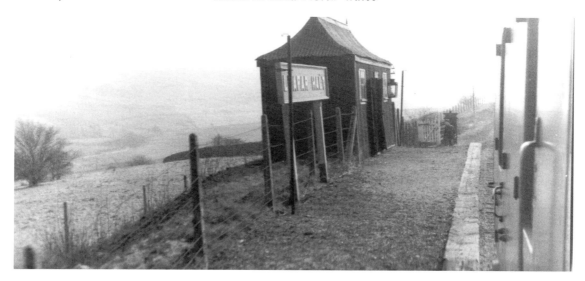

From Trawsfynydd, the branch ran through Llafar Halt, seen here on 20 March 1959 looking towards Blaenau Ffestiniog. (R. Casserley)

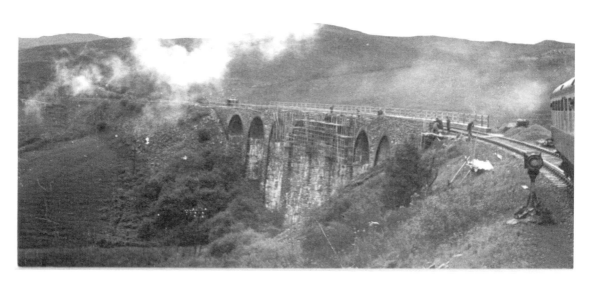

From Llafar Halt, the line continues to climb, passing through Bryn-Celynog Halt over a viaduct, seen here in August 1953, before arriving at Cwm Prysor. Cwm Prysor was the summit of the line and lay at 1,278 feet above sea level. As can be seen, the area around here was very remote and not served by a main road until the A4212 was opened in the early 1960s, just as the railway was closing. (R. Casserley)

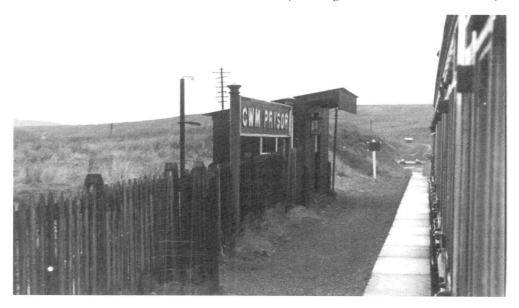

Right at the peak of the branch was the simple halt at Cwm Prysor, seen here in 1953. (R. Casserley)

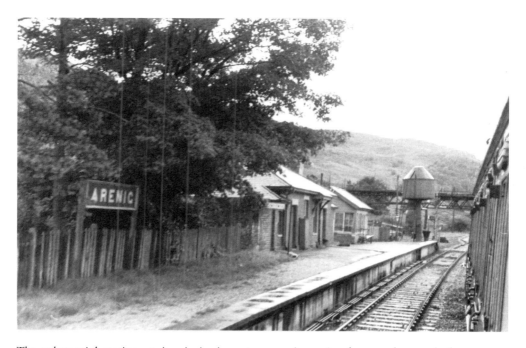

The substantial station at Arenig in August 1953. A passing loop and two platforms were provided here, along with a parachute water tank to supply locos before they attacked the climb to Cwm Prysor. (H. Casserley)

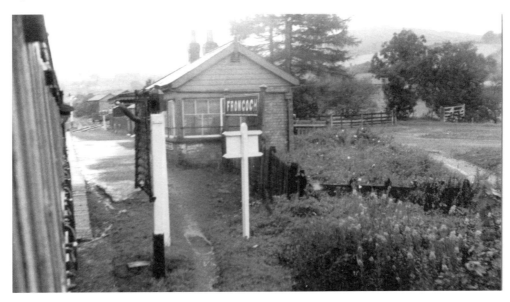

From Arenig, the branch ran through Capel Celyn Halt and Tyddyn Bridge Halt before arriving at Frongoch; the station is seen here on 15 August 1953 as a train from Blaenau Ffestiniog is departing. In 1957 plans were made to build a reservoir and flood the section of the branch just east of Capel Celyn Halt and just west of Frongoch. Construction of the Llyn Celyn reservoir effectively sealed the fate of the branch. Although there were proposals to divert the line around the lake, lack of passengers and freight meant that costs would be too high and the line was doomed. The only section of the line to remain open was the section between Bala and Bala Junction but this section was closed in 1965. (H. Casserley)

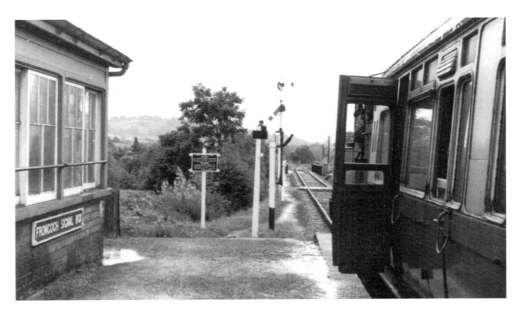

The signal box at Frongoch station in 1953 with a train waiting to depart for Bala. Frongoch was the home of the Welsh Distillery Company, who had premises that adjoined the railway, and the whiskey produced brought some revenue for the railway here. (H. Casserley)

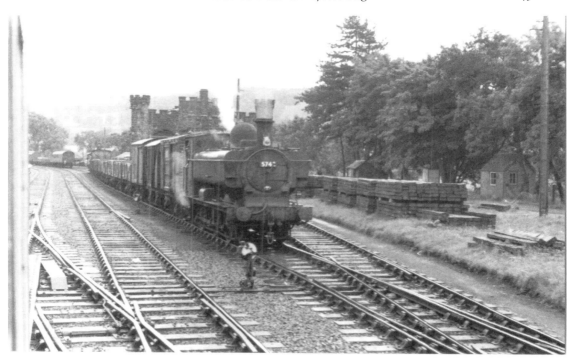

Approaching Bala station from Bala Junction is 57xx 0-6-0PT No. 5742 at the head of a goods train for Blaenau Ffestiniog on 15 August 1953. As the terminus of the original branch, a loco shed was provided here, another sub-shed of Croes Newydd; the castellated shed can be seen just to the right of the train. (H. Casserley)

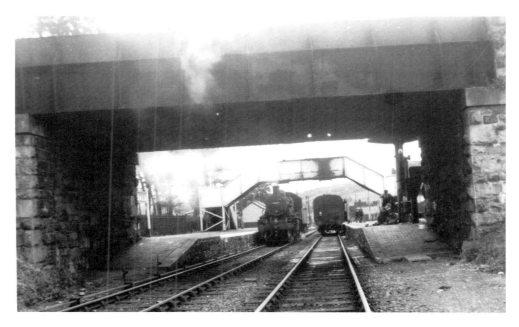

Only a year before closure and ex-LMS Ivatt Class 2 2-6-0 No. 46509 is running around its train at Bala station on 15 July 1963. (R. Casserley)

BALA and BLAENAU F

Miles.	Down.	Week Days only. mrn	mrn	Except Sats. mrn	Sats. only. mrn	aft	Except Saturdays. aft	af
	Bala .... dep.	6 55	9 20	1125	•1140	....	3 45	5 4
2¼	**Frongoch**	7 1	9 26	1130	•1146	....	3 55	5 4
7¾	Arenig	7 15	9 38	1144	12 1	....	4 15	5 5
10½	Cwm Prysor	a	a	a	a	....		a
16¼	Trawsfynydd	8 16	9 58	12 3	1220	3 5		6 1
19¼	Maentwrog Road	8 18	10 6	1212	1228	3 15		6 2
21¼	**Festiniog**	8 30	1013	1219	1234	3 30		6 3
23½	Manod 463, 584	8 40	1025	1226	1245	3 40		6 4
24¾	**Blaenau Festiniog** ‖ arr.	8 45	1031	1233	1252	3 55		6 5

a Stop when required; passengers wishing to alight

‖ ¼ mile to L.

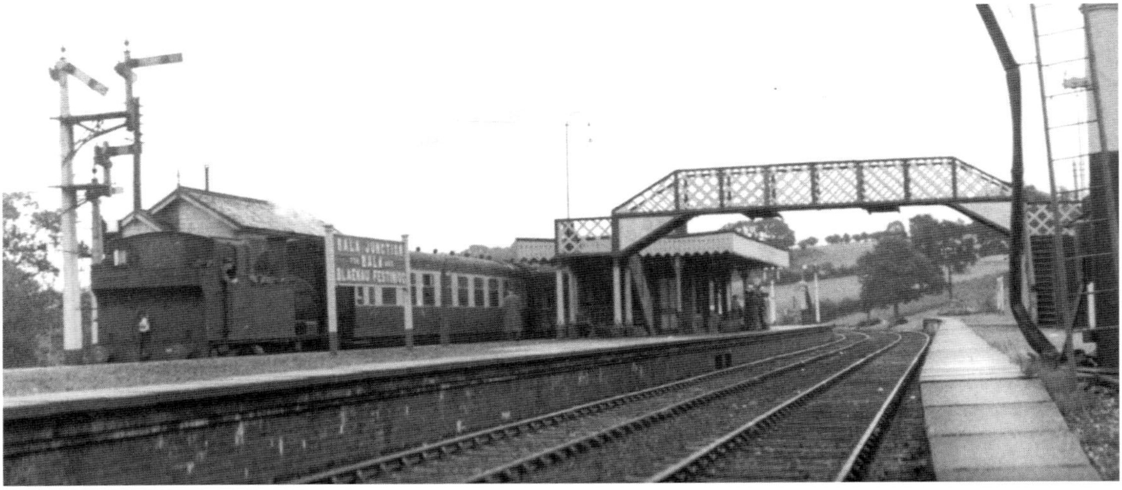

INIOG.—Great Western.

Up.	Week Days only.							
	mrn	mrn	aft	aft	aft	aft	aft	aft
Blaenau Festiniog....dep.	7 40	9 30	12 20		2 35	4 30		7 7
Manod.........	7 47	9 37	12 27		2 42	4 36		7 14
Festiniog............	7 57	9 47	12 40		2 52	4 46		7 21
Maentwrog Road......	8 2	9 52	12 47		2 57	4 51		7 29
Trawsfynydd	8 8	9 59	12 57		3 5	4 57		7 35
Cwm Prysor.........	a	a		a			a
Arenig................	8 28	10 18		12 35	3 24		5 5	7 54
Frongoch	8 41	10 30		12 47	3 36		5 20	8 8
Bala (above)......arr.	8 46	10 35		12 52	3 41		5 30	8 13

notify the Guard at either Arenig or Trawsfynydd.
W. Station.

Above: A 1922 timetable for GWR passenger services between Bala and Blaenau Ffestiniog. As can be seen, many of the halts seen earlier do not appear in the list – closure appears to have been their fate or they were request stops only. (Author's Collection)

Opposite below: Although the GWR branch finished at Bala, trains ran through to Bala Junction where connections could be made to Wrexham, Dolgellau and the Cambrian Coast line to Pwllheli and Aberystwyth. Here, ex-GWR 0-6-0PT No. 5810 is about to depart with the 10.50 a.m. train for Bala on 15 August 1953. (H. Casserley)

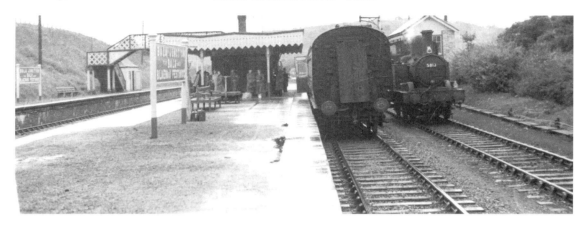

Running around its train after arriving at Bala Junction with the 9.15 a.m. from Blaenau Ffestiniog on 15 August 1953 is ex-GWR Collett 0-4-2T No. 5813. (H. Casserley)

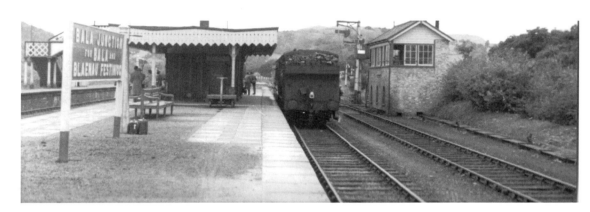

Looking west at Bala Junction and ex-GWR 0-6-0PT No. 7443 has arrived with the 11.45 a.m. train from Bala. (H. Casserley)

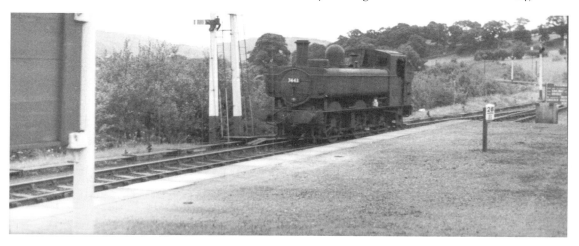

The same loco is seen running round at Bala Junction on 15 August 1953. (H. Casserley)

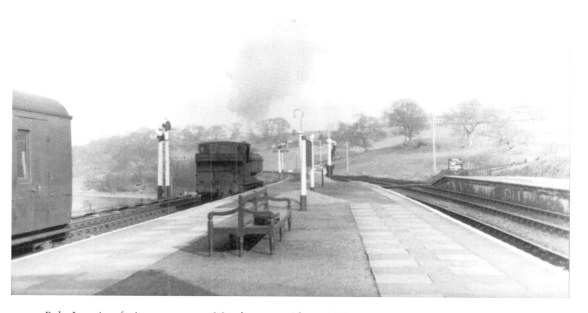

Bala Junction facing east on 20 March 1959 with ex-GWR 0-6-0PT No. 8727 running round after bringing in the 2.20 p.m. from Blaenau Ffestiniog. (R. Casserley)

THREE

THE GWR IN NORTH WALES

As previously mentioned, the GWR first arrived in the North Wales area around Wrexham over the metals of the Shrewsbury & Chester Railway, which had opened in 1846, its famous Paddington–Birkenhead expresses running through the town. The Paddington company also had another important line, from Ruabon to Barmouth, which connected Wrexham with the Cambrian Coast line and ran through the attractive Vale of Clwyd. This line closed in the mid-1960s but two sections have been reopened as preserved railways. The Llangollen Railway operates standard gauge steam trains from its headquarters at Llangollen to Carrog and there are plans to extend further to Corwen. The section between Bala and Llanuchllyn has also been reopened as the narrow gauge Bala Lake Railway.

Within Wrexham itself, the GWR served the many collieries, brickworks and steelworks that crowded the town, but there was competition for traffic from the Great Central Railway, who had taken control of the Wrexham, Mold & Connah's Quay Railway in 1905, its trains carrying freight to the docks at Connah's Quay for onward shipment. Both companies operated the many local passenger services from their stations at Wrexham General (GWR), Wrexham Exchange (GCR) and Wrexham Central (GCR & Cambrian, the latter company running from Ellesmere, Shropshire). To provide motive power, Wrexham was provided with two loco sheds, the first at Rhos Ddu (BR code 84K), which dealt with GCR/LNER locos. This shed closed in 1960 but remained in use to store withdrawn ex-GWR engines. The other shed was at Croes Newydd (BR code 84J), the GWR shed, which also had sub-sheds at Bala, Penmaenpool and Trawsfynydd.

Much of the railway system around Wrexham was closed in the late 1960s and early 1970s, with only the old GWR main line through to Chester remaining open, and that only a secondary route from Wolverhampton. The Rhos Ddu shed site is now occupied by factory units and Croes Newydd shed was demolished in 1974/5 and is now a traveller campsite.

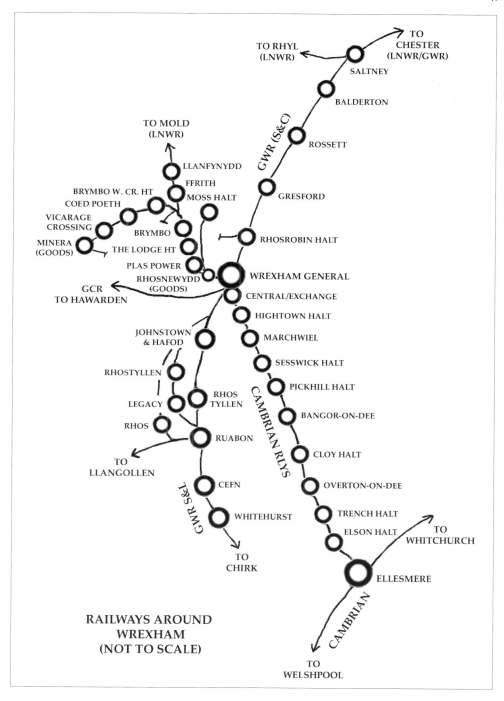

RAILWAYS AROUND
WREXHAM
(NOT TO SCALE)

The railway system around Wrexham. The main Shrewsbury & Chester Railway passes through Wrexham General station, while the small branches served local services and steelworks. As road transport expanded, these little lines were closed. Local trains were operated by steam railmotor trains, including the ex-Cambrian Railways line between Wrexham Central and Ellesmere. Along with the GWR, Wrexham was also served by the Great Central Railway from the Wirral and Connah's Quay. (Author's Collection)

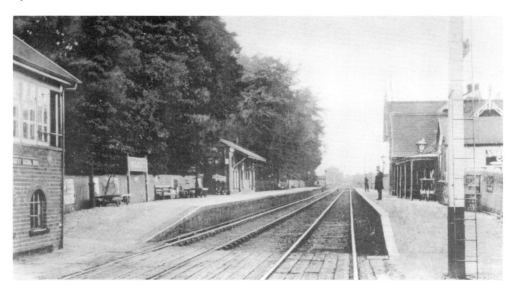

From Saltney, the first station on the line between Chester and Wrexham General was at Balderton with Rossett station coming next. The station is seen here in GWR days. (Author's Collection)

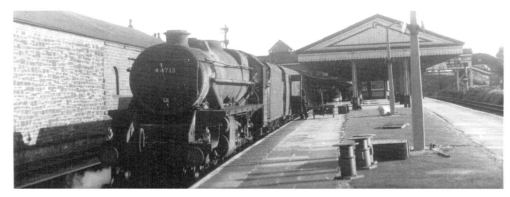

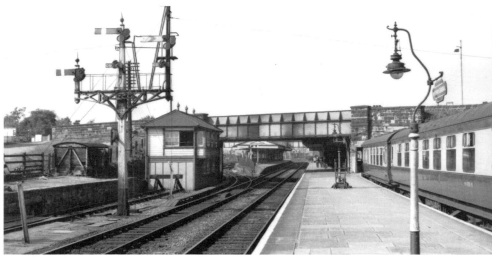

Opposite middle: Wrexham General station on 27 August 1964 with an ex-LMS Black Five 4-6-0 No. 44713 in charge of the 2.10 p.m. Paddington–Birkenhead express. Wrexham General, at this time, had become part of BR London-Midland Region a year before. Thus, much of the traffic through the station was in the hands of ex-LMS traction and ex-GWR engines were fast disappearing from the scene. (H. Casserley)

Opposite bottom: Wrexham General station in the 1950s. The station here was opened in 1846 as part of the Shrewsbury & Chester Railway, later becoming part of the GWR. As this was the main line between Paddington and Birkenhead, Wrexham became a busy freight centre. The town also provided freight from its collieries and steelworks, which made the town attractive to the railway companies. Indeed, the town was blessed with three important stations, at Central and Exchange as well as General. Exchange station was adjacent to the GWR station and was originally a terminus for Great Central Railway trains (later LNER) when opened in 1866. The GCR operated services from the Wirral and Connah's Quay to Wrexham, its local trains being operated by LNER Class N5 0-6-2Ts and C13 4-4-2Ts. Exchange became a through station in 1887 when an extension to Central was completed. Central station, itself, was opened in 1887 as an extension from Exchange. Services, operated by the Manchester, Sheffield & Lincolnshire Railway (GCR) from Chester Northgate, started in 1889. The Cambrian Railways also had a presence at Central, which became a through station in 1895 when the Wrexham & Ellesmere line opened. The Ellesmere line was closed in 1962 and the station then reverted to a terminus. Several branch lines were operated from Wrexham General and a roundhouse was built in 1902 to provide motive power. Known as Croes Newydd, this GWR roundhouse had a sub-shed at Penmaenpool as well as Bala and Trawsfynydd. (Author's Collection)

Coded CYND in GWR days and 84J in BR days, its allocation in the last year of private ownership was as follows:

Collett 0-4-2T (motor-fitted)	1401, 1411, 1416, 1457
Wolverhampton 0-6-0PT	1532, 1706, 1747, 1773, 1780, 2183, 2184, 2188, 2190, 2704, 2713, 2716, 2717
Collett Goods 0-6-0	2259, 2287, 3203, 3206
ROD Robinson 2-8-0	3026, 3028
Churchward 2-6-0	5315, 5319, 5334, 5365, 6303, 6316, 6327, 7305, 7310
Collett 0-4-2T non-motor-fitted)	5810, 5811
Collett 0-6-2T	6694, 6698
Collett 0-6-0PT	7403, 7409, 7414, 9656
Collett Manor 4-6-0	7817 *Garsington Manor*
WD 2-8-0	70808
	Total: 43

The allocation shows that most locomotives at the shed were for local passenger and freight traffic. Along with Croes Newydd, the GCR also had a loco shed at Rhos Ddu, which became a sub-shed of Chester's GWR shed at nationalisation. When Chester shed closed in 1960, all of its allocation was transferred to Rhos Ddu while awaiting their fate.

WREXHAM and BERWIG (Motor Cars—One class only).—Great Western.

Miles.	Down.	Week Days only. mrn	mrn	mrn	mrn	aft	aft	aft	aft	aft	aft	aft	aft	aft	aft	aft	aft	aft	Sats. aft
	Wrexham ....dep.	7 30	8 31	9 35	1140	12 23	1 58	3 15	4s23	4e40	5s10	5e45	5s50	6e48	7 s 5	7 50	8s35	8 55	9 55
2	Plas Power ¶	7 38	8 39	9 43	1148	12 31	2 6	3 23	4s31	4e48	5s18	5e53	5s58	6e56	7s13	7 58	....	9 3	10 3
3¼	Brymbo ¶ 457	7 45	8 46	9 50	1155	12 38	2 13	3 30	4s39	4e55	5s25	6 e 0	6 s 5	7 e 3	7s18	8 5	8s48	9 10	1010
6¼	Coed Poeth ¶	8 0	h	10 5	h	12 51	2 28	3 45	4s53	5 e 8	5s38	6e13	6s18	7e16	7s30	8e19	9 s 0	9e23	1023
6¾	Berwig Halt...........arr.	8 5	....	1010	....	....	2 33	3e50	4s58	....	....	....	....	....	7s35	....	....	....	....

Miles.	Up.	Week Days only. mrn	mrn	mrn	aft	aft	aft	aft	aft	aft	aft	aft	aft	aft	aft	aft	aft
	Berwig Halt ¶ ....dep.	8 17	....	1022	....	....	2 40	3e57	....	5 s 5	....	....	....	....	7s42	....	....
½	Coed Poeth ¶	8 25	k	1030	k	1 13	2 48	4 5	5e10	5s15	5s55	6e15	6s30	7e18	7s50	8e22	9 25
3½	Brymbo ¶ 457	8 36	8 55	1041	12 2	1 24	2 59	4 16	5e22	5s27	6 s 7	6e27	6s42	7e30	8 s 2	8e34	9 37
4¾	Plas Power ....[716	8 42	9 1	1047	12 8	1 30	3 5	4 22	5e28	5s33	6s13	6e33	6s48	7e36	8 s 8	8e40	9 43
6¾	Wrexham* **84, 87,** arr.	8 50	9 8	1055	1216	1 38	3 13	4 30	5e36	5s40	6s20	6e40	6s55	7e44	8s18	8e47	9 52

e Except Saturdays. **h** Runs to Brymbo West Crossing. **k** Leaves Brymbo West Crossing about 3 minutes *earlier*.
s Saturdays only. * Station for Holt (5½ miles).
¶ "**Halts**" at The Lodge, between Plas Power and Brymbo; Brymbo West Crossing and Pentresaeson (for Bwlchgwyn), between Brymbo and Coed Poeth; and Vicarage Crossing, between Coed Poeth and Berwig.

WREXHAM and RHOS (Motor Cars—One class only).—Great Western.

Miles	Down.	Week Days only. mrn	mrn	mrn	mrn	mrn	aft	aft	aft	Sats. aft	aft	Sats. aft	aft	aft	Sats. aft	aft	Sats. aft	aft
	Wrexham ....dep.	7 25	8 23	9 40	10 30	11 57	1 20	2 55	3 45	4 25	5 0	5 40	6 26	7 2	7 31	8 25	9 0	9 48
1¾	Rhostyllen	7 31	8 29	9 46	10 36	12 3	1 25	3 1	3 51	4 31	5 6	5 46	6 32	7 8	7 37	8 31	9 6	9 54
3	Legacy	7 36	8 34	9 51	10 41	12 8	1 31	3 6	3 56	4 36	5 11	5 51	6 37	7 13	7 42	8 36	9 11	9 59
4¼	Rhos	7 39	8 37	9 54	10 44	12 11	1 34	3 9	3 59	4 39	5 14	5 54	6 40	7 16	7 45	8 39	9 14	10 2

Miles.	Up.	Week Days only. mrn	mrn	mrn	mrn	aft	aft	aft	aft	Sats. aft	aft	Sats. aft	aft	aft	Sats. aft	aft	Sats. aft	aft
	Rhos ....dep.	7 57	8 40	10 0	1047	12 20	1 37	3 16	4 3	4 42	5 16	6 0	6 43	7 20	7 48	8 42	9 23	10 5
1¼	Legacy	8 1	8 44	10 4	1051	12 24	1 41	3 20	4 7	4 46	5 20	6 4	6 47	7 24	7 52	8 46	9 27	10 9
2½	Rhostyllen ....[716	8 4	8 47	10 7	1054	12 27	1 44	3 23	4 10	4 49	5 23	6 7	6 50	7 27	7 55	8 49	9 30	10 12
4¼	Wrexham* **84, 87,** arr.	8 10	8 53	1013	11 0	12 35	1 51	3 30	4 17	4 56	5 30	6 14	6 57	7 33	8 2	8 56	9 37	10 20

* Station for Holt (5½ miles).

WREXHAM and MOSS (Motor Cars—One class only).—Great Western.

Miles.	Down.	Week Days only. mrn	mrn	mrn	aft	aft	aft	aft	Sats. aft	aft	Sats. aft	aft	Sats. aft	aft	Sats. aft
	Wrexham ¶ ....dep.	7 45	9 0	11 5	1245	2 5	3 15	4 20	5 20	5e40	6 0	7 37	8 14	9 5	9 35
3¼	Moss Halt ....arr.	7 58	9 13	11 18	1258	2 18	3 28	4 33	5 33	5e53	6 13	7 50	8 27	9 18	9 48

Miles.	Up.	Week Days only. mrn	mrn	mrn	aft	aft	aft	aft	Sats. aft	aft	Sats. aft	aft	Sats. aft	aft	Sats. aft
	Moss Halt ¶......[716 dep	8 0	9 20	11 20	1 0	2 20	3 30	4 35	5 35	5e56	6 17	7 54	8 31	9 22	9 53
3¼	Wrexham * **84, 87,** arr.	8 13	9 33	11 33	1 15	2 36	3 43	4 48	5 50	6e11	6 32	8 8	8 44	9 35	10 6

e Except Saturdays. * Station for Holt (5½ miles).
¶ "**Halts**" at Gatewen, Pentre Broughton, and Gwersyllt Hill, between Wrexham and Moss.

Timetables from 1922 showing local services that operated out of General station. Virtually all of these services ceased by the late 1960s as road transport took away all of its business. The Wrexham–Berwig trains lasted for only twenty-six years, not making it unto the 1930s. As can be seen, these trains were 'motor cars', little 0-4-2Ts or 0-6-0PTs providing motive power. (Author's Collection)

LIVERPOOL, BIRKENHEAD, BIDSTON, CONNAH'S QUAY, HOPE, and WREXHAM.—Gt. Central.

Miles	Up.	Week Days.																			Suns.	
	Landing Stage.	mrn	mrn	mrn	mrn	mrn	mrn	aft	aft	aft	aft	aft	aft	aft	aft	aft	aft	aft	aft	aft	mrn	aft
—	**Liverpool** (By Boat) . . dep.	....	....	7 30	7 50	9 20	11 15	1s10	1e20	1 30	3 0	....	....	4 50	5 20	6e0	7 0	....	9 15	....	9 45	8 15
—	**Seacombe & Egremont** "	....	....	7 43	8 12	9 35	11 30	1s25	1e35	1 50	3 13	....	....	5 3	5 33	6e15	7 20	....	9 30	1045	1015	8 35
1½	Liscard and Poulton . . . "	....	....	7 47	....	9 39	....	....	1e40	1 55	....	....	....	....	....	....	7 24	....	9 34	....	1019	8 39
—	592 **Liverpool** (Cn., L.L.) dep.	....	....	6 22	....	8 55	11 5	1s3	1e15	Sats. only.	2 5	....		4e35	5s5	5e45	6 35		9 7	....	....	8 10
—	" (James St.) "	....	....	6 24	....	8 57	11 7	1s5	1e17		2 7	....		4e37	5s7	5e47	6 37		9 9	....	....	8 12
—	**Birkenhead*** . . . . . . "	....	....	6 27	....	9 0	11 10	1s8	1e20		2 10	....	Saturdays only.	4e40	5s10	5e50	6 40		9 12	....	....	8 15
—	" **Park** . . . "	....	....	6 35	8 9	9 9	11 18	1s18	1e27		2 18	....		4e46	5s18	5e57	6 47	Saturdays only.	9 19	1034	....	8 20
—	" **Docks** . . "	....	....	6 38	....	9 12	11 21	1s21	1e30		2 21	....		....	....	....	6 50		9 22	1037	....	8 23
3	**Bidston** . . . . dep.	....	....	7 52	8 19	9 44	11 38	1s34	1e46	2 1	3 20			5 10	5 40	6e22	7 30		9 39	1053	1024	8 44
4½	Upton	....	....	7 56	....	9 48	11 42	1s38	1e50	2 5	3 24			5 14	5 44	6e26	7 34		9 43	1057	1028	8 48
7½	Storeton, for Barnston	....	....	8 2	....	9 54	11 48	1s45	1e56	2 11	3 30	Except Saturdays.		5 20	5 50	6e32	7 40		9 49	11 3	1234	8 54
8¾	Heswall Hills	....	....	8 6	8 27	9 58	11 52	1s50	2e0	2 15	3 34			5 24	5 54	6e36	7 44		9 53	11 7	1038	8 58
11½	Neston and Parkgate	....	....	8 14	8 35	10 7	12 0	1s56	2e10	2 25	3 42			5 32	6 2	6e45	7 52		10 2	1112	1045	9 5
13½	Burton Point ‡	....	....	8 18	....	1011	12 4	2s1	2e15	2 30	3 46			5 36	6 6	6e49	7 56		10 6	1118	1049	9 9
17½	**Connah's Quay**† **464, 467, 717** arr.	....	....	8 26	8 46	1018	12 11	2s9	2e25	2 40	3 53			5 43	6 13	6e56	8 3		1013	1125	1056	9 16
	dep.	6 22	7 30	8 28	....	1020	12 13	2s11	2e27	2 42	3 54	4 8	4 33	5 45	6 14	7e0	8 5	9 33	1016		1058	9 20
19½	**Hawarden**	6 28	7 36	8 35	....	1027	12 20	2s18	2e35	2 50	4 0	4 14	4 39	5 51	6 20	7e6	8 11	9 39	1023		11 4	9 26
21½	Buckley Junction	6 34	7 42	8 41	....	1033	12 26	2s25	2e43	2 58		4 20	4 45	5 57	6 26	7e12	8 17	9 44	1030		1110	9 32
22¾	**Hope** (Exchange) **470**	....	7 44	8 43	....	1035	12 28	2s28	2e45	3 0		4 22	4 47	5 59	6 28	7e14	8 19	....	....		....	....
23	Pen-y-ffordd ‖	6 37	7 47	8 47	....	1039	12 31	2s31	2e50	3 5	Except Saturdays.	4 25	4 50	6 2	6 31	7e17	8 22	9 51	1036	Mons., Weds., and Sats.	1115	9 37
24¾	Hope Village	6 41	7 52	8 51	....	1043	12 35	2s35	2e55	3 10		4 30	4 54	6 6	6 35	7e21	8 26	9 55	1040		1119	....
25½	Caergwrle Castle and Wells	6 43	7 55	8 54	....	1046	12 38	2s38	2e59	3 14		4 33	4 57	6 9	6 38	7e24	8 29	9 58	1043		1121	9 42
26	Cefn-y-bedd	6 46	7 58	8 57	....	1049	12 41	2s41	3e2	3 17		4 36	5 0	6 12	6s41	7e27	8 32	10 1	1046		1125	9 46
28	Gwersyllt	6 50	8 3	9 2	....	1054	12 46	2s47	3e7	3 22		4 41	5 5	6 17	6 44	7e32	8 37	10 6	1051		1130	9 51
29¾	**Wrexham** (Exchange)	6 55	8 8	9 7	....	1059	12 51	2s52	3e12	3 27		4 46	5 10	6 22	6 49	7e37	8 42	1011	1056		....	....
30¾	" (Cen.) § **584** arr.	6 58	8 11	9 10	....	11 2	12 54	2s55	3e15	3 30		4 49	5 13	6 25	6 52	7e40	8 45	1014	1059		1135	9 56

Miles	Down.	Week Days.																			Suns.	
		mrn	mrn	mrn	mrn	mrn		aft	aft	aft	aft	aft	aft	aft		aft	aft	aft			mrn	aft
	Wrexham (Central) . . . . dep.	6 40	....	7 30	....	9 45	....	1242	1 35	2 35		4 5	4 30	5 20	....	7 10	9 0	....	....	....	8 15	5 10
½	" (Exchange)	6 43	....	7 33	....	9 48	....	1245	1 38	2 38		4 8	4 33	5 23	..	7 13	9 3	....	....	....	....	....
2¼	Gwersyllt	6 48	....	7 39	....	9 54	....	1251	1 45	2 46		4 13	4 38	5 29	....	7 18	9 10	....	....	....	8 21	5 16
4¼	Cefn-y-bedd	6 52	....	7 45	....	9 58	....	1255	1 49	2 50		4 17	4 42	5 33	....	7 22	9 14	....	....	....	8 27	5 23
5	Caergwrle Castle and Wells	6 55	....	7 49	....	10 1	....	1258	1 52	2 53	Except Saturdays.	4 20	4 45	5 36	....	7 24	9 17	....	....	....	8 30	5 25
5½	Hope Village	6 59	....	7 57	....	10 5	....	1 2	1 55	2 56		4 23	4 48	5 40	....	7 27	9 20	....	....	....	8 37	5 31
7½	Pen-y-ffordd ‖	7 4	....	8 5	....	10 10	....	1 7	2 0	3 1		4 28	4 53	5 45	....	7 32	9 25	....	....	....	8 44	5 38
7¾	**Hope** (Exchange) **470**	7 6	....	8 7	....	10 12	....	1 9	....	....		4 30	4 54	5 47	....	7 34	9 27	....	....	....	....	....
8¾	Buckley Junction	7 11	....	8 12	....	10 18	....	1 15	2 8	3 6		4 35	4 59	5 53	....	7 39	9 32	....	....	....	8 49	5 44
10¾	Hawarden	7 17	....	8 20	...	10 23	....	1 20	2 13	3 11	4 9	4 41	5 4	5 58	....	7 44	9 37	10 0	....	....	8 57	5 51
13	**Connah's Quay**† **464, 467, 717** arr.	7 22	....	8 25	....	10 28	....	1 25	2 18	3 16	4 14	4 46	5 9	6 3	....	7 49	9 42	10 5	....	....	9 2	5 56
	dep.	7 24	8 0	8 27	8 55	10 30	....	1 28		3 18	4 15			6 6	....	7 50	9 44	1010	....	....	9 5	5 59
16¾	Burton Point ‡	7 32	8 7	8 34	....	10 37	....	1 34		3 25	4 22			6 14	....	7 58	9 51		....	....	9 13	6 7
19	Neston and Parkgate	7 40	8 17	8 42	9 7	10 44	....	1 41		3 32	4 27		Except Saturdays.	6 21	....	8 4	9 59		....	....	9 20	6 14
21½	Heswall Hills	7 46	8 23	8 48	9 13	10 50	....	1 48	Saturdays only.	3 38	4 33	Saturdays only.		6 27	....	8 11	10 5		....	....	9 26	6 20
23	Storeton, for Barnston	7 50	8 27	8 52	....	10 54	....	1 52		3 42	4 37			6 31	....	8 14	10 9		....	....	9 30	6 24
25¾	Upton	7 55	8 32	8 57	....	10 59	....	1 57		3 47	4 42			6 36	....	8 19	10 14		....	....	9 35	6 29
27½	**Bidston 592** . . . . arr.	7 59	8 36	9 1	....	11 3	....	2 1		3 51	4 46			6 40	....	8 23	10 19		....	....	9 40	6 34
28½	593 **Birkenhead Docks** arr.	8 52	8 52	....	....	11 17	....	2 22		4 22	5 22		....	7 22	....	....	10 37	Except Saturdays.	....	....	....	6 57
29½	" **Park** . . . "	8 37	8 56	9 45	....	11 20	....	2 25		4 25	5 25		....	7 25	....	9 30	10 40		....	....	....	7 0
30½	" (Hamilton Sq.) "	8 44	9 4	9 52	....	11 32	....	2 32		4 32	5 32		....	7 32	....	9 38	10 53		....	....	....	7 13
31½	**Liverpool** (James St.) "	8 47	9 7	9 55	....	11 35	....	2 35		4 35	5 35		....	7 35	....	9 41	10 56		....	....	....	7 16
32	" (Cen., L. L.) "	8 49	9 9	9 57	....	11 37	....	2 37		4 37	5 37		....	7 37	....	9 43	10 58		....	....	....	7 18
28¾	Liscard & Poulton **592** arr.	....	....	....	....	11 8	...	2 6	....	3 56	4 50	....	....	6 45	....	8 28	10 23	....	....	....	9 45	6 39
30¼	**Seacombe & Egremont** "	8 6	8 43	9 8	9 30	11 12	....	2 11	....	4 0	4 55	....	....	6 49	....	8 32	10 27	....	....	....	9 49	6 43
31	**Liverpool** (Lan. Stage) "	8 16	8 56	9 26	9 46	11 36	....	2 26	....	4 16	5 6	....	....	7 6	....	8 48	10 46	....	....	....	10 6	7 6

e Except Saturdays.
s Saturdays only.
* Hamilton Square.

† Connah's Quay and Shotton.
‡ Station for Burton and Puddington.
‖ Station for Leeswood.
§ Station for Holt (5½ miles).

For other Trains BETWEEN Seacombe and Bidston . . . . PAGE 592

The GCR also operated local trains between Wrexham and Bidston, on the Wirral; this 1922 timetable shows the extent of these services from and to Wrexham Exchange. (Author's Collection)

WREXHAM a										
s	**Down.**	mrn	mrn	aft	aft	aft	aft			
.	Wrexham (Cen.)..dep.	8 10	9 55	1 35	3 50	6 30	9 20			
2½	Marchwiel...............	8 15	10 0	1 40	3 55	6 35	9 25			
5½	Bangor-on-Dee.........	8 22	10 7	1 47	4 2	6 42	9 32			
8½	Overton-on-Dee........	8 31	1016	1 56	4 11	6 51	9 41			
2½	Ellesmere 466,467 arr	8 40	1025	2 5	4 20	7 0	9 50			
3¼	467 WHITCHURCH .. arr.	9 25	1157	2 38	5 0	8 5	1025			
9	466 OSWESTRY .... ''	9 10	1050	2 35	5 13	7 30	....			

The Wrexham Central Railway, as the Cambrian, timetable of 1922 from Central station to Ellesmere where it joined the main Whitchurch–Welshpool line. (Author's Collection)

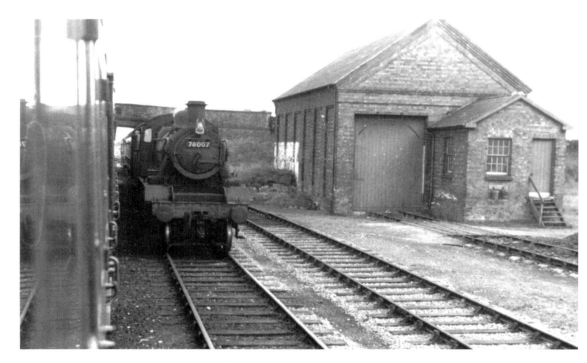

Arriving at Ellesmere on the Cambrian Railways line, is BR Standard Class 2 2-6-0 No. 78007 on the 2.05 p.m. service from Whitchurch to Welshpool on 15 August 1953. Ellesmere was served by the Oswestry, Ellesmere & Whitchurch Railway from 1863. The market town then became a junction with the opening of the Wrexham Central line in 1895. (H. Casserley)

LESMERE.—Cambrian.

	Up.	mrn	mrn	aft	aft	aft	aft				
	467 OSWESTRY ......dep.	8 35	1140	1 55	4 10	5 25	....	....	....	....	....
	466 WHITCHURCH... "	8 22	10 5	1 50	...·.	4 25	6 40	....	....	....	....
	Ellesmere.........dep.	9 0	12 0	2 25	4 35	5 47	7 15	....	....	....	....
1¼	Overton-on-Dee	9 9	12 9	2 34	4 44	5 56	7 24	....	....	....	....
7½	Bangor-on-Dee	9 16	1216	2 41	4 51	6 3	7 31	....	....	....	....
0½	Marchwiel........[671	9 25	1225	2 50	5 0	6 12	7 40	....	....	....	....
2¼	Wrexham (C.) **80**, arr.	9 30	1230	2 55	5 5	6 17	7 45	....	....	....	....

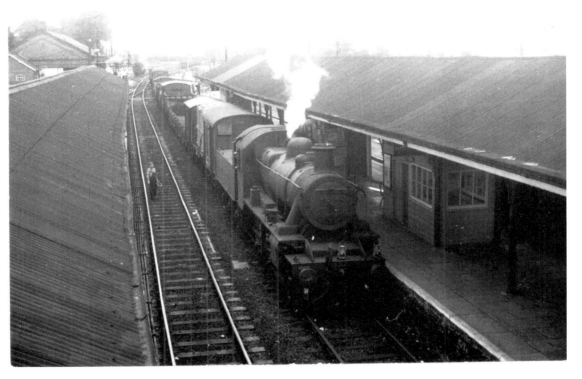

At the other end of the line, in Welshpool, ex-LMS Ivatt Class 2 2-6-0 No. 46510 runs through the station with a goods train on 28 August 1964. (H. Casserley)

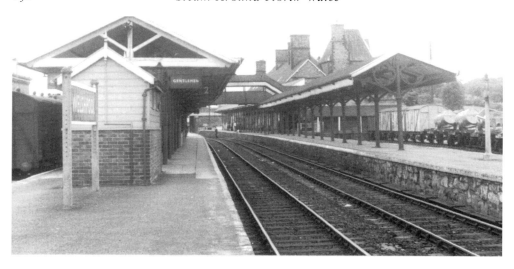

Welshpool station, looking west, on 28 August 1964. (H. Casserley)

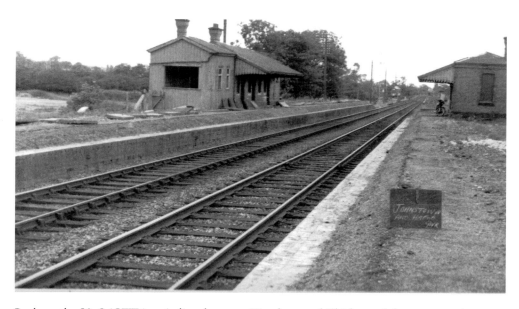

Back on the S&C (GWR) main line, between Wrexham and Chirk was Johnstown station, seen here in the late 1960s awaiting demolition. (Author's Collection)

Opposite below: A map of the GWR line from Ruabon to Barmouth Junction (Morfa Mawddach). Until 1922, when the Cambrian was absorbed by the GWR, the line from Ruabon to Dolgellau was operated by the GWR, while the section from Dolgellau to Barmouth Junction was operated by Cambrian Railways and a head-on connection was made at the Merionethshire market town. After the takeover, trains ran directly to Barmouth on the old Cambrian section. (Author's Collection)

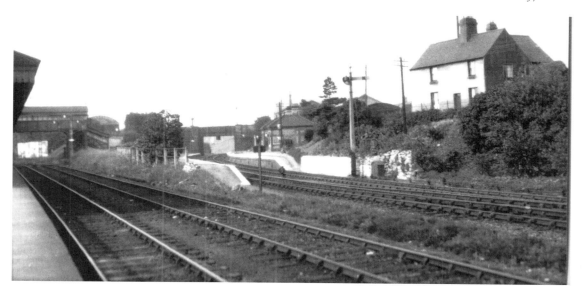

Next station was at Ruabon, the junction of the line to Llangollen and Dolgellau as well as a local branch to Rhos. (Author's Collection)

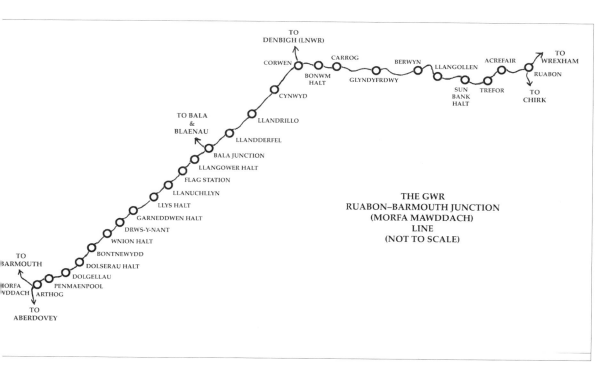

RUABON, LLANGOLLEN, CORWEN, BALA

Miles from Ruabon.	Down.	Week D										
	Paddington Station,	mrn	mrn	mrn	mrn	mrn	mrn	aft	mrn	aft	mrn	mrn
	74 London .... dep.	....	12¼h	....	....	....	....	....	6 30	....	9 50	1125
	74 Birmingham * .... "	....	3h53	....	6 0	8 30	m	....	1130	b	1248	1 50
	75 Shrewsbury .... "	....	6 30	....	8 0	10 5	1120	....	1241	b	2 13	3 2
	80 Manchester (Ex.) "	....	....	....	7 40	8 5	9 45	....	1045	....	1 5	....
	80 L'pool (Landing S.) "	....	6 0	....	8 0	10 0	1020	....	1140	....	1 20	2 20
	80 Chester (General) "	....	6 45	m	9 0	1045	1115	....	1245	....	2 15	3 5
—	**Ruabon** .... dep	....	7 48	8 32	9 40	1125	1230	....	1 40	....	3 10	3 50
1½	Acrefair..................	....	7 53	8 36	9 45	1130	1234	....	1 44	....	3 14	....
2½	Trevor ¶..................	....	7 56	8 40	9 49	1133	1237	....	1 48	....	3 18	....
6¼	**Llangollen**..............	....	8 5	8 52	10 2	1145	1248	....	2 1	....	3 28	....
7¾	Berwyn..................	....	8 9	8 59	10 6	m	1252	....	2 5	....	3 32	....
11½	Glyndyfrdwy	....	8 17	9 7	1013	....	1 0	....	2 14	....	3 40	....
13½	Carrog..................	....	8 21	9 13	1018	....	1 5	....	2 20	....	3 45	....
16¼	**Corwen 478**......... arr.	....	8 28	9 18	1026	....	1 10	....	2 25	....	3 50	4 20
	dep.	....	8 31	....	1029	....	....	1 20	m	....	4 0	4 22
18¼	Cynwyd	....	8 36	....	1034	....	....	1 27	....	....	4 6	....
21	Llandrillo	....	8 42	....	1040	....	....	1 35	....	....	4 16	n
23¾	Llandderfel..............	....	8 48	....	1046	....	....	1 45	....	....	4 22	n
28	**Bala** †.............. arr.	....	9 7	....	11 7	....	....	1 58	....	....	4 34	4 47
—	1 & 3 class. **Bala** .... dep.	7 35	9 30	....	1134	....	....	....	....	....	....	5 35
30½	Frongoch..................	7 40	9 35	....	1139	....	....	....	....	....	....	5 42
35¾	Arenig	7 52	9 47	....	1153	....	....	....	....	....	....	5 56
38½	Cwm Prysor	Sig.	Sig.	....	Sig.	....	....	....	....	....	....	Sig.
44¼	Trawsfynydd..............	8 11	10 6	....	1212	....	....	....	....	4 15	....	6 16
47¼	Maentwrog Road	8 21	1017	....	1220	....	....	....	....	4 25	....	6 25
49¼	**Festiniog**..............	8 27	1023	....	1225	....	....	....	....	4 50	....	6 30
51½	Manod ....[471, 477	8 35	1031	....	1233	....	....	....	....	4 57	....	6 37
52¾	**Blaenau Festiniog** arr.	8 43	1040	....	1240	....	....	....	....	5 5	....	6 45
--	**Bala** †.............. dep.	....	8 50	....	1047	....	....	....	....	....	....	4 30
32¼	Llanuwchllyn	....	9 8	....	11 5	....	....	....	....	....	....	4 48
38½	Drws-y-Nant..............	....	9 21	....	1121	....	....	....	....	....	....	5 1
42	Bontnewydd..............	....	9 30	....	1130	....	....	....	....	....	....	5 10
45¼	**Dolgelley 469**........ arr.	....	9 40	....	1140	....	....	....	....	....	....	5 20
54½	**469** Barmouth .... arr.	....	....	....	1220	....	....	....	....	....	....	5 53

A 1910 GWR timetable for trains from Ruabon to Dolgellau (then spelt Dolgelley on the timetable), the Cambrian taking over from there to Barmouth. (Author's Collection)

INIOG, and DOLGELLEY.—Great Western.

							Sundays.		
aft	aft	aft	m	aft			mrn		
....	2 13	m	4 55	....	...	...	1020	....	....
....	4 40	5 55	7 33	m	...	...	1 35	aft	....
....	5 55	7 23	7 40	8 38	...	...	2 58	mrn	....
3 40	4 55	5 10	7 15	....	...	...	7 50		....
4 50	5 10	6 20	7 20	8 40	...	...	2 50		....
5 23	6 5	7 37	8 40	9 50	...	...	3 40		..
6 12	7 8	8 18	9 30	1045	...	...	4 18	aft	....
6 16	7 13	8 22	9 34	1049	...	...	4 23		..
6 20	7 18	8 26	9 38	1053	...	...	4 27		....
6 32	7 30	8 38	9 50	11 5	.	...	4 35		....
6 37	7 34	....	....						
6 46	7 40	....	....	1119					
6 52	7 46	....	....	Sat.					
6 57	7 53	....	....	1130					
....	7 55								
....	8 0								
....	8 5								
....	8 14								
....	8 35								
....	8 15								
....	8 37								
....	8 51								
....	9 1								
....	9 10								

(Weds. & Sats.)

NOTES.

a Via Wrexham.

b 1st and 3rd class.

h Except Mondays.

i Leaves at 9 20 aft. on Saturdays.

m Motor Car, one class only.

n Sets down from London on notice being given to the Guard at Ruabon.

* Snow Hill.

† Passengers to and from Bala have to change at Bala Junction by most of the Trains.

¶ "Halt" at Sun Bank, between Trevor and Llangollen.

RUABON, LLANGOLLEN, CORWEN, BALA, and DOLGELLEY.—Great Western.

Down.

Miles from Ruabon	Station	Week Days						Sunday
		mrn mrn aft mrn	mrn mrn	mrn mrn aft aft aft aft aft				mrn mrn
84	London (Pad.) dep.	12·15 .... 12·15	9 10 9 10	10 15 10 40 .... 12·50 2 20 .... 4 0				.... 11·10
84	Birmingham * .... "	4·11 .... 6 0 8 20	11·20 11·20	12 50 1 17 3 4 26 .... 6 5				7 0 2 10·2
84	Shrewsbury (Gen) "	5 33 .... 7 45 11·25	12·27 12·50	2 1 2 45 4 28 5 39 .... 7 30				9 10 3 28·5
87	Manchester ‡ .... "	.... 7 30 9 45	11·20 11·20	12 51 3 52 4·53 4 0 4 45 6 30				10·10 ....
87	Liverpool § .... "	.... 6 45 8 0 10·20	11·50 12·30	1 0 2 20 4 50 5 10 6 20				10 0 2 40·3
87	Birkenhead (W.) "	.... 7 0 8 15 10·35	12·10 12·50	1 20 2 40 3 55 6 5 25 6 35				10·20 2 55·4
87	Chester (General) "	.... 7 40 8 55 11·15	12·48 1 30	2 0 3 12 4 20 5 35 8 0 7 45				2 15 2 46·5
—	Ruabon dep.	7 35 8 25 9 40 12·38	1 23 2 10	2 55 4 0 5 10 6 25 7 0 8 42				2 54 3 50·6
1¼	Acrefair .... "	7 40 8 30 9 45 12·43	.... 2 15	.... 4 5 5 15 6 30 7 5 8 45				2 59 4 35·6
2¾	Trevor ¶	7 44 8 34 9 48 12·46	.... 2 19	.... 4 8 5 18 6 33 7 8 8 49				3 2 4 39·6
6¼	Llangollen	7 55 8 45 10 0 1 0	1 38 2 33	3 10 4 13 5 28 6 45 7 18 9 0				3 10 4 46·6
7¾	Berwyn	8 1 .... 10 5 1 6	.... 2 39	.... 4 24 .... 7 24				
11¼	Glyndyfrdwy	8 9 .... 10 13 1 15	.... 2 47	.... 4 32 5 40 .... 7 34 9 13				
13¼	Carrog	8 15 .... 10 19 1 22	.... 2 55	.... 4 40 5 46 .... 7 40 9 20				
16¼	Corwen 470 { arr.	8 20 .... 10 25 1 30	1 50 3 ..	3 30 4 45 5 51 7 7 7 47 9 25				
	{ dep.	8 25 .... 10 28 1 35	2 0 m	3 34 4 50 5 53 7 12 7 50				
18¼	Cynwyd	8 31 .... 10 33 1 41	....	4 50 .... 7 55				
21	Llandrillo	8 36 .... 10 39 1 46	....	5 16 2 .... 8 0				
23¾	Llandderfel	8 42 .... 10 45 1 53	....	5 36 8 .... 8 6				
28	Bala † (below) { arr.	9 5 .... 11 0 2 0	....	4 5 5 27 6 25 7 49 8 12				
	{ dep.	9 48 .... 10 43 ₘ	....	3 45 5 16 6 57 25 8 ₘ				
32¼	Llanuwchllyn	9 5 .... 11 5	....	5 29 6 28 7 43 8 28				
38½	Drws-y-Nant	9 18 .... 11 20	....	5 40 6 41 9 1 8 51				
42	Bontnewydd	9 27 .... 11 29	....	5 54 .... 9 41				
45¾	Dolgelley 584 .... arr.	9 37 .... 11 40	3 0	4 55 5 6 56 8 2 29 A.m				
54¾	584 Barmouth .... arr.	10 5 .... 12 11	3 28	4 25 5 56 57 25 8 47				

Up.

Miles	Station	Week Days						Sunday
		mrn mrn mrn	mrn mrn mrn	mrn	mrn aft aft aft aft aft aft			aft aft a
	584 Barmouth .... dep.	....	7 45 9 50 10·15	11 23	11·55 12·40 .... 2 35 .... 5 37 7 10			
—	Dolgelley .... dep.	....	8 15 10·20 10·40		12·27 1 10 .... 3 10 .... 6 57 40			
3¼	Bontnewydd	....	8 25 10·28		.... 1 18 .... 3 19 .... 7 3			
6½	Drws-y-Nant	....	8 32 10·37		.... 1 27 .... 3 28 .... 8 3			
13	Llanuwchllyn	....	8 45 10·49 11·10		.... 1 40 .... 3 43 .... 3 13			
18	Bala † (below) { arr.	....	9 5 11 5 11·24		.... 1 55 ₘ 4 5 .... 6 52 8 25			
	{ dep.	.... 7 25	8 48 10·43 11·10		.... 2 7 2 55 3 48 .... 6 40 8 16			
21¼	Llandderfel	.... 7 34	9 5 11 7		.... 2 15 3 5 4 9 .... 8 23			
24½	Llandrillo	.... 7 40	9 10 11·13		.... 2 23 3 12 4 15 .... 8 45			
27	Cynwyd	.... 7 46	9 15 11·19		.... 2 29 3 20 4 21 .... 8 51			
29	Corwen 470 { arr.	.... 7 51	9 23 11·25 11·40		1 18 2 35 3 40 4 26 .... 7 10 8 56			
	{ dep.	.... 7 56	9 26 11·30 11·54		1 20 2 37 3 40 4 31 5 15 7 13 9 0			
31¾	Carrog	.... 8 2	9·40 11·36		.... 2 43 3 46 .... 5 24 7 19 9 6			
33¼	Glyndyfrdwy	.... 8 10	9·40 11·42		.... 2 48 3 55 .... 5 40 7 25 9 12			
37¾	Berwyn	.... 8 21 ₘ	9·40 11·51		.... 2 58 4 10 .... 5 53			
39	Llangollen ¶	.... 7 35 8 10 9 15	9 48 12 0 12·15		1 45 3 4 4 23 4 58 6 5 7 40 9 25	3 40 5 33·8		
42¼	Trevor	.... 7 45 8 44 9 26	9 59 12·12		.... 3 13 4 36 5 7 6 16 7 50 9 35	3 49 5 42·8		
43½	Acrefair	.... 7 49 8 48 9 30	9 59 12·12		.... 3 17 4 40 5 11 6 20 7 53 9 39	3 52 5 45·8		
45	Ruabon 84, 87	.... 7 55 8 50 9 35	10 3 12·16 12·35		.... 3 21 4 45 5 16 6 25 7 57 9 44	3 57 5 59·8		
62	84 Chester (Gen.) arr.	8 55 9 46	10·52 .... 1 32		2 35 3 55 4 49·6 5 7 25 8 35 10·15	4 40 7 5·8		
76¾	84 Birkenhead (W.) "	9 32 9 57	11·30 .... 2 5		3 15 4 50 5 20 7 10 8 39 9 15 11·10	6 33 1·39		
77	84 Liverpool § .... "	9 47 10 7	11·47 .... 2 17		3 25 5 7 6 37·7 27·8 57 9 27 11·22	6 17 8 27·1		
102	84 Manchester ‡ .... "	10 17 10·50	1 15 .... 3 30		3 55 4 57 5 9 29 2 10 43	6 15 9 10		
70½	87 Shrewsbury (Gen) "	8 52	10·54 .... 1 36		3 55 4 28 .... 6 23 7 58 9 8	4 57 7 10		
112¼	87 Birmingham * .... "	10·10	12 1 .... 2 46		5 48 .... 7 40 10·13	6 25 9 25		
223¼	87 London (Pad.) .... "	12·25	2 15 .... 5 0		8 5 .... 10·45 30	9 0		

A	Wednesdays and Saturdays.	k	Set down from Llanuwchllyn, Frongoch, and beyond on notice being given to the Guard.	*	Snow Hill.
b	Except Mondays.			†	Passengers to and from Bala have change at Bala Junction by mo
B	Arrives Paddington at 6 20 aft. on Saturdays.	ₘ	Motor Car, one class only.		of the Trains.
c	Except Saturdays.	o	Takes up for London on giving notice at Station.	‡	Exchange Station.
i	Mondays and Fridays.			§	Landing Stage.
				¶	"Halt" at Sun Bank, between Trevor and Llangollen.

By 1922, the GWR had absorbed the Cambrian and this timetable of the time shows trains now running through to Barmouth. (Author's Collection)

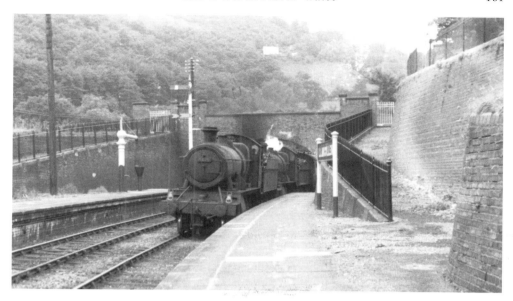

Llangollen station, on the line from Ruabon, on 15 August 1953 with a pair of Churchward 2-6-0s, Nos 4375 and 6344, at the head of the 8.45 a.m. from Pwllheli, on the ex-Cambrian line. The GWR line between Ruabon and Corwen opened in two stages. The Vale of Llangollen Railway was incorporated on 1 August 1859 and the line from Ruabon to Llangollen was opened to goods on 1 December 1861 and to passengers on 2 June 1862. The Vale of Llangollen Railway had stations at Acrefair, Trefor and Sun Bank Halt before reaching the famous market town. (H. Casserley)

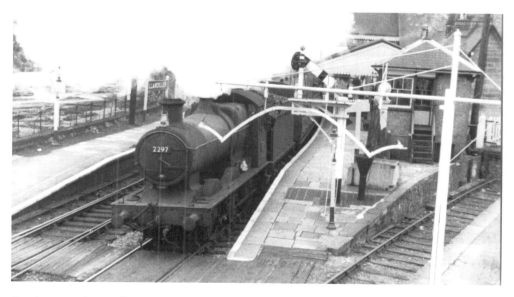

On the same day, Collett Goods 0-6-0 No. 2297 departs from Llangollen with the 10.25 a.m. service from Dolgellau. Llangollen became famous as the home of the International Eisteddfod, which brought many visitors to the railway during the festival and visitors to the town to see its attractions during the summer months, situated as it is next to the River Dee and the wooded Vale of Llangollen (H. Casserley)

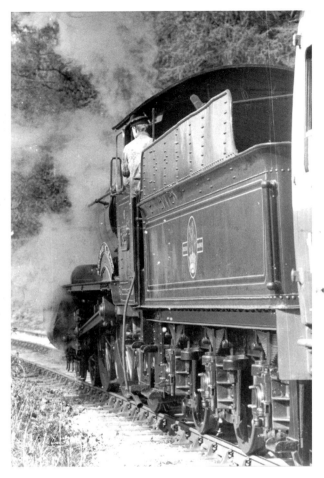

Ex-GWR Manor Class 4-6-0 No. 7822 *Foxcote Manor* is seen running between Llangollen and Berwyn. Although the scene appears to be in the 1950s, it is actually 10 April 1988, the loco operating its first service on the line since restoration. A plan to operate a steam railway between Llangollen and Corwen, the attractive location being popular with tourists, was begun when the Flint and Deeside Railway Society occupied the derelict and overgrown Llangollen station in 1975. In the same year, track had been laid within the station complex and a small engine shed and workshop had been established. By 1981, a mile-long section of track had been laid and, by 1985, the line reached the very attractive station at Berwyn, some 2 miles distant, and has since gone on to reach Carrog. It is still hoped to reach Corwen and the line is creeping ever closer, financial support having been gained from the Wales Tourist Board and the EU in recognition of its tourist potential. Indeed, the line does very well during the International Eisteddfod, recalling the days when the festival was served by the main-line railway. (G. Roberts)

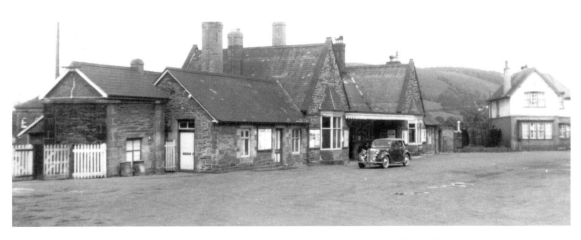

Exterior of Corwen station on 15 July 1963. The section from Llangollen to Corwen was incorporated as the Llangollen & Corwen Railway on 6 August 1860 and opened to both freight and passenger traffic on 1 May 1865. Corwen was a junction with the LNWR line to Ruthin and Denbigh, the station being jointly staffed, but the GWR always remained the senior partner. (R. Casserley)

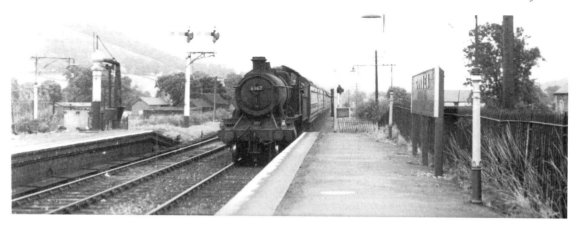

Arriving at Corwen station on 13 August 1953 is ex-GWR Churchward 2-6-0 No. 6367 at the head of the 3.45 p.m. Ruabon–Barmouth service. When established, Corwen was provided with a two-road engine shed with turntable, which provided all motive power in the early years of the line. Its importance, however, declined with the opening of Croes Newydd shed and the GWR abandoned Corwen shed in 1927. In 1921, Corwen shed had an allocation of six locos, four 0-6-0 saddle tanks, a 2-4-0 tender engine and a Dean Goods 0-6-0. (H. Casserley)

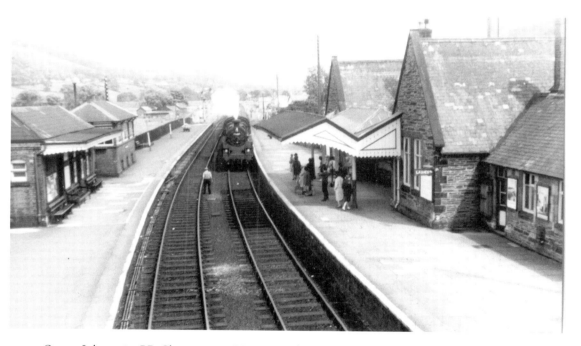

On 15 July 1963, BR Class 4 4-6-0 No. 75027 brings the 1.20 p.m. Chester–Barmouth train into Corwen station with passengers awaiting its arrival, and the signalman is waiting to receive the single-line token. Between Llangollen and Corwen, there were stations at Berwyn, Glyndyfrdwy, Carrog and Bonwm Halt. The majority of these stations are now preserved as part of the Llangollen Railway and have been beautifully restored. In GWR days, the station at Glyndyfrdwy handled significant quantities of slate from local quarries, linked to the station by a narrow gauge tramway. (R. Casserley)

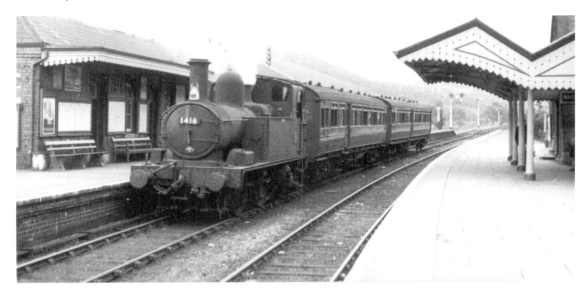

Motor-fitted ex-GWR 0-4-2T No. 1416 arrives at Corwen with the 3.30 p.m. Bala–Ruabon train on 13 August 1953. (H. Casserley)

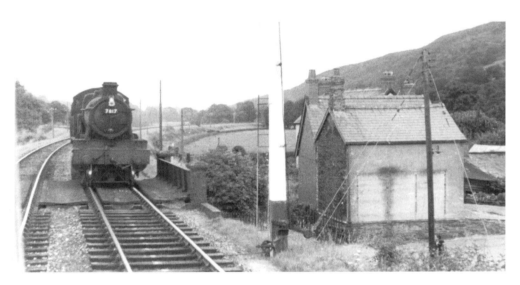

Approaching Corwen station on 13 August 1953 at the head of the 2.05 p.m. Ruabon–Barmouth service is ex-GWR Manor Class 4-6-0 No. 7817 *Garsington Manor*, which at that time was allocated to Croes Newydd shed. The LNWR line to Ruthin is on the left. (H. Casserley)

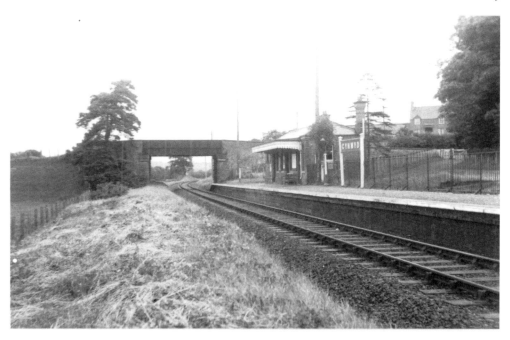

From Corwen, the line through to Dolgellau was built in stages between April and August 1868, the whole of the line coming under GWR control from 1 July 1896. The section from Dolgellau to Barmouth Junction belonged to Cambrian Railways until absorbed by the GWR in 1922. The first station on this section was at Cynwyd, seen here on 15 July 1963. (R. Casserley)

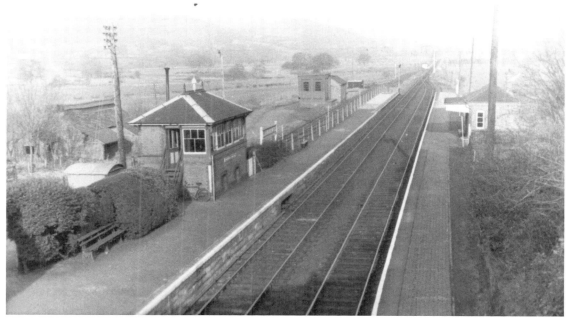

From Cynwyd, the line ran through Llandrillo before entering Llanderfel, seen here with its passing loop and two platforms. (R. Casserley)

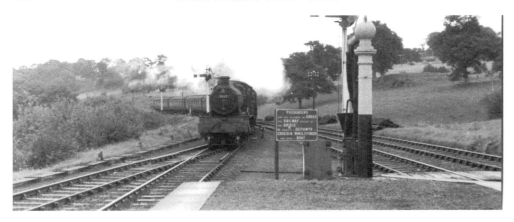

From Llanderfel, the line arrives at Bala Junction, connecting with the line to Bala and Blaenau Ffestiniog. Here, ex-GWR Manor Class 4-6-0 No. 7827 *Lydham Manor* arrives at Bala Junction with the 8.40 a.m. service from Chester to Pwlheli on 15 August 1953. (H. Casserley)

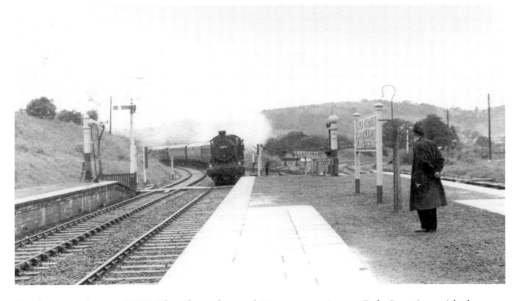

On the same day, ex-GWR Churchward mogul No. 7305 arrives at Bala Junction with the 9.20 a.m. Barmouth–Birmingham service. This train will run to Wrexham, thence to Shrewsbury, Wolverhampton (Low Level) and Birmingham (Snow Hill). (H. Casserley)

Opposite top: Arriving at Bala Junction on 15 July 1963, BR Standard Class 4 No. 75029 heads the 12.45 p.m. Pwllheli–Chester train. (R. Casserley)

Opposite middle: Bala Junction, looking west on 15 August 1953. The line between Llangollen Goods Junction and Bala Junction was closed on 13 December 1964, a few months earlier than planned, due to flooding at Dolgellau which prevented through running of all trains. Only four years later, on 1 April 1968, the whole of the line from Ruabon ceased to exist until the Llangollen Railway reopened its section. (H. Casserley)

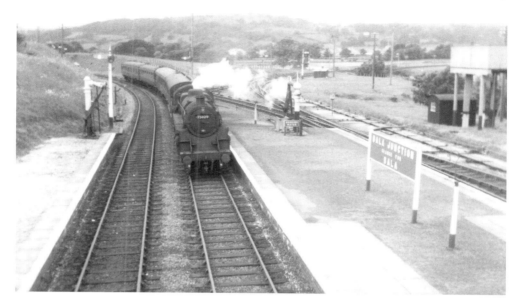

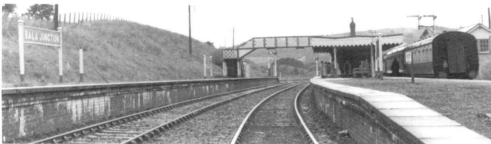

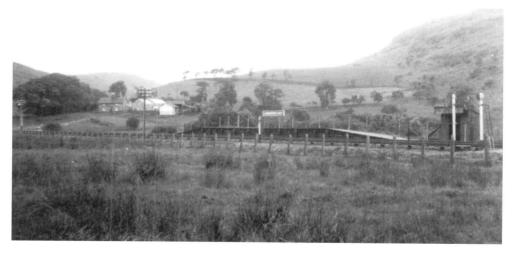

After leaving Bala Junction, the line ran through more rural country, passing Bala Lake as the line passed stations at Llangower Halt, Flag Station, Llanuchllyn and Llys Halt. The section between Llanuchllyn and Bala Junction now forms the narrow gauge Bala Lake Railway. From Llys Halt, the line entered Garneddwen Halt, seen here in its rural setting on 15 July 1963. (R. Casserley)

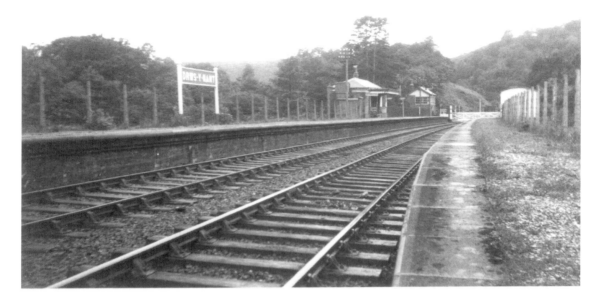

From Garneddwen, the line entered the little station of Drws-y-Nant, seen here on the same day and looking in the direction of Barmouth. (R. Casserley)

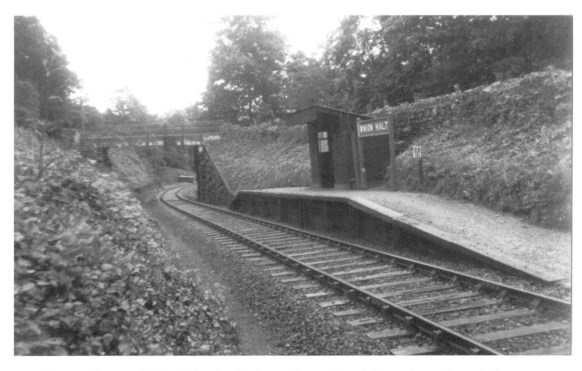

Next station was Wnion Halt – its simple wooden waiting shelter and very short platform are seen here on 16 July 1963. It would appear that very little traffic was likely to emanate from such a small, rural location. (R. Casserley)

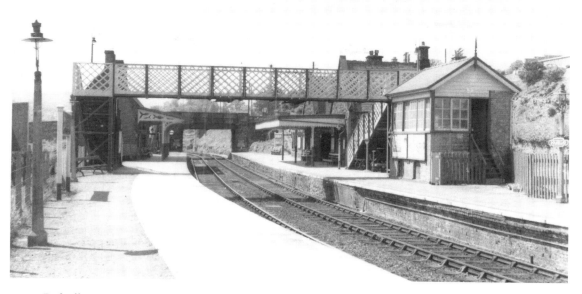

Dolgellau station on 5 June 1962. The station served the county town of Merionethshire and was the point where the GWR and Cambrian Railways met. It was flooding here that caused early closure of the line mentioned earlier. Dolgellau station itself was closed in 1965 and the old trackbed is now the A170, which bypasses the attractive little town. (G. Ellis)

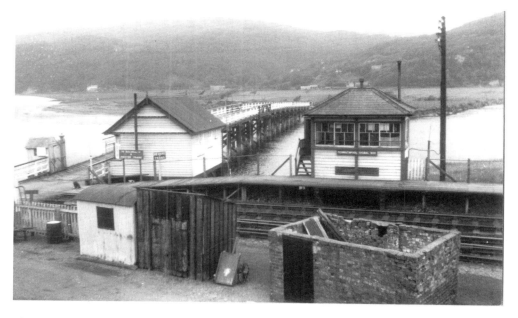

The section of line from Dolgellau was part of Cambrian Railways right through to Pwllheli in the west and Aberystwyth to the east. The station after Dolgellau was at Penmaenpool, seen here on 16 July 1963, set in attractive Snowdonia countryside with a jetty going down to the river here. (R. Casserley)

FOUR

THE CAMBRIAN COAST LINE

In an attempt to resurrect Vignoles's plan for a railway to Porth Dinllaen to compete with the LNWR for Irish traffic, plans were made for a line through Mid Wales from Shrewsbury to Porth Dinllaen.

The first section of the line through Mid Wales was part of the Shrewsbury & Chester Railway from Gobowen to Oswestry, followed by sections to Llanidloes and Newtown in 1859, and Oswestry, Ellsemere and Whitchurch in 1864. Further west, the Newtown & Machynlleth Railway was incorporated on 27 July 1857, its line opening on 3 January 1863. It was the Aberystwyth & Welsh Coast Railway that completed the line to Pwllheli. All of these lines were engineered by David Davies and Thomas Savin.

In 1865, these companies were merged to form the Cambrian Railways, who completed the line to Pwllheli. Although the Cambrian was never financially viable, almost becoming bankrupt on more than one occasion, it did open up Cardigan Bay to tourism, many visitors coming from the industrial West Midlands, travelling by train from GWR stations at Birmingham (Snow Hill) and Wolverhampton (Low Level) to Shrewsbury where they could board Cambrian trains to places like Barmouth, Criccieth and Pwllheli.

Despite threats to the line, including an invasion by teredo worm into the wooden structure of Barmouth Bridge, which forced BR to close it in 1980, and the Beeching Report of 1963, the line remains open to serve remote towns in the area and often plays host to steam excursions using preserved locos, some of which hauled trains over the Cambrian Coast line in GWR and BR days.

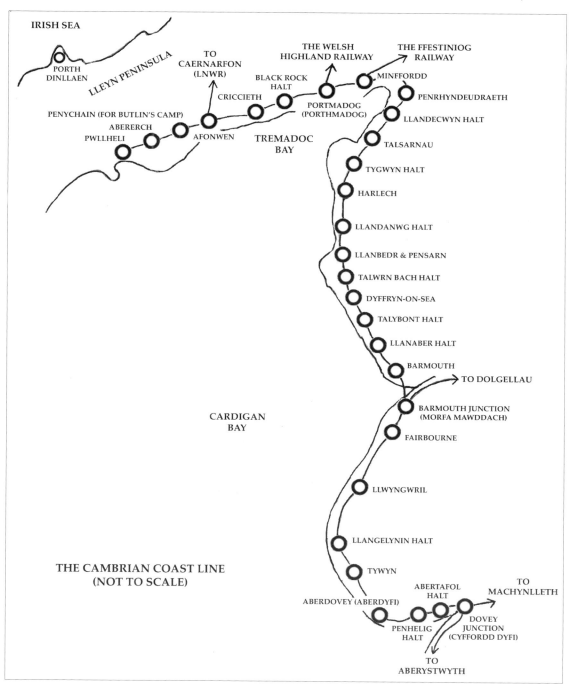

The Cambrian Railways line from Dovey Junction, where the line from Shrewsbury and Mid Wales met the Aberystwyth & Welsh Coast line to Pwllheli. This was the line that was planned to reach Porth Dinllaen for Ireland. The fact that this section was never built was due to pressure by the much more powerful LNWR who would allow no threat to its own port at Holyhead. (Author's Collection)

MACHYNLLETH, ABERDOVEY, BARMOUTH, HARLECH, and PWLLHELI.—Cambrian.

Miles	Down.	Week Days mrn	mrn	mrn	mrn	mrn	mrn	mrn	mrn	aft	aft	aft	aft	aft	Sundays mrn	mrn	aft
	466 WHITCHURCH ......dep.			2 25					10 5			1 50				2 25	
	466 OSWESTRY .... "			3 25				8 20	1056			2 42				6 15	
	466 WELSHPOOL......... "			4 12				9 5	1140			3 35				7 0	
—	**Machynlleth**..........dep			5 55			8 35	1048	1 25			5 5				8 55	
4	Dovey Junction ...... arr.						8 45	1055	1·33			5 13					
	dep.						8 50	11 0	1 40			5 15					
9¼	**Aberdovey**			6 15			9 4	1114	1 54			5 28				9 18	
13½	**Towyn * 465**			6 23			9 12	1122	2 2			5 36				9 26	
16	Tonfanau						9 17	1127	2 7			5 41				9 31	
20½	Llwyngwril			6 35			9 24	1134	2 17			5 48				9 39	
22¾	Fairbourne, for Friog......			6 44			9 33	1143	2 27			5 57				9 49	
23¾	Barmouth Junction			6 47			9 36	1146	2 30			6 0				9 52	5 2
—	**Barmouth** ....dep.	Mondays only.		7 50			10 0	12 7	2 55			5 55		7 5		1028	
—	Barmouth Junction ..			7 57			10 7	1218	3 5			6 5		7 15		1035	
24¾	Arthog			8 0			1010	1221	3 8			6 8		7 18		1038	
29¼	Penmaenpool			8 11			1025	1233	3 20			6 20		7 30		1050	
31½	**Dolgelley † 105**...arr.			8 16			1030	1238	3 25			6 25		7 35		1055	
25¼	**Barmouth** .... arr.			6 54			9 45	1155	2 38			6 8				10 0	5 8
	dep.						9 50	1225	2 48			6 15					5 10
30¼	Dyffryn						10 0	1235	2 58			6 25					5 20
33½	Llanbedr and Pensarn.....						10 6	1241	3 4			6 31					5 28
36	**Harlech**	5 30					1016	1250	3 13			6 40					5 36
39½	Talsarnau	5 40					1024	1257	3 21			6 49					5 45
41½	Penrhyndeudraeth						1029	1 1	3 26			6 54					5 50
42½	Minffordd **477**	5 50					1035	1 6	3 32			7 1					5 56
44¾	**Portmadoc**, for Beddgelert.	5 55			7 30		1040	1 10	3 36		6 50	7 5	8 40				6 0
49¾	Criccieth..........................				7 41		1057	1 27	3 53		7 2	7 22	8 52				6 14
53	Afonwen **471**		6 0		7 50	1045	11 5	1 36	4 0	6 10	7 10	7 30	9 0		8 49		6 22
55½	Abererch		Sig.		Sig.	Sig.	Sig.	Sig.	Sig.	Sig.		Sig.	Sig.		Sig.		Sig.
57¼	**Pwllheli**, for Nevin ....arr.		6 10		8 5	1055	1120	1 55	4 20	6 20		7 45	9 12		8 58		6 32

Miles	Up.	Week Days mrn	mrn	mrn	mrn	mrn	mrn	aft	aft	aft	aft	aft	aft	Sundays mrn	aft	aft
	Pwllheli ....dep.		6 15		7 40	1030	11 0	1 25	4 0	5 55		7 0	8 50	9 0		6 40
1¼	Abererch........................		Sig.		Sig.	Sig.	a	Sig.	Sig.	Sig.		Sig.	Sig.	Sig.		Sig.
1¾	Afonwen **471**................		6 27		7 55	1045	1110	1 40	4 20	6 10		7 10	9 5	9 10		6 49
7¼	Criccieth		6 38		8 7	1056		1 50	4 30	6 20			9 15	9 20		
12¼	**Portmadoc**, for Beddgelert	5 5	6 50		8 20	1110		2 3	4 45	6 30			9 25	9 33		
14¾	Minffordd **477**		6 54		8 25	1115		2 7	4 50					9 37		
15¾	Penrhyndeudraeth		6 58			1121		2 12	4 55					9 42		
17¾	Talsarnau........................		7 3			1126		2 16	5 0					9 46		
21¼	**Harlech**	5 25	7 10			1133		2 23	5 7					9 53		
23¾	Llanbedr and Pensarn	Mondays only.	7 18			1143		2 31	5 17					10 3		
26½	Dyffryn..............................		7 25			1154		2 38	5 27					1012		
31½	**Barmouth** .... arr.		7 35			12 4		2 48	5 37					1022		
	dep.		7 40			12 7		3 10	5 55		7 55			1028	5 55	
—	Mls **Dolgelley** ....dep.		7 15	9 10		1150		2 5	5 25		7 20				4 40	
—	2¼ Penmaenpool..........		7 20	9 15		1155		2 10	5 30		7 28				4 45	
—	6½ Arthog..................		7 30	9 25		12 5		2 20	5 40		7 38				4 55	
—	7¾ Barmouth Junc.*(above)*		7 33	9 29		1210		2 23	5 43		7 41				5 0	
—	9½ **Barmouth** ......arr.		7 40	9 36		1220		2 31	5 53		7 48				5 8	
33¼	Barmouth Junction *(above)*		7 48			1220		3 17	6 5		8 1			1034	6 1	
34¼	Fairbourne, for Friog......		7 51			1223		3 20	6 8		8 5				6 4	
37	Llwyngwril......................		8 0			1233		3 30	6 18		8 15				6 12	
41¼	Tonfanau.........................		8 8			1241		3 38	6 25		8 26				Sig.	
43¼	**Towyn * 465**		8 12			1246		3 43	6 30		8 33				6 24	
47¼	**Aberdovey**		8 23			1256		3 51	6 42		8 43				6 35	
53¼	Dovey Junction **466** . arr.		8 37			1 10		4 5	6 54		9 0					
	dep.		8 45			1 13		4 8	7 6		9 2					
57¼	**Machynlleth 466, 467** arr.		8 53			1 20		4 15	7 13		9 15				7 0	
98¼	467 WELSHPOOL.........arr.		1032			3 3		6 24	8 54						8 43	
114¼	467 OSWESTRY .... "		1135			4 6		7 13	9 35						9 33	
132¼	467 WHITCHURCH....... "		1220			5 0		8 5	1025						1025	

a Stop by signal to take up or set down Passengers booked from or to Stations on other Companies' Lines, notice to be given to the Guard to set down.

* ½ mile to the Tal-y-llyn Company's Station.
† Station for Cader Idris.

A 1910 Cambrian Railways timetable for services between Machynlleth, Barmouth and Pwllheli as well as its own section between Dolgellau (Dolgelley) and Barmouth Junction. (Author's Collection)

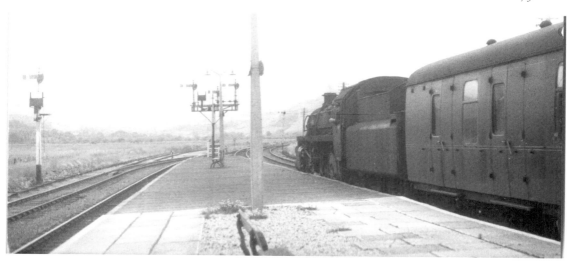

Dovey Junction (Cyffordd Dyfi) on 20 June 1966 with BR Standard Class 4 4-6-0 No. 75048 with the 6.00 p.m. express from Aberystwyth to Shrewsbury. Although Dovey Junction is really in Mid Wales, it was the point where the famous 'Cambrian Coast Express' from Paddington was divided, one section going to Aberystwyth while the other went north to Barmouth, Harlech and Pwllheli. (H. Casserley)

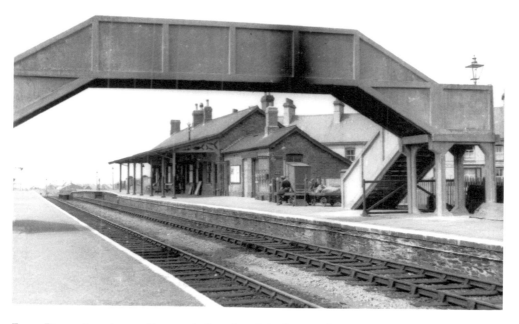

From Dovey Junction to Barmouth Junction (Morfa Mawddach) the A&WCR ran through some difficult and mountainous country and at Friog rockfalls were often a problem, causing an accident in 1883 when a landslide derailed engine No. 25 *Pegasus*, it landing on the beach below. A similar incident occurred in 1933, the GWR constructing a rock shelter over this dangerous section of line to prevent further incidents. There were several stations on this section, which served seaside resorts in the area, including Tywyn, seen here on 8 July 1955, and Fairbourne, which now connects with the Fairbourne narrow gauge railway. (G. Ellis)

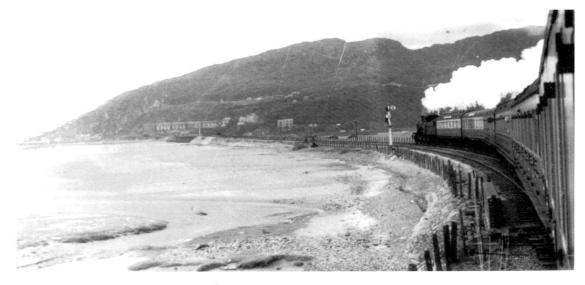

Approaching Barmouth and the Barmouth Bridge (Bont-y-Bermo) is the 3.45 p.m. train from Ruabon on 13 August 1955, with ex-GWR Churchward mogul No. 6367. When Barmouth Bridge was about to open, in 1867, a local man had said that he would eat the engine of the first train to cross the River Mawddach, over which the Barmouth Bridge crossed, such was his disbelief in the ability of any train to cross the estuary. When the bridge was opened, he was on the first train to cross. On arrival at Barmouth, he was approached by the official party, taken to the end of the station platform where a table was laid and asked whether he would like his engine baked or boiled. His reply was not recorded, but perhaps he had a sense of humour. (H. Casserley)

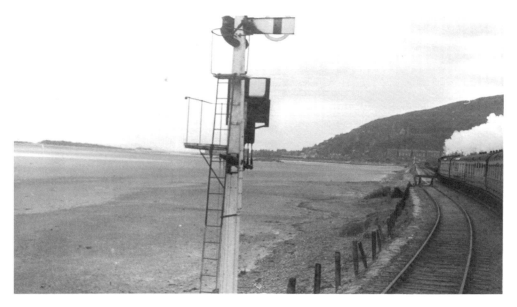

Further along the line toward Barmouth on the same day and the town has come into clearer view, with the Cader Idris brooding above. (H. Casserley)

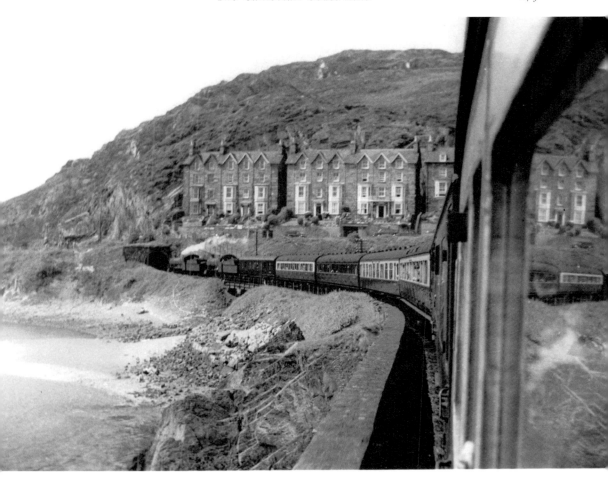

A special train, headed by a Manor 4-6-0 piloting a mogul, enters the tunnel under the Cader Idris in 1958 as it nears Barmouth. Lodging houses for visitors to the town are now clearly visible. From here, the train will cross the Barmouth Bridge before entering the seaside resort. (D. Ibbotson)

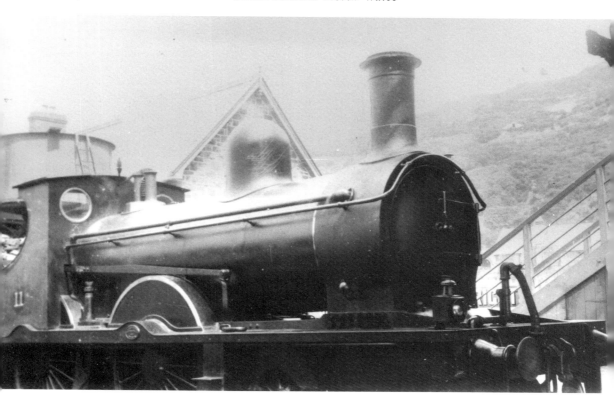

Standing at Barmouth station early in the twentieth century is Cambrian Railways 4-4-0 No. 11, built by Sharp-Stewart in 1895. The GWR inherited some thirty-five of these 4-4-0s when the Cambrian was absorbed by the Paddington company and they were all gone by the early 1930s. The section of the line between Barmouth and Pwllheli was opened in 1867 after a difficult gestation period. In July 1866, the Cambrian informed the Board of Trade that certain sections of the line were ready for inspection, which included that between Barmouth and Portmadoc. However, by September the Cambrian had to ask for a delay in opening due to bad weather, gales and high tides having done much damage to the coastal section of the line. Repairs were undertaken and the Cambrian, on 28 November, contacted the Board of Trade to let them know that the line was once again ready for inspection. The following day, however, the Cambrian informed them that this only referred to the section between Barmouth and Portmadoc. Only by February 1867 was the section between Barmouth and Portmadoc, along with the section from Portmadoc to Pwllheli, available for inspection. The Board of Trade inspector was not impressed, with almost everything wrong with the line from thin and patchy ballast under the tracks, through lack of fencing and inadequate guard rails, along with other problems with the permanent way. There were also issues with dangerous steps, footbridges that were needed and waterlogged cuttings. Such were the problems that under no circumstances was the line to be opened. As late as May 1867, the inspector still refused to allow opening and it was not until September that permission was finally given but with a proviso that a man should be constantly employed to patrol the Harlech cutting and no train was allowed to pass without his sanction. Barmouth station itself, therefore, opened in 1867 after completion of the Barmouth Bridge, and stood on the north side of a level crossing. The town was a tourist destination even before the railway arrived and the station was provided with a passing loop and two platforms, its buildings constructed of stone. The town itself had been a busy seaport, and materials for construction of the railway were often delivered here. After the railway had opened, sea trade virtually disappeared and Barmouth was left to concentrate on tourism, many of the old seamen finding employment on the new railway. (Author's Collection)

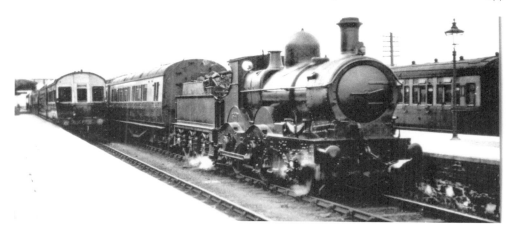

Barmouth station on 1 June 1932 with GWR 3201 Class 2-4-0 No. 3207, a conversion from a broad gauge tank loco near the end of its working life, at the head of the 12.09 p.m. service to Pwllheli with a local 'railmotor' service standing on the opposite platform, probably on an all-stations service to Wrexham or Dovey Junction. By this time, Barmouth had developed into a major seaside resort, the station lying between seafront houses and the expanding town. The GWR, in 1929, noted that Barmouth had a population of some 3,000 people and was an important tourist attraction on the Cambrian line. During the summer months traffic would be rather heavy with holidaymakers and day excursionists visiting the resort. At the station, the Up line was the more important with the spacious waiting rooms and offices situated on that platform, and some twenty-three men were employed here with many trains starting and terminating here and engines for local trains based at Penmaenpool. In those days, the best GWR train left Paddington at 11.05 a.m. and arrived in Barmouth at 5.25 p.m., having run via Ruabon and Llangollen. (H. Casserley)

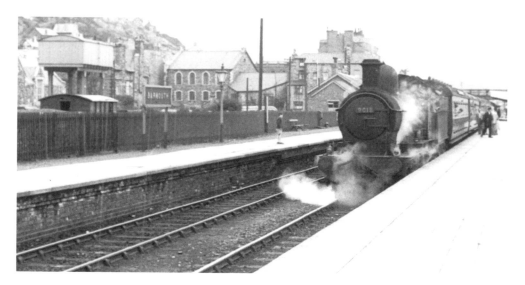

Some twenty-one years later, on 13 August 1953, and ex-GWR double-framed Dukedog 4-4-0 No. 9018 arrives at Barmouth station with the 5.55 p.m. train to Pwllheli. Although classed as new engines, C. B. Collett took the boilers from withdrawn Duke of Cornwall Class locos and the frames of Bulldog engines to reconstruct these rather ancient-looking locomotives, which were lightweight enough for the Cambrian system, allowing withdrawal of old Cambrian types. Many of these engines were to last well into the 1950s and up to 1960. (R. Casserley)

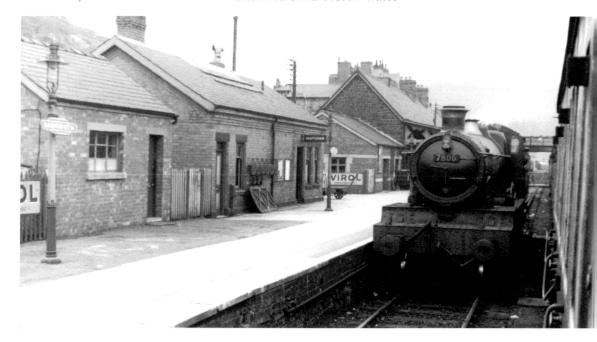

Running light on the Up line at Barmouth is ex-GWR Manor Class 4-6-0 No. 7800 *Torquay Manor* on 24 August 1954. This was the first member of a class of thirty engines built by the GWR just before the outbreak of the Second World War. Again these engines were of lightweight construction for use on cross-country and main lines, which were not suitable for heavier engines, and were ideal for use on the Cambrian section. These engines were often a feature of the Cambrian Coast Express between Shrewsbury and Aberystwyth. (H. Casserley)

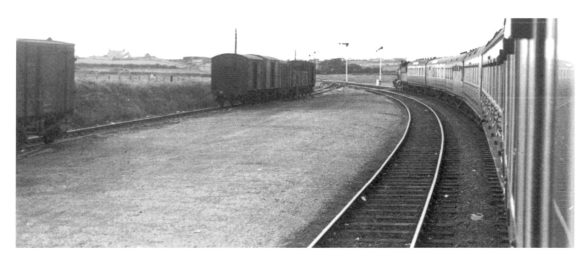

Lying between Barmouth and Harlech was the station of Llanbedr and Pensarn, seen here on 13 August 1953 with ex-GWR Dukedog 4-4-0 No. 9018 departing at the head of the 5.55 p.m. Barmouth–Pwllheli service. (R. Casserley)

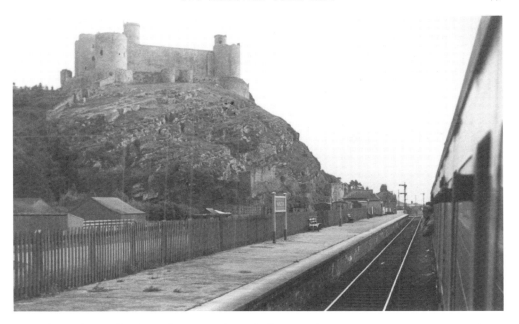

Harlech Castle stands above the station here, looking south on 13 August 1953. In Cambrian Railways days, punctuality was not a feature of the line and a story goes that, in 1911, a tourist arrived at Harlech station at around 6.00 p.m. and asked the stationmaster if the approaching train from the south was the 5.20, only to be told that it was probably the 4.10, which, indeed, it was. (R. Casserley)

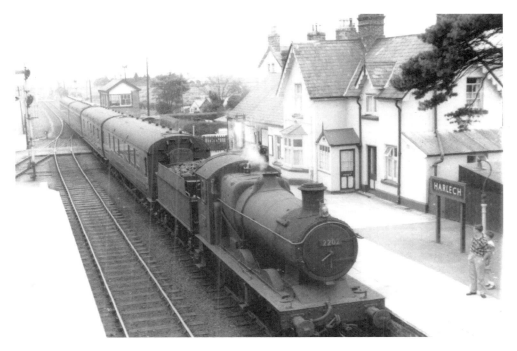

Harlech station on 25 August 1959 with ex-GWR Collett Goods 0-6-0 No. 2202 arriving with a train from Barmouth and going forward to Pwllheli. (G. Ellis)

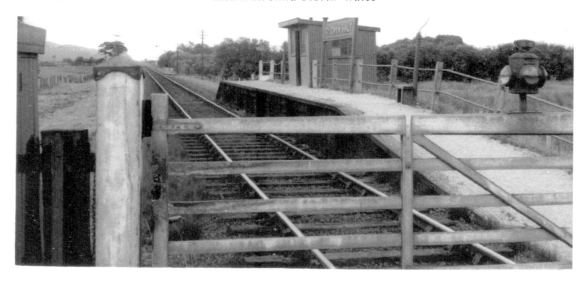

From Harlech, the Cambrian Coast line passed through the tiny Ty Gwyn Halt, seen here on 11 July 1954 with its simple waiting shelter and short platform. (G. Ellis)

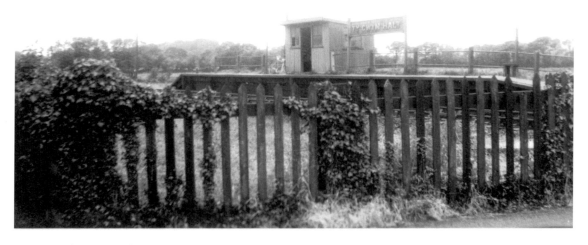

Another view of Ty Gwyn Halt on 20 June 1963. Many of the small halts on the line were similar to this one. (R. Casserley)

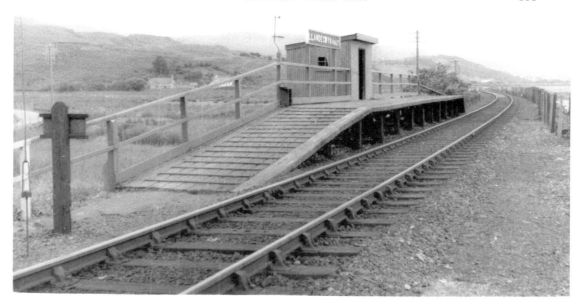

Heading north, before approaching Penrhyndeudraeth, lay Llandegwyn Halt, seen here on 11 July 1954. (G. Ellis)

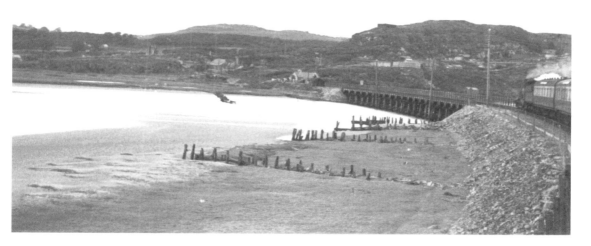

Just south of Penrhyndeudraeth, 9018 runs along the shore of Cardigan Bay with its train for Pwllheli on 13 August 1953. (R. Casserley)

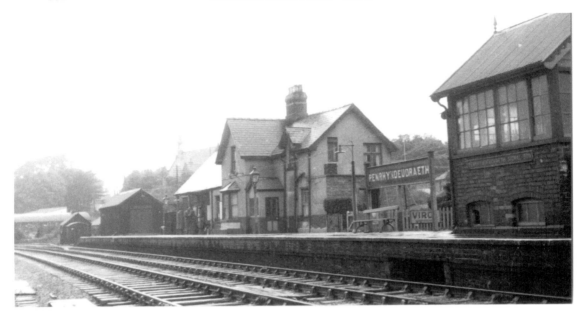

The station and signal box at Penrhyndeudraeth, looking towards Pwllheli, as it appeared on 28 June 1956. As the area had many slate and granite quarries, an explosives factory was situated here, which brought a lot of business to the Cambrian system, and there were sidings to deal with such traffic. (H. Casserley)

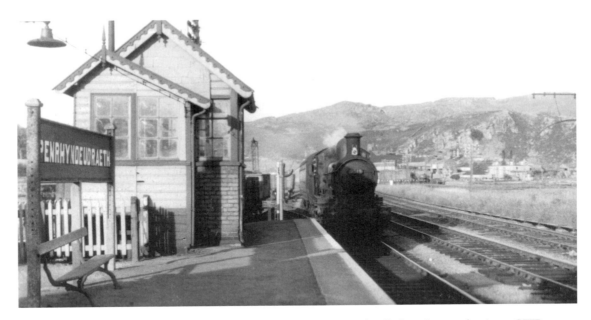

Arriving at Penrhyndeudraeth with the 5.40 p.m. from Machynlleth to Portmadoc is ex-GWR Dukedog 4-4-0 No. 9018 on 27 June 1956. (H. Casserley)

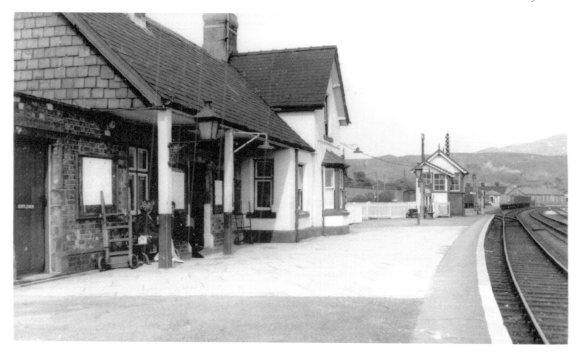

Penrhyndeudraeth station, looking towards Harlech, as it appeared on 4 June 1962. (G. Ellis)

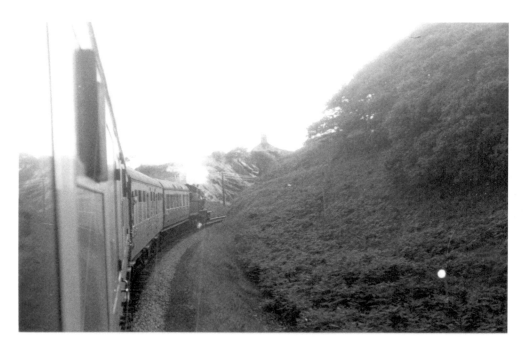

Between Penrhyndeudraeth and Minffordd, 9018 heads its train to Portmadoc on 27 June 1956. After leaving Penrhyndeudraeth, the Cambrian Coast line turns west as it heads towards Pwllheli. (H. Casserley)

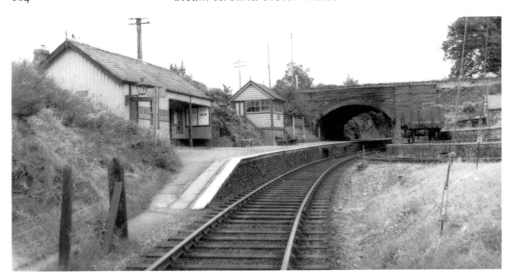

Minffordd station on 11 July 1954. The narrow gauge Ffestiniog Railway had interchange sidings with the Cambrian system here, which allowed the Oswestry company to tap slate traffic from the quarries at Blaenau Ffestiniog. These sidings are just visible on the right. (G. Ellis)

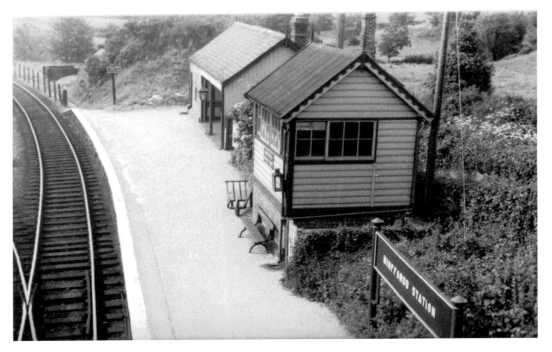

The signal box and simple waiting shelter at Minffordd station, looking towards Pwllheli, on 27 June 1956. (H. Casserley)

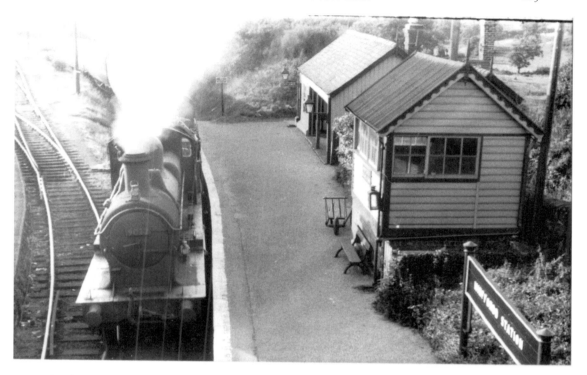

On the same day, another ex-GWR Dukedog 4-4-0 No. 9022 arrives at Minffordd station with the 7.45 p.m. Portmadoc–Barmouth train. (H. Casserley)

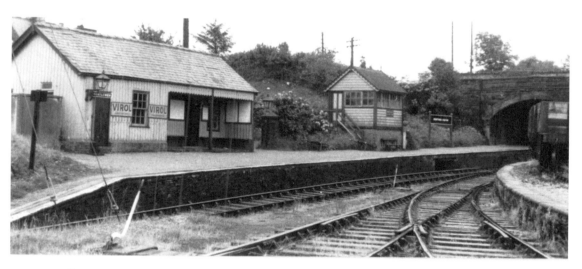

Minffordd station, facing Barmouth, on 28 June 1956 with the exchange sidings on the right. The ground lever gave access to the sidings. (H. Casserley)

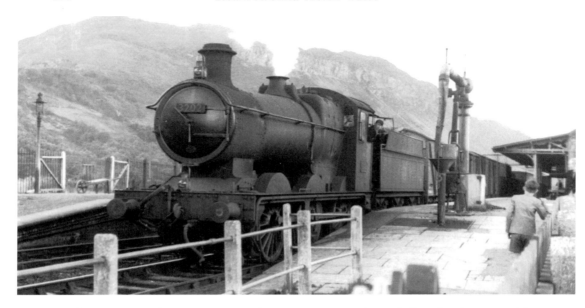

Standing at Portmadoc station on 24 August 1954 is ex-GWR Collett Goods 0-6-0 with a freight train. Portmadoc was a major centre for slate traffic emanating from the many quarries in Snowdonia, much traffic being brought in by the narrow gauge Welsh Highland Railway, which ran from the LNWR Caernarfon line and through the mountains to the port town. (H. Casserley)

As much traffic was generated here, Portmadoc, along with Pwllheli, was provided with a loco shed, both being sub-sheds of Machynlleth (coded 89C in BR days), whose allocation in 1950 was as follows:

GWR 14xx 0-4-2T	1465, 1474
GWR 2251 0-6-0	2200, 2206, 2219, 2223, 2260, 2283, 2292, 2298, 3200, 3201, 3202, 3207
GWR 2301 0-6-0	2323
GWR 4500 2-6-2T	4501, 4512, 4530, 4549, 4555, 4560, 4571, 4575, 4581, 5560, 5570
GWR 78xx 4-6-0	7802 *Bradley Manor*, 7803 *Barcote Manor*
GWR 9000 4-4-0	9000, 9002, 9004, 9005, 9009, 9012, 9013, 9014, 9017, 9024, 9027
Cambrian 0-6-0	864, 894
	Total: 41

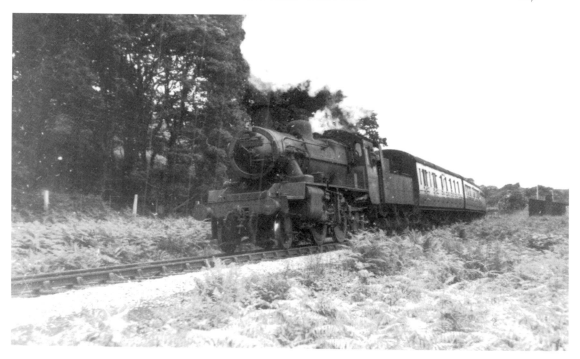

Heading towards Portmadoc from Criccieth on 9 July 1954 is BR Standard Class 2 2-6-0 No. 78007 with a train for Barmouth. (G. Ellis)

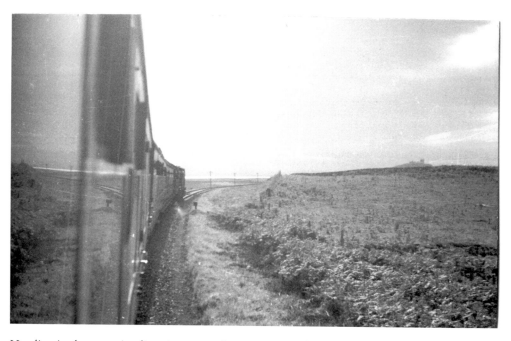

Heading in the opposite direction on 24 August 1954 is the 3.45 p.m. Barmouth–Pwllheli train double-headed by ex-GWR Dukedog 4-4-0 and BR mogul No. 78002. Criccieth Castle is visible on the right. (H. Casserley)

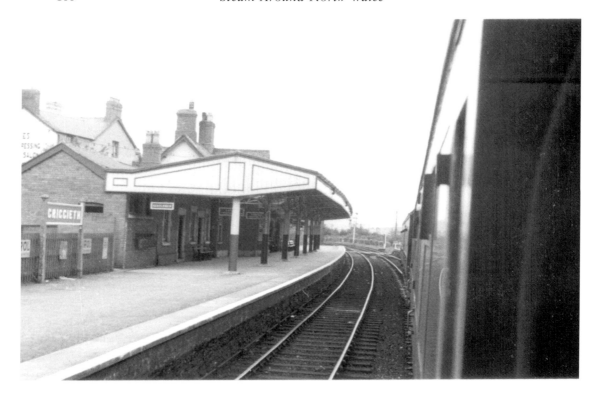

The very smart station at Criccieth, looking east, on 24 August 1954. Much business at the station was derived from tourism, as the resort here was quite popular. (H. Casserley)

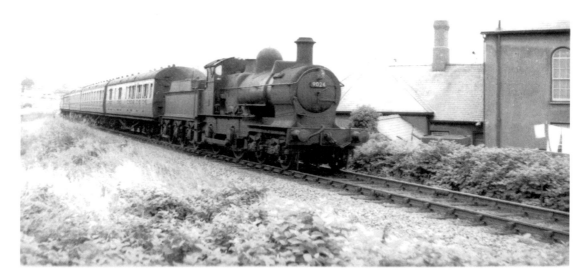

Approaching Criccieth station on 15 July 1955 is ex-GWR Dukedog 4-4-0 No. 9024 with a train for Pwllheli. (G. Ellis)

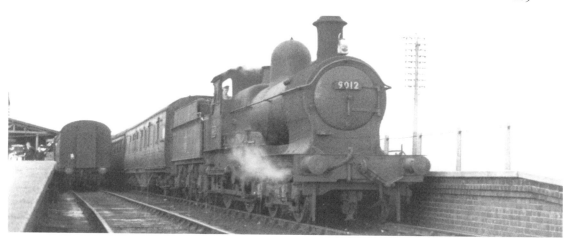

Coming full circle, Dukedog 4-4-0 No. 9012 arrives at Afonwen on 13 August 1953 with the 8.15 a.m. Portmadoc–Pwllheli service. This is the point where the LNWR Bangor–Caernarfon–Afonwen met the Cambrian Coast line. Afonwen station itself was closed when the LNWR line ceased to exist in 1964 and no trace of the station now remains. (H. Casserley)

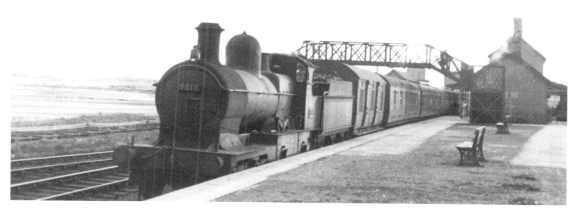

Waiting at Afonwen station on 13 August 1953 is Dukedog No. 9018 with the 8.15 a.m. Pwllheli–Portmadoc service. (H. Casserley)

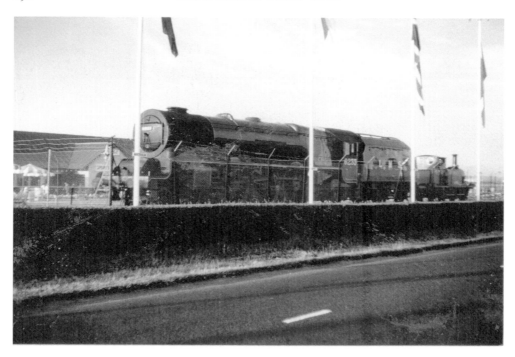

From Afonwen, the Cambrian Coast line arrives at Penychain, which served Butlin's holiday camp. Billy Butlin had built his first holiday camp at Skegness in 1936 followed by another at Clacton, both in LNER territory, and they shared advertising costs with Butlin's. In 1938, the Holidays with Pay Act had come into law, which gave workers a week's holiday with pay and allowed the possibility of increasing demand for seaside holidays. With this in mind, a new camp was planned at Filey in North Yorkshire (also in LNER territory) but war intervened and the camp was turned over to the RAF for the duration. While the Filey camp was under construction, Butlin was asked to build something similar for the Navy on the south coast. However, before a site could be found on the south coast, Dunkirk evacuations had occurred and the Admiralty requested a site in North Wales. A suitable site was found on the Lleyn Peninsula, near the village of Penychain, the camp becoming HMS *Glendower* and being used for training of both Navy and Merchant Navy personnel. When hostilities were over, the camp was returned to Butlin's and it opened on 29 March 1947. In that year, the camp played host to some 5,000 campers, many coming by rail from Lancashire, Merseyside and the West Midlands. In 1990, after many improvements, the camp was renamed Starcoast World and by 1995 the site occupied some 47 acres and employed 1,200 staff to cater for 8,000 visitors. By November 1998, the camp was closed and became a Haven Holiday Park from April 1999 called Hafan-y-Mor (Sea Haven). This was the last of Butlin's camps to have a narrow gauge or miniature railway. In happier days, Butlin's brought ex-BR locos to Pwllheli camp. Ex-LMS Duchess Class Pacific No. 6233 *Duchess of Sutherland* is visible at the entrance to the camp. The engine had been retired from Edge Hill shed in 1963–64 and was bought by Butlin's and displayed at the camp. In 1970, the loco went to Bressingham, finally going to the Midland Railway Centre at Butterley, Derbyshire. Another ex-LMS Pacific also found its way to Pwllheli in September 1962 when No. 46203 *Princess Margaret Rose* arrived at the camp. She went on to be restored to working order at Butterley. (Author's Collection)

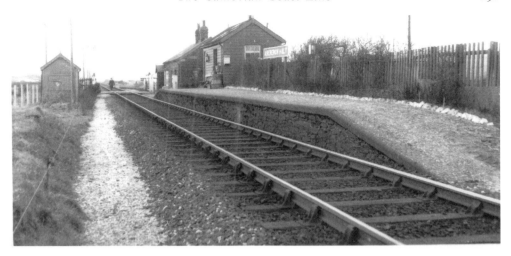

Between Penychain and the terminus at Pwllheli, there was a halt at Abererch, seen here on 6 February 1961. (G. Ellis)

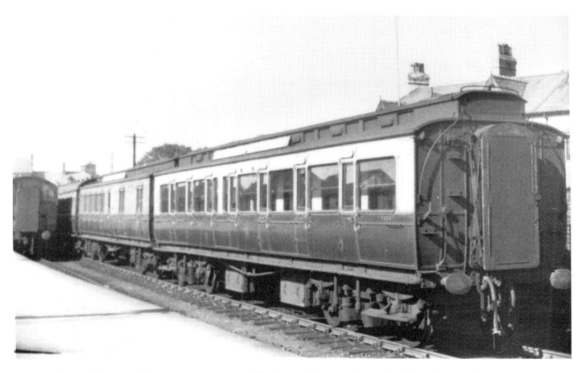

The Cambrian Railways terminus at Pwllheli, seen here with coaches from the Cambrian Coast Express on 10 September 1937. The original station at Pwllheli was opened near the harbour in 1867 but passengers were constantly complaining about the lingering smell of fish and it was replaced by a new one in 1909. This new station was more conveniently sited than the old one had been. Had the original plan to Porth Dinllaen gone through, the line would have turned north from Pwllheli to reach the port. An aerodrome is now located there. (Author's Collection)

ACKNOWLEDGEMENTS

This work would have proved very difficult to complete without the assistance of several people, including Gwyn Roberts, Peter Owen, R. Casserley, Roger Carpenter, G. Ellis and David Ibbotson. Bernard Unsworth took the trouble to sort out shed allocations, which did save me a fair bit of time, and Bourne Leisure provided background to the story of Butlin's camp at Pwllheli. To all of those mentioned and to others I may have omitted, I offer my sincere thanks for their efforts on my behalf. My thanks also go to Alwen, who was an inspiration to me on many occasions, and she is still missed.

Finally, my thanks to my wife, Hilary, who is a constant support and still makes a good cup of tea, and to my sons, Gary and Keith, who also provide their support.

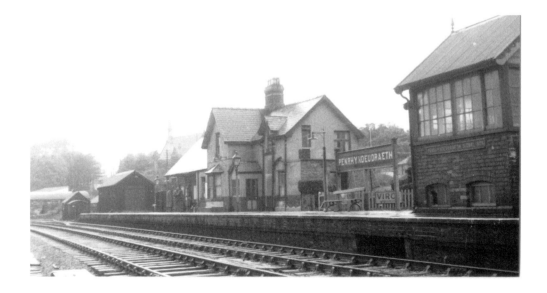